Lives Less Ordinary

About the Author

Andrew Hughes is an archivist and historian, and the author of *The Convictions of John Delahunt* and *The Coroner's Daughter*, which was chosen as the prestigious 'One Dublin One Book' for 2023.

LIVES LESS ORDINARY

Dublin's Fitzwilliam Square, 1798-1922

Revised and Updated Edition

Andrew Hughes

The Liffey Press

Published by
The Liffey Press
'Clareville', 307 Clontarf Road
Dublin D03 PO46, Ireland
www.theliffeypress.com

© 2023 Andrew Hughes
Revised and Updated Edition
Originally published 2011

A catalogue record of this book is
available from the British Library.

ISBN 978-1-7397892-7-5

Printed in Northern Ireland by W&G Baird

Contents

Acknowledgements

Not so long ago, when purse strings were a little looser, I would on occasion receive commissions to carry out research into the history of individual Georgian houses. Proud owners were keen to know the historical context in which their businesses or institutions were placed, and I scoured street directories, deeds, census returns and newspaper archives to discover all their previous residents.

The seed of this book lay in the fact that I was separately asked to examine three houses in Fitzwilliam Square in quick succession: No. 57, the office of Lyons Kenny Solicitors; No. 11, the home of the Italian Cultural Institute in Dublin; and No. 61, once the building of Eugene F. Collins Solicitors, originally of Eustace Street, now of Burlington Road. Among the lives unearthed for those three houses was a Polish philosopher exiled from Stalinist Warsaw; a young man who grew up to be British ambassador to the Soviet Union on the eve of World War II; a lawyer, the Recorder of Singapore, who appeared as a character in the fictional book *Anna and the King of Siam*; and a well-known Dublin medium who held twice-weekly séances with members of Dublin's literary circle. Each of the three houses had a further ensemble of distinguished lawyers and doctors, academics and soldiers.

It occurred that if those three houses could contain such a diverse array of inhabitants, whose lives were swept up in both domestic and international events, then perhaps the entire sixty-nine houses of Fitzwilliam Square would contain lives enough to fill a book. Therefore, I'd like to thank those who gave me a foothold in the square:

Graham Kenny and Barry Lyons of Lyons Kenny Solicitors, Naoise Mac Fheorais of the Italian Cultural Institute and Barry O'Neill of Eugene F. Collins Solicitors.

In the course of the research I received a great deal of assistance from individuals, privately and in public institutions, all much appreciated. In particular, I'd like to thank Dr. Michael Purser and Anthony O'Brien, who both went out of their way to provide me with very useful information and beautiful images.

I'm very grateful to The Liffey Press and David Givens for taking on the project and all the excellent work that made the book a reality.

Thanks to my siblings for reading drafts, making suggestions, use of office facilities, lending laptops during computer crashes. A special word of thanks to my uncle Jack Downes, who was even more keen than the publisher to see completed chapters and whose enthusiasm for the book was a great encouragement. And most of all thanks to my parents, Margaret and Kevin, for their constant support.

Foreword to Revised Edition

This time last year I was in Tullynally Castle, surveying the archives of the Earls of Longford. While sitting in a magnificent archives room, with huge bay windows overlooking the estate, I received an email from the Dublin UNESCO City of Literature Office, letting me know that my novel *The Coroner's Daughter* had been chosen as the One Dublin One Book for 2023. In a way it was fitting that I should hear the news while surrounded by archives, and while staying at a beautiful historic house, for those things have very much inspired my writing.

Lives Less Ordinary stemmed from my fascination with the people who lived in Dublin's Georgian houses, and the fragments of history they left behind: a coat of arms hidden in a stained-glass fanlight; a letter from a young lady to her mother describing her first dinner party; a simple childhood drawing of infant brothers playing in a nursery, while knowing one of their lives would end on a battlefield. I didn't realise it at the time, but all of the research I was doing for the book was providing me with a fantastic setting for historical fiction, as well as a readymade cast of characters.

My first novel *The Convictions of John Delahunt* was a fictional account of a true life murderer and Dublin Castle informer, a character I stumbled upon while researching the career of Chief Justice Edward Pennefather, who resided in No. 5. Even bit-part players in that novel such as Professor Lloyd, Dr Moore, and Captain Dickenson, were all, in reality, Fitzwilliam Square inhabitants, plucked from the pages of *Lives Less Ordinary*. Some of Delahunt's memories of childhood were based on the autobiography of A.P. Graves, Robert Graves's father, who grew up in the square in the 1840s, and who features in Chapter 4 of this book.

Abigail Lawless of *The Coroner's Daughter* was a completely fictional character, a young lady sleuth in Regency Dublin, operating at the dawn of forensic science. However, the research for *Lives Less Ordinary* still informed much of her world. The layout of a Georgian house, for instance, with the upstairs downstairs dynamic of family members and servants. The social pursuits of the upper classes, with their salons and promenades and balls. Also, the antagonists of the novel, the evangelical Brethren, were loosely based on the Plymouth Brethren, and their founder John Nelson Darby, who first began meeting in Fitzwilliam Square in the late 1820s.

And so it's particularly pleasing that the choice of *The Coroner's Daughter* for One Dublin One Book 2023 should lead to a new and updated edition of *Lives Less Ordinary*. For one, it has been possible to include new stories only recently uncovered, particularly tales relating to the revolutionary period of Irish history. But also, the setting, the atmosphere, and the characters of my novels can very much be traced to the Georgian houses of Fitzwilliam Square.

Andrew Hughes
September 2023

1

The Setting

Tʜᴇ ʜɪsᴛᴏʀʏ ᴏғ Fɪᴛᴢᴡɪʟʟɪᴀᴍ Sǫᴜᴀʀᴇ begins with a Fitzgerald squire – James Fitzgerald (1722-73), the twentieth Earl of Kildare, subsequently the first Duke of Leinster. In 1745, construction began on his stately Georgian mansion (where the Dáil now sits) built on the very south-eastern edge of Dublin city, in an area dubbed Molesworth's Fields. To walk beyond Kildare House then would involve traipsing the pasture in the adjoining estate of the Viscounts Fitzwilliam. Keeping the meandering route of Gallows Road (now Baggot Street) to your right, you would pass the ruins of Baggotsrath Castle before coming upon Ballsbridge village after an old English mile of countryside.

It was a trend-bucking choice of site for Fitzgerald as at the time the most fashionable developments were occurring north of the river within the Gardiner estates. Luke Gardiner (d. 1755) had commenced construction of Henrietta Street in 1730, and had also developed the northern end of Sackville Street together with its central mall. Fitzgerald supposedly remarked on the prudence of his own site with confidence: 'Wherever I go, fashion will follow me', and time it seems has proved him right. However, the notion that developers skedaddled across the river in the earl's wake is misleading. When Kildare House was completed in 1751, construction of the great squares of north Dublin (Rutland, we'll call it Parnell, and Mountjoy) had not even commenced. Parnell Square would envelop the Lying-in (Rotunda) Hospital and gardens, laid out and developed by Dr. Bartholomew Mosse between 1748 and 1757. Luke Gardiner let the first plots of what is now Parnell

Square east in April 1753 and the square was completed some thirty odd years later. Gardiner's grandson, also Luke (1745-1798), became Baron Mountjoy in 1789 and was the force behind the development of Mountjoy Square, laid out in 1791 with building commenced in 1793. Meanwhile, several other streets and terraces were constructed in and around these set-piece developments north of the river. What this simply demonstrates is that there was life in the Gardiner estate for several decades following Fitzgerald's notion to bring his sphere of influence to the south.

There's no doubt, however, that Fitzgerald's decision spurred the Viscounts Fitzwilliam to emulate the Gardiners and plan the layout of a series of streets and squares on their own holdings. Peter Pearson described the extent of the Fitzwilliam estates which:

> ... ran eastward from Leinster House as far as Blackrock and Ringsend on the shore of Dublin Bay ... included most of the present day Roebuck and Dundrum and ran up to the Dublin mountains, where the family opened a quarry that provided granite for their various building projects.[1]

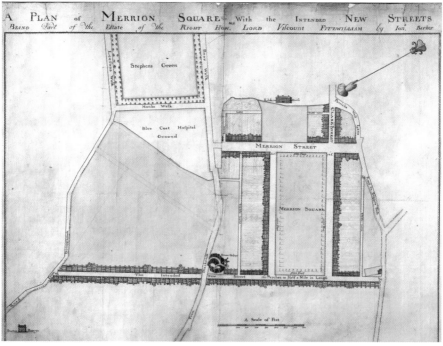

A plan of Merrion Square with intended new streets (Jonathan Baker, 1764)

Plans were first initiated by Richard, sixth Viscount Fitzwilliam of Merrion (1711-1776), who commissioned Jonathan Barker to carry out a series of surveys and preliminary plot outlines in 1762.

A survey of 1764 (see previous page) shows a projected complete layout of Merrion Square together with an intended new street, which would correspond to Fitzwilliam Street and (eventually) the east side of Fitzwilliam Square. As such, the survey is the first indication of plans to develop in this direction. The house designs in the plan are irregular – many taking the older architectural form of the Dutch Billy. They were merely figurative, for a decision had already been taken to build the houses in the uniform fashion and limited scale that we now know as the Georgian style – just as they were then being constructed in Parnell Square, and had already commenced in Merrion Street.

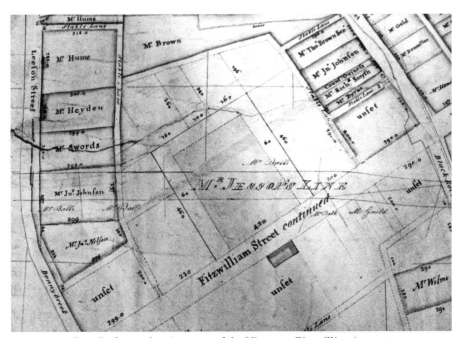

Detail of map showing part of the Viscount Fitzwilliam's estate
(Pat and John Roe, 1789)

Building commenced on the north side of Merrion Square in 1762, but the square would not be completely finished until 1833. In the meantime, another more modest residential square was planned, leased and constructed along the axis of Fitzwilliam Street, between Baggot Street to the north, and Leeson Street to the south. The intended Fitzwilliam Square was first seen laid out in a survey map by Pat and John Roe in 1789.

Mary Bryan quoted the *Dublin Evening Post* from 18 June 1791:

> A new square is planned at the rere of Baggot Street, in which lots are rapidly taken and the buildings are to be immediately commenced. The design is not without elegance and the execution, it is believed, will be correspondent.[2]

The first leases for plots on Fitzwilliam Square were granted by Richard, seventh Viscount Fitzwilliam (1745-1816) in 1791, however building got off to a slow start. An economic slump caused by revolutionary wars in Europe and political unrest at home, culminating in the Act of Union in 1800, meant that only four houses in the new square were constructed in the late eighteenth century. These were built on the north side in 1796 and 1797 and are now No.'s 56 to 59 Fitzwilliam

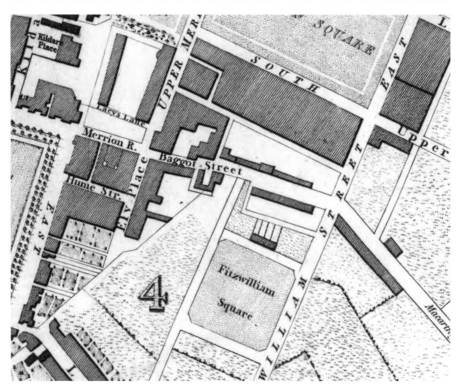

Detail, Plan of the City of Dublin (William Faden, 1797)

Square. This remote outpost of houses was pleasingly captured by William Faden in his 1797 *Plan of the City of Dublin*.

IMAGINE A YOUNG MESSENGER WALKING from the north-east corner of St. Stephen's Green towards Baggot Street in 1797. Soldiers in scarlet coats regard him with suspicion as he shuffles towards the outskirts of a city on the brink of rebellion. But turning right he enters a newly cleared roadway through empty ground. The back of a new row of houses on Leeson Street is visible in the distance, but otherwise the vista is clear to the Dublin mountains. Walking a little further the side elevation of an incongruous terrace of four houses begins to loom on his left. He sees that they front on to roads that outline a square cut through the farmland but eerily bereft of houses. Here and there plots are staked out and range walls built, but otherwise the four houses huddle with their backs to the city. Pausing, he tries to picture the square with houses complete on every side, securely hemming in a central park enclosed by an iron railing and containing trees, shrubs and gravel pathways. But the loneliness of the square's current situation makes that seem unlikely. As he moves on, the door of the third house opens and a young man in military attire hurriedly descends the steps and heads towards the city. The messenger notices that he clutches a bayonet beneath his arm as their paths cross. This is the student Peter Roe, rushing to attend manoeuvres of his Trinity College yeomanry corps, formed to combat the threat of the United Irishmen – but we'll catch up with him in Chapter 6.

Richard, Seventh Viscount Fitzwilliam

The Landlord

Richard, seventh Viscount Fitzwilliam, was born in Richmond, Surrey in 1745. An accomplished draughtsman and harpsichordist, he was educated at Trinity Hall, Cambridge, receiving an MA in 1764. While at college he fell in love with a local barmaid and was determined to marry her. His father, aghast, packed young Richard off on a 'grand tour' of Europe to finish his education in the hopes that he would forget about the girl. Peter Pearson wrote: 'He returned some years later to find her settled down and with her own children and he swore never to marry. The young man instead devoted his energies to music and art.'[3]

During his travels he built up an impressive collection of illuminated manuscripts, paintings and prints. He had succeeded to his father's titles in 1776, and while he made frequent visits to his Irish seat, Mount Merrion, Richard lived mainly at Fitzwilliam House in Surrey, where he curated his large art collection.

Richard, 7th Viscount Fitzwilliam (1745-1816)

The Setting

He was something of a libertine. In Paris in the years before the French Revolution, Richard embarked on a long and scandalous affair with a teenaged Opéra dancer named Marie Anne Bernard, stage name: Mademoiselle Zacharie. Three hundred letters from the French ballerina to the Irish peer survive in the Fitzwilliam Museum in Cambridge, tracing the depth and closeness of their relationship, and revealing that the couple had three children together, a girl who died in infancy, and two boys, Fitz and Bily.

'Oh! Che Boccone!' or 'Oh! What a Mouthful!': 1789 print purporting to show Richard Fitzwilliam in the garb of a clown in the dressing room of Mademoiselle Zacharie

The unmarried Fitzwilliam divided his time between his house in Surrey, his estates in Dublin, and his family in Paris. There are no letters from Zacharie after December 1790, and it's assumed that she died following a bout of ill-health. Likewise, no trace remains of Bily in historical records, so he too may have predeceased his father. Fitz, on the other hand, was alive and well and living in Surrey with his wife and family at the time of Richard's death in 1816. Richard made sure that they were amply provided for in his will.

Having been born out of wedlock, Fitz was not entitled to inherit his father's vast estates, and so it fell to Richard to choose a legitimate heir from his extended family. The story goes that there were two candidates: Charles Wentworth, 5th Earl Fitzwilliam of Wentworth House, and George Augustus Herbert, 11th Earl of Pembroke (Richard's first-cousin once removed). Richard invited both men to his home with a view to forming an opinion as to their character. Tea was served. Young Charles, finding his beverage a little hot, poured the tea into his saucer to cool it down and slurped from the dish. His fate was sealed. Richard later remarked, 'No one who drinks his tea like a washerwoman will be my heir!'[4]

That is why in 1816, George Augustus Herbert Pembroke inherited the streets and squares of his cousin's estates in Dublin. From then on, it was known as the Pembroke Estate.

Richard Fitzwilliam served as the MP for Wilton from 1790 to 1806. He continued his development of Georgian Dublin with an Act for enclosing Merrion Square in 1791, his plans for Fitzwilliam Square, as well as a new church at Booterstown built in 1812 for his Catholic tenants. He died on 4 February 1816 in Bond Street, London, aged 70. Today, he his best known for the bequest of his art works and music library to the University of Cambridge, as well as £100,000 for the establishment of a gallery, now the world-renowned Fitzwilliam Museum.

THE DIFFICULTIES IN BUILDING (in both Merrion Square, Fitzwilliam Square and the adjoining streets) caused severe problems for Richard Fitzwilliam's land agent, Barbara Verschoyle. In Fitzwilliam Square seven of the original leases reverted back to the estate due to rent arrears and the inability to build. One leaseholder wrote to Verschoyle saying, 'eject me if you will, I will be glad to get rid of my bargain'. Verschoyle described the condition of the country in a letter to Lord Fitzwilliam in 1797, expressing sentiments uncannily similar to those in Ireland at the time of writing:

> The situation in the country is truly melancholy – where it will end, God knows. Our bankers have stopped circulating cash which has occasioned great confusion – you may suppose that in all this distress that rents are not getting paid ... the Union is the terror of everyone and I am sorry to say I am sure it will be ... I fear the present buildings will fall into decay or at least not be kept in the style they ought.[5]

Verschoyle's fears proved ultimately unfounded as building recommenced in the first decade of the nineteenth century. The Act of Union in 1800 did lead to an inevitable decline, exaggerated perhaps slightly by Maurice Craig:

> On the last stroke of midnight, December 31, 1800, the gaily caparisoned horses turned into mice, the coaches into pumpkins, the silks and brocades into rags, and Ireland was once again the Cinderella among the nations.[6]

But gradually, as Dublin's peers and gentry relocated to London, members of the 'liberal' professional classes (doctors and lawyers, as well as soldiers and academics) took up residence in the fashionable squares of the Fitzwilliam estate. F.O.C. Meenan wrote, 'the history of the Georgian squares is the history of the professional classes in Dublin'.[7] The houses of Fitzwilliam Square were particularly suited to this influx, having been built at a slightly more modest, and therefore affordable, scale.

Leases were initially acquired by speculators who would erect houses on their own particular plots – adhering to strict building conditions contained within. Another fine survey completed in 1822 by John Roe (see below) named the early leaseholders in Fitzwilliam Square. (The survey was carried out for the eleventh Earl of Pembroke, who inherited the estate after Richard Fitzwilliam's death in 1816. From then on it was known as the Pembroke Estate.)

Among the names visible we see Nathaniel Calwell, a stationer and lottery office keeper at College Green, and Price Blackwood, a lieutenant in the Royal Navy. The south side was developed by the architect firm Henry, Mullins and McMahon and a Wexford merchant named Clement Codd. The unmarked plots were later built on by architect John Vance. The west side was dominated by tradesmen and builders, namely the Dixons, James Doyle and George Gibson. Gibson and Doyle also had plots on the north side together with James Donovan, who operated as a wholesale china and crystal glass broker out of 23 George's Quay. We can also see from the survey that the square is far from complete, despite its late date. The north east section is unbuilt together with most of the south side. The plot adjoining Pembroke Street Upper on the west side is also empty.

The sequence of building on the north side was the most uneven. As noted, the first houses were built there in 1796. All but three houses on the north side were built before 1822, but the row was only completed

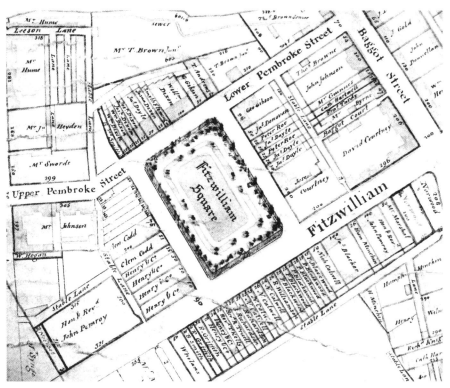

Detail, a map of part of the estate of the Earl of Pembroke (John Roe, 1822)

in 1828. Mary Bryan has shown that building continued in a fairly orderly progression on the other three sides of the square. Houses on the west were constructed between 1807 and 1815; on the east mostly between 1816 and 1822; and on the south between 1823 and 1828.[8] The construction of the south side had the (for some) regrettable effect of closing off the view to the Dublin mountains enjoyed by the houses already in situ. George Newenham Wright described the open-ended square in 1821:

> This beautiful little square is at the south side of the city, not far from [Merrion square]; the flagged walk around it measures 1 fur. 31 per. 4 yds., and that close to the railing is only eight perches less.
>
> The interior is enclosed by an iron-railing, resting on a dwarf wall, and ornamented by lamp-supporters at equal intervals.
>
> The interior area, which is laid out in gravel-walks, shrubberies, and flower-plats, is below the level of the street, and consequently the foot-passenger has a perfect view of the whole garden at one glance. The houses here are not so large as those in Merrion-square, but remarkably well finished, and produce a large rent. Only three sides are erected, and from this circumstance is derived the principal advantage this square possesses; namely, the magnificent mountain view on the south side, which will be shut out if that side be ever completed.[9]

The garden had been created and enclosed by an 1813 act of parliament which charged fourteen commissioners (residents and early leaseholders) with its upkeep. The garden is unique in Dublin as its layout remains unchanged nearly 200 years later.

So in 1828 the square was complete with its sixty-nine houses. There are seventeen houses on each of the east, west and north sides and eighteen on the south. The square shape is compressed to a rectangle because access is restricted to two roads. Fitzwilliam Square West connects Upper and Lower Pembroke Street. Fitzwilliam Square East connects Fitzwilliam Street and Fitzwilliam Place. The north and south sides are book-ended by these main routes which gives the square a sense of enclosure and seclusion. Each house in Fitzwilliam Square seems connected with all the others, lending a far greater sense of community compared to the other Georgian squares in Dublin. This is enhanced by the relationship each house has to the enclosed, and still private, central garden.

Early Reports

BUT CASTING OUR MINDS BACK TO THE first decades of the square we can consider again its frontier location. We noted above the lonely position of the original four houses (No.'s 56-59) seen in Faden's map of 1797. A security feature for two of those first four abodes was an additional fan-shaped railing placed between the front door and the ground floor window – no doubt designed to hamper unauthorised access from thieves and vagabonds lurking in the darkness.

Fan-shaped railing outside No. 57

The square's early proximity to open ground was referred to in a *Freeman's Journal* article dated July 1809, reporting an organised bare-knuckle fist-fight:

> Tuesday morning, in consequence of a dispute which arose on the preceding night between the parties, one Owen Dodd, who is the owner of one of the cars or jingles which ply on the road between Dublin and the Blackrock, and one Dollard a bricklayer, met in a field in the neighbourhood of Fitzwilliam-square to decide the contest in a pugilistic combat, when after a few rounds, shocking to relate, Dollard was killed upon the spot by his antagonist, against whom

informations have been lodged in the Police Divisional Office, Duke-street.[10]

Poor Dollard. As a brick-layer he was probably employed in the construction work on the estate.

Mary Bryan quoted a letter from an early resident, a Miss Charlotte Burgh of what is now No. 42, to a cousin living in Paris in 1814, five years after Dollard's demise:

> Our Landlord died and we found it not the same thing under his successor. We therefore resolved to depart and have got a new house in a new part of Dublin – a very pretty square called Fitzwilliam Square – we have bought it, not hired it, come and look and tell me how you like it.

Bryan commented:

> Fitzwilliam Square at this stage must in reality have been a large busy building site and anything but 'pretty' – except in the eyes of the proud new owner.[11]

By 1827, nearly all the houses on the south side of the square were complete. But their situation was still remote and not particularly safe. Consider this tale of a young shop assistant delivering silk gowns to the daughters of Rev. Truell in No. 15. *The Freeman's Journal* on 5 March 1827 reported:

> Daring Highway Robbery. – On Saturday night, as a servant girl, belonging to Miss Healy, dress maker, of Grafton-street, was passing along the south side of Fitzwilliam-square, between nine and ten o'clock, she was stopped by a low sized man, and a lad, who took from her a box, containing some silk dresses, which she was taking home to the family of Dr. Truell; both the man and the lad were respectably dressed, and had no appearance of persons who could have been suspected of such an offence.[12]

Imagine those scoundrel opportunists preying on the young woman. By their description they could almost be pictured as gentlemen thieves, charming the poor girl as they fleece her, escaping with the swish of a cloak and all as part of some jape. Far more likely they were cold and menacing and the shop girl terrified. One can also imagine the disappointment in the Truell household when the eagerly awaited dresses failed to arrive.

A more positive picture of the square and outlying Dublin suburbs was given by William Makepeace Thackeray in his 1843 *Irish Sketch Book*:

> The entrance to the capital is very handsome. There is no bustle and throng of carriages, as in London; but you pass by numerous rows of neat houses, fronted with gardens, and adorned with all sorts of gay-looking creepers. Pretty market gardens, with trim beds of plants, and shining glass-houses, give the suburbs a riante and cheerful look; and passing under the arch of the railway, we are in the city itself. Hence you come upon several old-fashioned, well-built, airy, stately streets, and through Fitzwilliam Square, a noble place, the garden of which is full of flowers and foliage. The leaves are green, and not black as in similar places in London; the red brick houses tall and handsome.[13]

Lives Less Ordinary

BUT OF COURSE THIS BOOK IS CHIEFLY concerned with the residents of these handsome houses. Members of the learned professions, the military and academia, as well as writers, artists, politicians and the landed gentry. These hundreds of lives provide a cast of characters and hopefully Irish political and social history can be retold through their perspectives. To varying degrees the residents of Fitzwilliam Square had wealth enough to provide the uncommon privilege of expanded horizons: the opportunities given by education and career advancement, and the leisure time for travel and artistic expression. With just a little digging, lives seemingly respectable and humdrum are shown to contain remarkable tales. Take for example Augustine and Emily Barton who married on 12 October 1853. Four days later, Augustine's mother died and he inherited her fine house at No. 23 Fitzwilliam Square South, where the newly married couple immediately took up residence.

A picture of Victorian domesticity, but both bride and groom had intriguing back-stories. This had not been Emily's first marriage. Mrs.

Barton was born Emily Martin on 2 January 1827, daughter of James Martin of Ross, County Galway. Emily's mother, Anne née Higinbotham, later died giving birth to a fifth daughter. Young Emily was raised by her widowed father who was keen to see his daughters married off so he could remarry and beget an heir. In the winter of 1842 fifteen-year-old Emily and her sister Mary were packed off to live with a maternal aunt in Inver, County Antrim. This woman had also married a James Martin, completely unrelated to Emily's father, and he was rector of that small parish. Raymond Brooke takes up the tale:

> During that visit to Inver Rectory the Barklies gave a dinner-party at Inver House, which developed into an informal dance in the drawing-room....The two girls – Emily and Mary – did not dine, but came in afterwards for the dancing. While they were sitting alone in the drawing-room waiting for the diners to come in, two young men, James McCalmont and Hugh McCalmont Cairns [afterwards Lord Chancellor of England] walked into the room. James McCalmont glanced at Emily and made some remark to Cairns, which the girls did not catch, but which seemed to amuse him [James later told Emily he whispered he at once intended to marry her]. As soon as possible, James McCalmont had himself introduced and of course Emily Martin danced with him.[14]

Two days later, McCalmont sent a letter to the rectory saying he wished to propose marriage to Emily, causing great consternation. Emily was surprised a man would wish to marry a girl after one meeting and apparently 'treated the whole affair as a great joke'. Her aunt and uncle were shocked at her levity and wrote to her father in Galway informing him of the proposal, and the manner in which it was entertained. Martin immediately travelled from Galway and severely insisted that Emily accept McCalmont's offer. Emily finally consented and was brought back to Ross to await the ceremony.

However, while there she met John Burke, a soldier in the 'The Buffs' (East Kent Regiment). He fell in love with Emily and persuaded the reluctant bride-to-be to elope with him instead.

All arrangements were made, as to the date and meeting place, and a message was to be sent at the last moment to Emily telling her the exact hour at which she was to meet Burke. John sent the message by an old servant who somehow found out what it was all about and, fearing the wrath that would fall on his head afterwards, took it to John Burke's mother. She immediately told the Martins what was hatching.

James Martin flew into a rage with his daughter who retaliated by saying nothing would now induce her to marry James McCalmont.

Her father said he would soon bring her to reason, and following the practice of the day, locked her up in her room where she was fed on bread and water. The siege went on for some time.

Caricature of Hugh McCalmont Cairns

Emily only relented when an appeal was made to her by her beloved grandfather Robert. She insisted on being allowed to tell McCalmont the whole story but he maintained that he wished to marry her. The wedding took place on 27 April 1843, the bride and groom setting off on their wedding tour in a beautiful phaeton, 'the bride literally howling'.

A beginning worthy of some romantic novel, but the marriage was ultimately a happy one. When James McCalmont died suddenly six years later Emily was left with two small boys. She took a house in Dublin and eventually met with Augustine Barton.

Augustine was born in 1814 to Dunbar Barton who had come into possession of Rochestown House, County Tipperary through his wife. Augustine was a sickly young man and spent time in the warmer climates of the Mediterranean and eventually Australia where his health improved. He got his hands on a portion of £10,000 which had been set aside for his inheritance and invested it all in real estate.

> [He] continually wrote home to his father and elder brother imploring them to send him out money which he could put out at ten, twelve and even more per cent 'and safe as the Bank of England'.

Reckless lending was as ill-judged then as it is now and it seems he lost it all.

> He always said that at one time he owned all the land on which Melbourne was afterwards built, but he could not hold on, and told [his daughters] – 'If everything had gone right with me, you two would be the richest heiresses in Ireland to-day'.

> However that might have been, he came home across Canada, and when he got to Ireland, his possessions consisted of a case of Australian butterflies, a piece of gold quartz in a crystal locket which he wore on his watch-chain, and the full outfit of a Red Indian Brave. This last he acquired in Canada, and wearing it at a fancy dress ball in Dublin he completely captivated Mrs James McCalmont who consented to become Mrs Augustine Barton.

So this was the newly married couple who took up residence in No. 23 Fitzwilliam Square in October 1853. Augustine secured a position as registrar in the Four Courts and was quite comfortably off. Emily was able to entertain guests lavishly in the house and had a great reputation as a witty conversationalist. Perfectly respectable and conventional, but I wonder how many neighbours knew of their curious histories.

One of the Barton daughters, Rose, was a well-known townscape painter and we shall look at her career in Chapter 5. Augustine died in 1874 and in later life Emily divided her time between London, Scotland and Antrim (her sister had married one of the Barklies, hosts of that fateful party in 1842). However she spent each winter 'season' back in Dublin. A Fitzwilliam Square cabman recalled her fondness for card playing, and an incident that took place on the night of the 'Big Wind', a great storm that swept across Ireland on the night of 26 February 1903:

> Well, that night, I had her over the other side of the Square, playin' cards, and she came out and says she, 'Farrell', says she 'go back home and tell Kate to give you me glasses, off the table in me room. I'm after losing five pounds and I don't want to lose any more'. So I got the glasses and when she came back out to go home she said 'I'm after winnin' back me fiver and a bit more, for when I had me glasses I could see the cards'. And the wind blew th'ould cab around the Square and I took her out of it in me arms and the wind blew the two of us down the Square and I had Hell's delight to get her into the house.

Emily (Martin McCalmont) Barton died in 1907.

Drawing Rooms

THROUGHOUT THE NINETEENTH CENTURY Fitzwilliam Square was at its busiest during the Dublin Castle Season, which began with an audience and reception with the Lord Lieutenant, the Queen's representative, in the first week of February and ended with the St. Patrick's Ball on March 17. This was also when young aristocratic women who had come of age were presented at court. Thackeray was very contemptuous of the whole business (and one finds it hard to disagree):

> There is no aristocracy in Dublin. Its magistrates are tradesmen.... Brass plates are their titles of honour, and they live by their boluses or briefs. What call have these worthy people to be dangling and grinning at lord lieutenants' levees, and playing sham aristocracy before a sham sovereign? Oh, that old humbug of a castle! It is the greatest sham of all the shams in Ireland.[15]

Charles Dickens thought the court gave the city a much needed social boost, but he was aware of Thackeray's opinion. Dickens wrote:

> At the proper time in the 'season' the show begins, the grand rooms are thrown open, the Viceroy and the Vicereine are ready to see their subjects, to feast them in their halls. Then Irish paterfamilias, delighting in his beeves and his fields,

with a sigh gives way. Mamma and the three daughters (they are like mothers and daughters everywhere else) have joined to persuade and intimidate. And paterfamilias, like his kind elsewhere, is not strong enough to withstand such pressure. He is reminded of what his duty is to his 'girls,' under the just penalty of being stigmatised as a 'brute.' And thus, when the season sets in, the country families come flocking up, and take houses in 'Fitzwilliam-street' and 'Fitzwilliam-square,' in 'Pembroke-place,' and other genteel and genteelly-named localities.

We may suppose it to be the beginning of the season, and the night of the first drawing-room; for levees and drawing-rooms have been going on here for centuries; and, with a sensible eye to picturesque effect, the drawing-rooms are always held at night. Towards ten o'clock carriages are converging to the little hill from half-a-dozen different points, and form into one line; inside of which, fluttering young girls, all trains and lappets, are folded up somehow. A crowd is at the gates, laughing, jesting, criticising, half satirically, but mostly with respect, the charms that pass them by.[16]

We can recall paterfamilias Rev. Truell of No. 15 ordering silk dresses for his daughters from a Grafton Street boutique, only for the gowns to be carried off as booty. A travelogue writer in 1843 briefly recalled staying with friends in Fitzwilliam Square, arriving after an exhausting journey into a household preparing for one such castle reception:

> On our arrival in Fitzwilliam-square, we found our friends preparing to attend a drawing-room at the Castle, and after having tried to smile for a few minutes at the contrast between our woe-begone appearance, and their gay courtly array, we gladly retired to rest, and hailed the coming darkness that called – 'Earth's weary children to repose'.[17]

The equivalent of a 'best dressed' list, which we might read following some gaudy awards ceremony, appeared in the *Freeman's Journal* following a Dublin Castle drawing room in April 1828, the year of the square's completion. Several Fitzwilliam Square damsels and matrons were described in their finery:

Mrs Pittar, [No. 62] Fitzwilliam Square – An extremely elegant dress of pearl white Piedmont satin, richly trimmed in bouillons of Normandy blond lace, over a slip of pearl white ducape [stout silk fabric]; train of rich satin, corresponding with the corsage of the dress, also elegantly trimmed with Normandy lace. Head dress, diamonds, rich real blond lappets, and ostrich feathers.

Miss Waring [her niece], Fitzwilliam Square – A beautiful dress of pearl white ducape gauze, with pearl white satin body, richly trimmed in blond lace; train of pearl white ducape, tastefully ornamented with satin noeuds, edged with blond. Head dress, feathers, pearls, and topazes, with rich blond lappets ...

Mrs Purcell, [No. 27] Fitzwilliam Square – Rich black satin dress, fully trimmed with real blond lace; train of cerise rep des Indes edged with blond. Head dress, superb turban of gold lama, pearls and feathers.

Miss Purcell – Rich dress of pink ossis gauze, over pink satin slip, trimmed with tulle and blond lace; train of rich figured white gros royale. Ornaments, rich suit of aquamarine in gold, lappets and feathers.

Miss M Purcell – Dress of richly figured white ducape, tastefully trimmed with satin, tulle and blonde; train of superb pink marabout gauze ducape, edged with blond lace. Head dress, pink topazes and ornaments to correspond, feathers and lappets.[18]

All very understated. It appears blond lace trim was in. This author was going to include only a couple of those descriptions, but then it occurred to him that those omitted would have been sorely disappointed, if they could know. Indeed, the *Freeman's Journal* article ended with the following disclaimer: 'Ladies whose Dresses are omitted, must blame their Milliners, not us.'

Of course, the square played host to less formal gatherings all year round: salons and afternoons, balls and dinner parties. The Clarkes of Graiguenoe Park, County Tipperary took up residence in No. 11 Fitzwilliam Square on the east side in 1864, the year of their marriage. Marshal

Neville Clarke was described in a pamphlet entitled *The Remarkable Mr Clarke*:

> Marshal, the only son, on his marriage was a strikingly handsome man of 37, firm but delicate features and an intellectual forehead. Educated at Kilkenny College and T.C.D. (fellow commoner) he was called to the Irish Bar and bought a big house, No.11 Fitzwilliam Square. He did not do a great deal in the legal way, but kept a coachman and carriages, gave dinner parties, was a member of the Kildare Street Club; and had a large circle of friends.[19]

Marshal Neville Clarke of No. 11

Marshal's wife was Mary, née Pearson, from Cheltenham. On 28 March 1873, she wrote to her parents from No. 11, describing the typically Victorian social engagements within the house:

> We have charming weather at last. The easterly winds have departed for a season and my cough has gone with them. We were at a very pleasant tea at Lady King's yesterday and are going to another at Lady Nithervilles this afternoon. The Henry Shakerleys are quartered in Dublin. We have exchanged visits and I asked them to our first dinner party next week, they were pre-engaged, the only people who were so. On the 1st we expect the Granby Burkes, Laws, Boyles, Hemphills, Swiftes, Quinans, Mrs Atkinson, Mr Kenniens (an elderly bachelor of good fortune and family), Capt Sandes (ditto but not so old), Mr Codd the best amateur singer in Dublin and Mr Thompson, an agreeably rich and slightly musical young man. On the 3rd we expect Sir Arthur Phayre, Count d'Altore who professes the combined attractions of being a Tipperary squire and a Count of the Holy Roman Empire, Colonel Meadow Taylor and daughters, Mr and Mrs Ormsby, the Galweys, Moore Tabershams, and Mr Walsh. On the 4th we dine with the Jessops and on the 5th Marshal goes to Graiguenoe. Such is our programme for next week.

Mary Clarke née Pearson of No. 11

Consider the houses hosting dinner parties as described above. Guests arriving by carriage and greeted in the front parlour; a long dining table laden with the finest fare and dinnerware; the basement abuzz with the preparation of food and the logistics of service; then entertainment and conversation in front of open fires on the first floor piano nobile. We'll meet the Clarkes again in Chapter 6 when we follow the fortunes of their soldier sons.

Upstairs Downstairs

Naturally, not all Fitzwilliam Square residents would have had the time, money or inclination to host such engagements. Also, considering the way of life in the square as a whole, there were the parallel worlds of the maids, cooks, butlers, coachmen, tutors and governesses residing in the smaller rooms of the upper floors and the basement. The census returns of 1901 and 1911 allow us to see the proportion of residents in the square who were principal owners as opposed to domestic servants and their respective families. They also demonstrate the religious make-up of the denizens. Let's look in detail at the 1901 census as being most analogous with the preceding Victorian era.

Counting up each return we find there were 499 souls living in Fitzwilliam Square on 31 March 1901 – quite a community. Of those, 300 were Protestants (how precise) and 199 Roman Catholic, perhaps a larger proportion than would be imagined. However, only 21 of those Catholics were principal house owners and their families. On the other hand, there were 175 Catholic domestic servants, coachmen, caretakers and their family members. The remaining few RCs were visitors at the time of the census. Of the 300 Protestant residents, 108 were domestic servants (or coachmen or caretakers) and their families. Overall, the principal residents of the square were outnumbered by their staff 283 to 216, which hopefully was an incentive to treat them well.

Coachmen would have resided in rooms above the stables within the mews at the rear of the houses adjacent to the stable-lanes. What might be a surprise, considering our modern estimation of these genteel locations, was that livestock was also kept in some of those back gardens. Around Christmas 1878 there was an outbreak of typhoid in Fitzwilliam Square and outlying districts due to the common use of milk from an infected Dublin dairy. Dr. C.A. Cameron carried out a survey of the square in order to determine where each household sourced its milk. He found that four houses on the square got their supply from the dairy in question, and only those houses suffered with cases of the sickness (including one male servant who died at Baggot Street Hospital on 10 January 1879). However, he also noted that three houses on the square got their milk from cows kept on the premises. If there were cows, why not pigs and hens? The keeping of livestock may not have been pervasive, but it adds a rustic quality to our perceptions of the square as a whole which is quite pleasing.

As an aside, the Clarke family of No. 11, noted above, were one of those affected by the outbreak. In the week after Christmas 1878 three children and one housemaid began showing symptoms of fever. The maid was packed off to hospital. The three children were attended to by Dr. Moore, who lived across the square in No. 40, and who diagnosed all four cases as undoubtedly typhoid. Marshal Clarke informed the doctor that the maid and stricken children had all drunk the infected milk uncooked daily. The remainder of the household, including two other children, only used the tainted milk to colour their tea, and so escaped infection. Everyone in the house made a full recovery, including the maid.

Parables of the Wicked Servant

UNFORTUNATELY, TALES INVOLVING THE lives of the domestic servants tend only to have been reported when they did something immoral or illegal, allowing newspapers to tut at their apparent corruptness and ingratitude. The alleged crimes ranged in seriousness from petty larceny to attempts at murder. So let's take a look, beginning with the more innocuous.

In 1878, Charles Kelly QC, a county court judge, was residing in No. 34, the second to last house on the south side. When Mr. Kelly had to travel to the west of Ireland on business, he hired John O'Connell, an ex-member of the Dublin Metropolitan Police, and his wife Lucy to look after the house. An *Irish Times* article reported on his choice:

> Mr Charles Kelly, Queen's Counsel, of Fitzwilliam-square, decided, for the better security of his goods and chattels while he himself was out of town, to put a caretaker in his house. He selected – one would have thought prudently enough – an ex-police constable, who, with his wife, was left in possession. When Mr Kelly returned to town he found that his confidence had been grossly abused. A large quantity of valuable property, including plate, window curtains, and bed-covering, had been removed, and of the ex-policeman there was no account.[20]

The items were recovered from pawnbrokers throughout the city, Sebastian Dangerfield as caretaker. Judge Kelly had yet more misfortune with caretakers in 1887. He was again absent from Dublin when on 15 July a fire broke out in No. 34 in 'a lady's bedroom, a governess's bedroom, and servants' bedrooms' on the upper floors. A total of £400 worth of damage was done. A report stated:

> An extraordinary circumstance in connection with the occurrence is the mystery as to its origin. The bedrooms in question were locked up, and neither the man in charge nor his daughter nor anybody else approached them. The men of the brigade and the police appear at a loss to form a theory as to the cause of the fire.[21]

Whenever Mr. Kelly was subsequently abroad in the country he must have returned to Fitzwilliam Square each time with some trepidation.

Crimes of a far more serious nature involving Fitzwilliam Square servants were reported in 1862 and 1878. The first story appeared in the *Freeman's Journal* on 16 July:

> Desperate Attempt At Murder –
>
> Yesterday morning, between seven and eight o'clock, a man named Norton Haugh [he was actually Martin Hough], alias

> O'Leary, a servant in the house of 62, Fitzwilliam-square
> North, attempted to murder a young woman named Maria
> Mitcham, a servant in the employment of Dr Athill, 11, Up-
> per Merrion-street, by cutting her throat with a razor.[22]

Hough, under the name O'Leary, had for some time 'been paying his addresses' to Mitcham, who it seems had agreed to marry him pending her mother's approval. This was not forthcoming. The mother had not been impressed with Hough's character, which turned out to be a shrewd assessment. Three days before the attack Maria wrote him a letter, saying she had to break off the engagement. The envelope contained the ring.

That morning he followed her to the residence of Dr. Athill's coachman, a man named Patrick Neill, in Lacy's Lane off Merrion Street. In a final stab, Hough beseeched Maria to elope with him but she refused. She had discovered that he had courted her under an assumed name and became contemptuous, saying he had no home to take her to, and that he should buy clothes, 'as she had never seen a change of clothes on him yet'. The coachman Neill met Hough in the stairwell and commiserated, saying he was a young man and would soon settle. The men shook hands and Neill went outside, but Hough returned to the chamber. Maria was stooped over the bed of a sick child and Hough locked the door. Maria later testified at his trial:

> As I was stooping over the child the prisoner caught me by
> the back hair and drew a razor across my throat; I called out
> 'O'Leary;' the prisoner then tripped me up; I fell and the
> prisoner still cut my throat kneeling on my body; I took the
> razor out of his hand and flung it away some distance.[23]

Maria's screams alerted Neill who rushed back up and tried to break down the door of his room. Hough himself unlocked the door, and then went back to kneel over his bloody victim. Neill surveyed the scene and said, 'If you strike her again I won't let you up'. Hough stood up and opened out his hands. 'Look at my hands with blood. I have put her from having another man, so you may put up the gallows and hang me.' Neill replied angrily, 'I will hang you, you rascal', and dragged Hough into custody.

Both Neill and Mitcham worked for Dr. Athill of Merrion Street. He attended the unfortunate girl at the scene, but 'she was so dreadfully mangled that I found it impossible to do anything for her'. Maria suffered severe slashes to her neck and forehead and a report the day after the incident said that 'the poor creature's hands are also frightfully cut, caused, no doubt, by her attempts to save herself from the murderous onslaught'. However she survived the ordeal and was a witness at Hough's trial that October.

Hough's employer at the time was the wife of Conolly McCausland Lecky from Derry. The Lecky's lived in No. 62 Fitzwilliam Square from 1849 to 1866. During the trial Hough was described as a good servant, but a former employer described some disquieting habits. He said, 'I observed that the prisoner was very flighty in manner. I frequently saw him walk up the garden and stop suddenly, and then turn back.' Also, 'I have known him go up to the parlour and drawing-room, stare deliberately at those present, and go out'. Hough's defence of homicidal monomania was discounted and he was found guilty of 'intent to do grievous bodily harm, and to maim the prosecutrix'. He was sentenced to penal servitude for life.

A murderous attack that took place within Fitzwilliam Square itself occurred in the stables of No. 21 on the south side in April 1878. The incident was a seemingly random and unprovoked assault on the coachman by one of the stable boys employed by Sir Gilbert King (1812-1895), third baronet of Charlestown, County Roscommon. The Kings were long-term residents of No. 21, moving there in 1864 (Lady King was one of the neighbours mentioned in Mary Clarke's letter from No. 11, quoted above). In this incident the attacker immediately attempted to take his own life as well. *The Irish Times* reported:

> On Saturday morning the residence of Sir Gilbert King, 21 Fitzwilliam Square south, was the scene of a murderous outrage and a desperate attempt at suicide. About half past eight o'clock two of the servants – a coachman named Joseph Turner and a stable boy named [Patrick] Connor – were engaged in the stable attached to their master's house, when, as far as at present can be learned, Connor suddenly seized a long triangular shaped piece of rough wood, [in later reports

the weapon was found to be a pitchfork] and violently struck Turner with it on the left side of the head, seriously fracturing the skull. The wounded man fell to the ground insensible. The stable boy then, it is supposed overwhelmed with remorse for the seemingly fatal injury he had inflicted, drew a gardener's horn hafted knife from his pocket, opened one of the blades, and plunged it into his own throat, inflicting a terrible gash. Both men bled profusely, and the straw on the floor of the stable was in a few minutes covered in blood.[24]

One of the sons in No. 21, Hosias Rowley King, was awakened by Turner's groans when he partially regained consciousness. He called from his window to the prostrate Turner who cried out, 'Pat has killed me!' King went down to the stables and sent for the police. Turner was brought into the house and from there conveyed to the City of Dublin Hospital in Baggot Street. It seems Connor was left lying in the straw for some time, face down and moaning now and then. It strikes one as odd that he would be so disregarded as it could not have been immediately clear how he had come by his injuries. A Dr. Butcher was driving by and he attended Connor when informed of the attack by onlookers. He managed to staunch the blood from the self-inflicted wounds and accompanied Connor's stretcher to the hospital where his victim had preceded him. The paper tried to discern a motive for the attack:

> No cause can at present with any degree of certainty be assigned for the attempted murder, as the men, both natives of County Roscommon, were known to have been generally on friendly terms. However, it is stated that Connor lately had in some measure betrayed symptoms of aberration of intellect, and it is believed that on the morning of the lamentable occurrence some ill-feeling had arisen between the men resulting in a quarrel.

At a future hearing Turner was asked how he had got on with his attacker in general:

> Like two brothers, until he struck me the blow. On coming to my senses I saw the prisoner dimly in the corner of the stall, but could not tell what he was doing. On the morning in ques-

tion I noticed a very wild look about the prisoner, and made a remark to himself to that effect, but he laughed at me.[25]

Whatever drove young Connor to carry out such a brutal assault? The attempt at suicide would suggest a complete mental breakdown, rather than an opportunistic and premeditated attack fuelled by some long-nursed resentment. Indeed, a jury found that Connor was of unsound mind and he was ordered to be detained during the pleasure of the Lord Lieutenant.

The grim history of No. 21 Fitzwilliam Square continued with another tragic case in 1927. At this point the house belonged to Lady Louise King, widow of the fourth baronet Sir Gilbert King (1846-1920). In May 1927, the household butler, 27-year-old Edward Vaughan, took his own life in No. 21 by putting his head in a gas oven. Lady King gave evidence at an inquest.

> Lady Louise King stated that about the beginning of the present month Vaughan complained of being ill, but after staying with his parents for ten days returned, and continued his work as usual. On last Tuesday morning he again complained of being unwell. He had his meals in bed and was told that members of the family were going out for the evening. When they returned at about 10.00 p.m. they found him lying with his head in the gas stove in the kitchen [the gas being fully turned on and the doors and windows of the kitchen closed]. The doctor and police were immediately notified.... He was a strong man and a good servant.[26]

How remarkable that these last two macabre incidents would occur in the same house and involve servants employed by the same family. It would seem of all the houses on Fitzwilliam Square, No. 21 has the most chilling past.

The preceding has hardly been a catalogue of blissful domestic service, but as mentioned earlier, only stories involving the wrongdoing or misfortune of Fitzwilliam Square staff tended to be those recorded, at least in the newspapers. Of course, there must have been countless examples of happy relationships between house owners and trusted staff members. Children in particular would have had very close bonds with nannies and governesses. In Chapter 5 we shall look at the Jellett household in No. 36, in particular the career of artist Mainie Jellett. But it is cited now as an example, for that household contained a nanny, called Nannie Skerritt, who was a mainstay of the house for several decades and much beloved.

Fitzwilliam Square Women

LOOKING AT JELLETT'S CAREER WILL ALSO be welcome in regards highlighting the achievements of Fitzwilliam Square women. Much of the book is concerned with the chauvinistic worlds of nineteenth century political, legal and military affairs, so it will be a respite to examine the square's women artists: Rose Barton, Mary Kate Benson, Jellett, Kitty Wilmer O'Brien and Norah McGuinness. Other women prominent in the book include Lady Branden of No. 3, whose affair with Viscount Melbourne scandalised Dublin; Margaret McGarry of No. 5, who operated a safe-house for members of the Dáil and their associates on the run during the War of Independence; and Emma Naher, a Swiss immigrant who ran the Swiss Private Hotel at No. 34, despite being mentally and financially undermined by the destructive presence of her husband. No. 21 (our own particular house of horrors) was owned by Captain William French of French Park House, County Roscommon in the 1840s. His daughter was Charlotte Despard (1844-1939), a renowned suffragist and Sinn Féin activist, though she grew up in Kent and had no real association with the square. Other residents of the square were rather more of a hindrance to the advancement of women. The following was the report on a meeting of the National League for Opposing Woman Suffrage, held in No. 13 Fitzwilliam Square in January 1911:

> A very successful drawing-room meeting in connection with this League was held on Tuesday, at 13 Fitzwilliam Square, the residence of Mr G.C. May. The meeting was largely attended.... Mrs A.E. Murray pointed out that adult suffrage must be the inevitable result of extending the Parliamentary franchise to women. She also spoke on woman's position under man-made laws as the facts exist, as they are often misrepresented by many suffragists...The Secre-

tary, Miss Morton emphasised two evils likely to follow the giving of votes to woman – first the injurious effect on themselves by placing on them new responsibilities, and secondly the depreciation in the validity of the law likely to follow female legislation.[27]

After 1915, No. 35 was a residence house for Alexandra College and a boarding school for girls run by a Miss Esther Fletcher, which seems very evocative of Miss Brodie in her prime. Such a house no doubt contained its own dramas, intrigues and cliques, which all add to the character of the square. Having just spoken of remarkable women, one of the 'Fletcher set', a young boarder at No. 35, was Fay Taylour (1904-1983), who was later known as 'Flying Fay'. She was an expert motorcyclist, a champion speedway racer throughout the 1920s and motorcar racer after 1931. And just to stretch the Miss Brodie analogies, Taylour was interned throughout the Second World War because of her association with the British Union of Fascists.

Fay Taylour, racing at Brooklands, 1938

Neighbourhood Watch

THE EXCLUSIVELY RESIDENTIAL CHARACTER of Fitzwilliam Square was waning at the start of the twentieth century. There was an inevitable influx of flats and rented rooms, guesthouses and hotels, doctors' consulting rooms and other offices. Throughout the century, Fitzwilliam Square flat dwellers were an eclectic bunch, including W.B. Yeats, Orson Welles and Malcolm MacArthur. The practice of converting certain houses into flats in Fitzwilliam Square led to a remarkable case heard in the Court of Chancery in August 1913. John Johnston Cooney of No. 42 Fitzwilliam Square was the owner of a number of properties in the neighbourhood and spent considerable sums converting them into flats, including No. 25 Fitzwilliam Square South. At the beginning of February a young lady introducing herself as May Terry, daughter of Charles Terry, well-known manager of the Theatre Royal, approached Mrs. Cooney with a view to renting one of these flats. Mrs. Cooney was charmed by the girl and on 19 February she met with Mr. Terry and an agreement to rent the top flat of No. 25 was signed. Mrs. Cooney suggested May should witness the agreement. May turned to Charles and asked, 'How will I sign it?', and he replied, 'Write your usual signature, May Terry.'

However in the following months Mr. and Mrs. Cooney became concerned at rumours surrounding the goings on at No. 25. It appeared that at various times Mr. Terry had introduced May as his niece, then his housekeeper, and finally it was discovered May and her sister were in fact barmaids at the Theatre Royal and of no relation to Mr. Terry whatsoever. Cooney sought an order of court rescinding the agreement on the grounds of fraud and misrepresentation and also sued for damages.

Mr. Terry's defence argued that although May's signature was a false representation, crucially, it was not a fraudulent one. They said in no wise had Mr. Cooney suffered harm, financial or otherwise, from the agreement; that Mr. Terry had pretended May was his daughter simply to protect the girl's reputation and 'stop tongues wagging'. Leaving the plausibility of that to one side, it fell to Mr. Cooney and his team to prove that improper relations had occurred in No. 25 between Terry, a married man, and this lady, which might have damaged Cooney's reputation and the value of the flat in subsequent lettings. To achieve this Mr. Cooney admitted to a remarkable investigation that he took upon himself. He unblushingly testified to spying on the supposed adulterers, audaciously atop a ladder at the rear of the house. He was examined by his own counsel:

He added that on the 23rd or 24th March he received some information, in consequence of which he watched three nights
at the back of the house. There was a contractor's ladder there.
About 12.30 at night he went up the ladder. He saw Mr and
Miss Terry enter the bedroom of the flat. Witness said Mr
Terry and the lady occupied the same bed. He saw that occurring on three nights. Witness then went to his solicitor.[28]

One would wonder what stayed him from going to the solicitor
after the first night.

Naturally, defence counsel were derisive of this supposed evidence,
questioning the character of Mr. Cooney, asking what manner of gentleman would admit to such voyeurism. Mr. Terry completely denied
that he shared a bed with May, but in any case his team argued that it
would have been impossible to view the bedroom from where Cooney
said he placed the ladder. He would have found himself between two
windows, they claimed, 7 feet and 16 inches apart. Defence counsel
Gibson remarked:

> Mr Cooney might possibly be as good an acrobat on the
> ladder as he had shown himself to be in the witness box in
> regard to facts.

Cooney was re-examined and was adamant the window was only
20 inches distant from the top of the ladder. He turned to the judge,
'Your Lordship can come and inspect it yourself,' which caused some
mirth in the courtroom. Even Cooney's own counsel seemed to mock
him when he interjected, 'There would be no attraction now,' to much
laughter.

Mr. Gibson had great fun at Cooney's expense when summing up
for his client, Mr. Terry:

> Mr Cooney must be one of the most extraordinary Peeping
> Toms of the century. They had not been long in the flat un-
> til Cooney said he developed suspicions, and, according to
> his own tale, in those cold winter nights in March, encamp-
> ed himself for several nights in the garden of 25 Fitzwilliam
> Square ... his patience was rewarded. He left the garden,
> got into the house, crept up the stairs, and got on the top of

the return lead roof, where there was a ladder. He crawled up the ladder, and with an acrobatic ability that would do credit to a politician, he leant out and watched what was, he said, going on in the bedroom between Mr Terry and this lady. Why, unless he had the eyes of a gimlet he could not have seen into the room from the ladder. The whole story told by the plaintiff was so saturated with improbability that no Court, not even a Divorce Court, would believe it.

In giving his verdict, Justice Barton stated that if the case had simply been a rescission of contract there would have been no difficulty. He found that the misrepresentation in the signing of the contract was material, and the plaintiff was entitled to have it nullified. He said that very unsavoury elements had been introduced to the proceedings but he found there was no evidence that any damage had accrued to Mr. Cooney from Mr. Terry's tenancy. He accordingly made an order rescinding the contract but he awarded no damages to the plaintiff, nor would he allow Cooney any costs of the action. Thus concluded that sordid little tale. We shall examine other cases of scandals and scoundrels in Fitzwilliam Square in Chapter 3.

So THAT'S OUR SETTING. SIXTY-NINE houses, four corners of Georgian Dublin but just one address. Scope enough for some remarkable tales and extraordinary lives. Homes that displayed at times salubrious, at times shabby, grandeur provide a backdrop for drawing room intrigue, revelry and temperance, devilry and romance; the abandon of artistic expression and the restraint of social convention; residents loyal and seditious, doctors medical and religious and gentlemen who attained the highest offices in legal, political and military circles. We'll endeavour to follow them all, so follow me dear reader, into Fitzwilliam Square.

Endnotes

1. Peter Pearson, *The Heart of Dublin*, p. 312.

2. Mary Bryan, *The Georgian Squares of Dublin*, p. 91.

3. Peter Pearson, Between the Mountains and the Sea (1998), p. 12.

4. Ibid.

5. Mary Bryan, *Fitzwilliam Square, Dublin* thesis. Vol., 1, p. 22.

6. Maurice Craig, *Dublin 1660-1860*, p. 259.

7 F.O.C. Meenan, 'The Georgian Squares of Dublin and the Professions', in *Studies: An Irish Quarterly Review,* Vol. 58, No. 232 (Winter, 1969), p. 407.

8 Bryan, *Georgian Squares of Dublin*, p. 92.

9 George N. Wright, *An Historical Guide to Ancient and Modern Dublin*, p. 262.

10. *The Freeman's Journal*, 27 July 1809.

11. Bryan, *Georgian Squares of Dublin*, p. 91.

12. *The Freeman's Journal*, 5 March 1827.

13. W.M. Thackeray, *The Irish Sketch Book of 1842*, p. 5.

14. The following passages regarding the Bartons of No. 23 are taken from Richard Brooke's *The Brimming River*, pp. 64-85.

15. Thackeray, *Irish Sketch Book*, p. 339.

16. Charles Dickens, *All the Year Round, Vol. 15*, p. 462.

17. Frances S. Parker, *Irish Scenes Eighteen Years Ago* (1847), p. 2.

18. *The Freeman's Journal*, 18 April 1828.

19. Ralph Lionel Clarke, 'The Remarkable Mr Clarke', www.marshalclarke.com.

20. *The Irish Times*, 4 October 1878.

21. *The Irish Times*, 16 July 1887.

22. *The Freeman's Journal*, 16 July 1862.

23. This and subsequent testimony taken from a report in *The Freeman's Journal*, 29 October 1862.

24. *The Irish Times*, 8 April 1878.

25. Ibid., 10 May 1878.

26. Ibid., 20 May 1927.

27. Ibid., 19 January 1911.

28. This and subsequent testimony taken from *The Irish Times* reports on 31 July and 1 August 1913.

2

Law and Order

$\mathbf{F}$ROM ADVOCATES TO MAGISTRATES, LAW clerks to lord chief justices, the houses of Fitzwilliam Square have forever attracted members of the legal profession. The elegance of the homes and cachet of the address proved ideal for these emergent middle class professionals after the Act of Union. Indeed, if one was to stroll around the square today, the brass name plaques of solicitors' offices would still outnumber those of any other. The sense of prestige is conveyed concisely by a character in Morgan Llewelyn's *1916: A Novel of the Irish Rebellion*:

> ... then the name and address scrawled below: 'Robert H. Beauchamp, solicitor, 25 Fitzwilliam Square South.' He gave a low whistle. 'Very posh.'[1]

Since the barrister Edward Carroll occupied No. 59 by deed dated 24 October 1797 (one of the first four houses to be built on the square), the buildings have generally evolved from being primarily places of abode for lawyers to places of business for law firms. However, we know of at least one early example of a home on the square containing a legal office, that of the solicitor Thomas Leland who occupied No. 47 from 1811 to around 1837 (it seems that legal practice didn't qualify as an 'offensive or noisy trade, business or profession', which were barred by the terms of the lease).

The reputation of an employee rather than the practice has endured longer. The poet James Clarence Mangan worked as a law clerk and scrivener in Leland's Fitzwilliam Square offices from 1829. At this point he was 26 years old and had already completed his apprenticeship in Kendrick's of York Street, and had worked for four years for Matthew Franks, solicitor, in Merrion Square. His tortuous life was vividly described by Louise Imogen Guiney in her introduction to *James Clarence Mangan: His Selected Poems* (1897):

> Mangan's is such a memory, captive and overborne. It may be unjust to lend him the epitaph of defeat, for he never strove at all. One can think of no other, in the long disastrous annals of English literature, cursed with so monotonous a misery, so much hopelessness and stagnant grief. He had no public; he was poor, infirm, homeless, loveless; travel and adventure were cut off from him, and he had no minor risks to run; the cruel necessities of labour sapped his dreams from a boy; morbid fancies mastered him as the rider masters his horse; the demon of opium, then the demon of alcohol, pulled him under, body and soul, despite a persistent and heart-breaking struggle, and he perished ignobly in his prime.[2]

The tormented soul of the poet was ill-suited for the drudgery of his reluctant vocation, working daily 'in close air and among vulgar associates, so tortured in every sentient fibre of his being that he affirmed nothing but a special Providence preserved him from suicide'. Mangan himself would later wonder at the toil he endured in his years as an attorney's apprentice and the sacrifices he made in order to support his family:

> I would frequently inquire, though I scarcely acknowledged the inquiry to myself, how or why it was that I should be called upon to sacrifice the immortal for the mortal; to give away irredeemably the Promethean fire within me, for the cooking of a beefsteak; to destroy and damn my own soul that I might preserve for a few miserable months or years the bodies of others. Often would I wander out into the fields, and groan to God for help.[3]

Perhaps a sentiment known to breadwinners everywhere, though hopefully not so keenly felt. Mangan's features are quite well known, thanks mainly to his bust in St. Stephen's Green, so we can picture him: wretchedly bent over a parchment in a candle-lit office overlooking the just completed Fitzwilliam Square, fingers ink-stained, meticulously copying out deeds of assignment, mortgages and marriage settlements, as if in a monastic scriptorium. We shall briefly look again at Mangan's poetic output at this time in the chapter on writers connected with the square.

As we sketch the careers of the most prominent legal minds to have resided in Fitzwilliam Square, hopefully we will get a sense of the evolution of the practice of law in Ireland. However, the legal discipline is one so steeped in tradition that many of the formalities and procedures we encounter, even from the early nineteenth century, will be immediately familiar to us. As we flit through the decades we'll occasionally snag on events and trials involving our residents that were of national significance, or at least

*James Clarence Mangan,
scrivener in No. 47*

captured the public imagination. For instance, Fitzwilliam Square dwellers past, present and future were together in court for the state trial of Daniel O'Connell in 1844; James Henry Monahan (of No. 5) was attorney general during the trials of the Young Irelanders as well as judge in the cause célèbre of the Yelverton case in 1861; while a host of the square's residents were investigators, prosecutors, victims and spoilers of Fenian plots. Of course, the majority of the square's lawyers weren't quite so noteworthy, but we shall try to include as many of them as possible in our narrative.

Casting back to the first decade of the 1800s, the most prominent lawyer residing on the square was Charles Burton (1760-1847). He lived in No. 56 from 1808 until 1822, when he removed to St. Stephen's Green after the death of his wife, Anna, née Andrews. Burton was born in Northamptonshire and attended school with Henry Addington, Prime Minister from 1801-1804. William Ferguson wrote, 'it redounds much to the independence of spirit and manly self-reliance which led Mr. Burton to look for advancement in life to his own unaided exertions rather than to the patronage of his influential schoolfellow'.[4] Initially, he studied for entry to the English bar but in 1787 he came to Ireland and began his studentship at the King's Inn. It's generally believed he did so under the influence of the celebrated John Philpot Curran, who took Burton under his wing and engaged him to assist in his briefs. Curran was a famous orator, politician and wit. It was he who coined the phrase, 'The condition upon which God hath given liberty to man is eternal vigilance'. The following less exalted exchange was also at- tributed to him:

> 'Curran,' said a judge to him, whose wig being a little awry, caused some laughter in court, 'do you see anything ridicu- lous in this wig?' 'Nothing but the head, my lord,' was the reply.[5]

It was at Curran's suggestion that Burton be appointed king's coun- sel in 1806, but James Whiteside, in his *Early Sketches of Eminent Persons*, dispelled the notion that Burton owed his rise solely to his eminent benefactor:

> Some people imagine that his professional advancement was entirely owing to the friendship of Curran. Unques- tionably it redounds to his credit to have acquired and pre- served to the last the friendship of that remarkable man; but his friendship, however ardent and sincere, could no more have gained practice for Mr. Burton at the bar than it could have made him Emperor of China.[6]

For some years Burton's practice was not particularly extensive and he was often overlooked as he went on the circuit. Whiteside wrote, 'he toiled on for a considerable period without business, and almost without hope'. However, his ability in various trials came to the fore and his reputation was cemented when he acted as counsel for the de- fendant in the cause of *King v O'Grady* in 1816, in which, according to

Ball, 'he made for his client a speech which was pronounced a master-piece in legal eloquence'.[7] Indeed, the trial was celebrated as a stage for the performance of the opposing counsel, Saurin and Bushe for the crown, Plunket and Burton for O'Grady. The case itself, while no doubt dealing with important constitutional issues, was a rather dry question as to the validity of the appointment by the Chief Baron of the Court of Exchequer of his son, Waller O'Grady, to the office of Clerk of the Pleas. However, in the course of the argument:

> ... there was no authority, however ancient, that was not ransacked; no principle, however apparently remote, which, if useful, was not applied; no source of legal learning, that was not explored and exhausted for the subject.... On the trial before the jury, Saurin was profound and luminous, Plunket bitter and severe, Bushe brilliant as ever, avenging himself upon his powerful opponent with many a splendid sarcasm, while he dazzled his fascinated audience. Burton shone not so brightly, but with a steadier light, neither heated by passion, nor led astray by fancy, he reasoned with powerful effect, in an argument compressed and vigorous.... If he did not soar to the highest flights of genius, he fathomed the utmost depths of reason.[8]

Following the O'Grady trial, Burton emerged from Curran's shadow and became one of the most respected members of the bar. He was appointed a justice of the King's Bench in 1820 and would sit there for over 25 years. His great friend Curran died in London in October 1817 and Burton would eventually move into his old house at No. 80 St. Stephen's Green. We shall encounter him again when examining the state trial of O'Connell and others in 1844.

As an aside, it's worth mentioning that Philpot Curran took part in five pistol duels during his career, to highlight the rather commonplace nature of this practice in legal disputes throughout the eighteenth century and on into the middle of the nineteenth century. As J.E. Walsh noted in his *Ireland Sixty Years Ago* (1847):

> No gentleman had taken his proper station in life till he had 'smelt powder', as it was called; no barrister could go circuit till he had obtained a reputation in this way; no election, and

scarcely an assizes, passed without a number of duels; and many men of the bar, practising half a century ago, owed their eminence, not to powers of eloquence or to legal ability, but to a daring spirit and the number of duels they had fought.[9]

Dr. Francis Hodgkinson (d. 1840), a professor of modern history and vice-provost of Trinity College, Dublin, lived in No. 40 Fitzwilliam Square on the west side from 1826 to 1833. Hodgkinson, in his old age, had some unusual advice for a startled law student. Walsh continued:

> Some years since, a young friend, going to the bar, consulted the late Dr. Hodgkinson, Vice-Provost of Trinity College, then a very old man, as to the best course of study to pursue, and whether he should begin with [Charles] Fearne or [Joseph] Chitty. The doctor, who had long been secluded from the world, and whose observation was beginning to fail, immediately reverted to the time when he had been himself a young barrister; and his advice was – 'My young friend, practise four hours a day at Rigby's pistol gallery, and it will advance you to the woolsack faster than all the Fearnes and Chittys in the library.'

Returning to the square, there were two other barristers who would become king's counsel residing just after the time of Burton. They were Edward William Scott of No. 61 and John Schoales of No. 21. In fact they both took silk in the same year, 1827, two years before Catholic emancipation. Their appointments prompted Daniel O'Connell, incredulous at their selection over more qualified Catholics, to write to Richard Newton Bennett:

> Lord Manners is disposed to play and is playing the devil. No less than six new King's Counsel and Perrin [Louis Perrin, 1782-1864] passed over. Edward Scott!!! Schoales!!! Tickell!!! inter alia. But this is merely crowding the inner Bar least by possibility any Catholic should get even the benefit of the existing laws.[10]

> – Daniel O'Connell, Merrion Square, 23 June 1827

The times, legal and political, were dominated by O'Connell and his pursuit of Catholic emancipation and then repeal of the Act of Union. Courts throughout the land were inundated with cases involving members of oath-bound societies, perpetrators of agrarian outrages such as the Whiteboys and Rockites, or offshoots of the United Irishmen such as the Defenders and Ribbonmen. In the courtroom, O'Connell was their foremost defender. Donnelly wrote:

> O'Connell appeared to be the chief political beneficiary of all this ferment. With some reason Protestants believed that in spite of his repeated condemnations of Ribbonism and Whiteboyism, the peasantry flocked to the standard of his Catholic Association believing that he was about to lead an armed revolt.... After all, no other contemporary barrister defended half as many accused Whiteboys, or saved half as many from the gibbet. No Rockite brief was so atrocious that O'Connell refused to take it.[11]

A Fitzwilliam Square resident and crown solicitor, James Perceval Graves (1811-1882), gave some interesting testimony on the subject of Ribbonism to a House of Lords select committee on the state of Ireland in 1839. More particularly, he described the subtly threatening demeanour of a Catholic clergyman towards prosecution witnesses in County Longford. Graves was raised in No. 41 Fitzwilliam Square and later lived in No. 30 from 1848 to 1853. At the time of his testimony, Graves was assistant to crown solicitor Tierney in the north-west circuit, and he stated that he himself had examined witnesses in Riband cases in Counties Cavan, Tyrone and Fermanagh. He was asked about a certain case in the Longford assizes:

> A Man named Michael Kenny was on Trial at the Time for a very bad Murder; he has been since executed; when a Witness named Thomas Farrell came upon the Table to be sworn (or at least he was called by the Crown for the Purpose of being sworn) he refused to give Evidence. I happened to be at the Foot of the Table opposite to the Judge, and it was suggested to me by the Gaoler that the Cause of Farrell's not giving Evidence was that a Priest, whom he pointed out to me, had nodded at the Witness when he

came on the Table. I looked at the Priest, and I saw him looking rather sharply at the Witness, but I did not see him nod to
him. The Witness still refused to be sworn, and some parley-
ing took place, upon which the Gaoler went forward openly
and stated to the Judge that he believed the Cause of the Witness not giving Evidence was that that Clergyman (pointing
to the Roman Catholic Priest) had nodded Twice to the Witness; that he had seen him do it. The Judge said that it was a
Contempt of Court to interfere with a Witness who was called
on the Table to be sworn, and that if the Matter was brought
before him by Affidavit he would take cognizance of it. At this
Time the Priest stood up, and said positively that he had not
looked more sharply at Farrell than at any other Witness, and
it was therefore not considered right to carry the Matter further. The Priest was desired to leave the Court.

– The Judge ordered the Priest to leave the Court?

I forget whether the Judge ordered it, or Mr Tierney, the
Crown Solicitor, but I know the Priest was told to leave the
Court and he did so.

– Did the Witness afterwards give Evidence?

No, he did not. I think there would have been a Conviction
if he had. The Jury did not agree at that Assizes. The Man
was tried over again at the last Assizes and was found guilty
and executed.[12]

Lords Chief Justice

IN 1835, THE FIRST OF TWO LORD CHIEF Justices moved into No. 5 Fitzwilliam Square. Edward Pennefather was born in 1775 in County Tipperary. Both he and his elder brother Richard were eminent members of
the bench and bar. O'Flanagan wrote: 'Rarely has any family produced
more estimable men, more distinguished lawyers or famous judges,
than the two brothers of the house of Pennefather'.[13] They both had lu-
minous university careers in Trinity College and together were called
to the bar in 1795. Richard's career advanced more quickly. He was appointed a Baron of the Court of Exchequer in 1821. Wills' biographical
sketch of Edward noted:

> ... it is said that [Edward's] further elevation was delayed
> by his refusing to preside over a commission appointed un-
> der the Insurrection Act.... Mr Pennefather, like Lord Plun-
> ket in his earlier bar life, eschewed politics, and refused in
> anywise to embarrass his hands, which were generally well
> filled with briefs, with any extraneous business.[14]

Of course, the two brothers often met as adversaries in the courtroom though:

> ... it never caused jealousy or collision between them, al-
> though they often met on opposite sides of a case, with
> various fortunes. It was remarked, that the public seemed
> to relish this brotherly contest.

Wills quoted the following description of Edward:

> In Court, his language and appearance bespeak the scholar
> and the gentleman. His forehead is smooth and open, yet
> somewhat over anxious; his expressive and intelligent
> countenance indicates deep meditation, but seems to say
> that all is peace within; his manner is artless and candid, his
> deportment erect and independent. When he commences
> his address, your attention is at once arrested; you perceive
> at a glance that he is master of his subject, and feels himself
> to be so; with perfect self-possession.

His advancement was further complicated by the succession of Whig and Tory governments in the 1830s. The Whig Prime Minister, Lord Grey, offered Pennefather the position of attorney general in 1830, but he declined, saying a government should have an attorney general that could happily co-operate in its policies, and that it was common knowledge his political principles differed from those of Lord Grey. He suggested Francis Blackburne

Edward Pennefather

should be offered the post instead and he was duly chosen. In 1835, the Tory Robert Peel was Prime Minister and Pennefather was informed that once again the post of attorney general was his if he wished to claim it. However, it was intimated to him that the government was mindful of the delicate matter of demoting Blackburne to the inferior office of solicitor general in order to accommodate Pennefather's appointment. Pennefather quite nobly agreed to accept the lesser post. O'Connell was less generous in his analysis:

> What shall I say of Edward Pennefather? All I shall say is, he refused to be Attorney-General for the Whigs, but condescended to be Solicitor-General of the Tories.[15]

This was the year Pennefather moved into No. 5 Fitzwilliam Square. In 1841, Peel was beginning his second term as Prime Minister. That autumn, upon the resignation of Charles Kendal Bushe, Pennefather was appointed Lord Chief Justice of the King's Bench.

It would seem Pennefather was a man of principle when considering his career moves, but he came to those conservative principles quite late in life. Wills wrote:

> Before the Act [of Union] passed, Mr Pennefather considered nothing could be more disastrous to the country than its passing – after it had passed, nothing more disastrous than its repeal; and in that opinion he remained firm to the last. He was in favour of emancipation all his life till the year 1828, and his opinion on this subject gave offence to Mr Saurin, long the Attorney-General for Ireland, a great personal friend of Mr Pennefather. Shortly before the passing of the Emancipation Act, he read much on the subject, and the result was he changed his opinion, and he signed the petition of the bar of Ireland against the Catholic claims. His name, I believe, headed the signatures.[16]

The Trial of O'Connell and Others, 1844

PENNEFATHER'S POSITION ON THE BENCH meant he presided over the state trial of Daniel O'Connell and others in 1844. In October 1843, Peel's government banned a monster meeting of the National Repeal Association scheduled for 8 October in Clontarf, County Dublin. The organisers acquiesced and the marchers were turned away. However the government went further by drawing up a series of indictments against O'Connell and other repeal leaders based on their speeches and newspaper articles, and in the same month they were arrested for conspiracy. Ball wrote:

> The state trial of O'Connell and his chief adherents for conspiracy to effect the repeal of the Act of Union was the great legal event in Ireland during Peel's administration. Apart from their political importance, the proceedings are memorable for their magnitude and strange incidents. They were spread over nearly a year, from the autumn of 1843 to the end of the summer of 1844, beginning in the Irish Queen's Bench and ending in the house of lords.... The crown led the way with an indictment, which was eighty feet in length, and described as endless, voluminous, unintelligible and unwieldy.... At the trial eleven counsel appeared for the crown and sixteen for the traversers.[17]

Among O'Connell's co-defendants were his son, John; Charles Gavan Duffy (editor of *The Nation* newspaper); and 'Honest Tom' Steele. The trial caused a sensation in Dublin where the roads to the Four Courts were thronged, the courtrooms packed, and newspapers carried verbatim reports of the speeches of the various parties. If we look to the list of dramatis personae in the almost 900 page report of the trial, we can see several Fitzwilliam Square inhabitants. As mentioned, Chief Justice Pennefather presided. He was joined on the bench by our old friend Judge Charles Burton. Judges Philip Crampton and Louis

John and Daniel O'Connell, 1844

Perrin completed that panel. William Daunt wrote that O'Connell later recalled the aspects of some of the judges in the trial:

> The Chief Justice (Pennefather) had the air of being counsel for the prosecution. Only for the seat he occupied, he might have been easily mistaken for the counsel for the prosecution.... Judge Crampton used to squeeze up his face at me, as if he wanted to terrify me with his lion aspect.... Judge Perrin seemed to be asleep during a great part of the trial.[18]

Of the sixteen counsels for the traversers, we find a James Henry Monahan QC who acted for John O'Connell. Monahan was born in Portumna, County Galway, in 1804. During his exchanges with Pennefather, neither man could have guessed that Monahan would not only follow the Chief Justice on to the bench, he would also follow him into his townhouse. Monahan moved into No. 5 Fitzwilliam Square in 1850, just a few years after Pennefather's death. At the bottom of the list we find Walter Bourne, clerk of the crown. He lived in No. 36 from 1853 to 1856.

Anthony Trollope gave a fictional account of the trial in the first chapter of his book *The Kelly's and the O'Kelly's*:

> 'The Traversers' were in everybody's mouth – a term heretofore confined to law courts, and lawyers' rooms. The Attorney General, the Commander-in-Chief of the Government forces, was most virulently assailed; every legal step which he took was scrutinised and abused; every measure which he used was base enough of itself to hand down his name to everlasting infamy. Such were the tenets of the Repealers. And O'Connell and his counsel, their base artifices, falsehoods, delays and unprofessional proceedings, were declared by the Saxon party to be equally abominable.[19]

The characters John and Martin Kelly gained entry to the courtroom and John described the crown solicitor and judges for his brother:

> 'There's old Kemmis,' as they caught a glimpse of the Crown agent; 'he's the boy that doctored the jury list. Fancy a jury chosen out of all Dublin, and not one Catholic! As if that could be fair!' And then he named the different judg-

es. 'Look at that big headed, pig faced fellow on the right – that's Pennefather! He's the blackest sheep of the lot – and the head of them! He's a thoroughbred Tory, and as fit to be a judge as I am to be a general. That queer little fellow with the long chin, he's Burton – he's a hundred if he's a day – he was fifty when he was called, seventy when they benched him, and I'm sure he's a judge thirty years. But he's the sharpest judge of the whole twelve, and no end of a boy afther the girls. If you only saw him walking in his robes – I'm sure he's not three feet high! That next, with the skinny neck, he's Crampton – he's one of Father Mathew's lads, an out and out teetotaller and he looks it; he's a desperate cross fellow sometimes. The other one, you can't see, he's Perrin. There, he's leaning over – you can just catch the side of his face – he's Perrin. It's he'll acquit the traversers av' anything does – he's a fair fellow, is Perrin, and not a red-hot thorough-going Tory like the rest of 'em.'[20]

Daniel O'Connell speaking during his state trial, 1844

We can recall that O'Connell was all for Perrin's advancement in 1827. Unfortunately, the author found no evidence of Judge Burton chasing 'afther the girls' in the course of the research. The initial excitement of the trial waned as the interminable procedures and speeches took their course. 'A Nut for the State Trials', writing in *The Dublin University Magazine,* welcomed their conclusion.

> The state trials are over. Thank heaven for that same! They were tiresome and dull.

His bias was against the defendants:

> The defence was simply this: the traversers did all that was imputed to them, but they did it professionally.

And he suggested their counsel should have appealed to the jury on the grounds that so daring an indictment could not be made against so humdrum a cadre of conspirators:

> Trust me, if such an appeal as this had been made, the jury would have slept at home on Saturday night. Walter Bourne, clerk of the crown, would not have caught cold walking to his house at four in the morning. There would have been neither charge nor conviction.[21]

The jury returned a guilty verdict and among the sentences, O'Connell was given a year's imprisonment. It is said Judge Burton shed tears as he read out the punishment. The conviction was quashed on appeal to the House of Lords and O'Connell was released that September.

Before we move on to Mr. Monahan's involvement with the trials of the Young Irelanders, we should catch up with other legal residents of Fitzwilliam Square. The two youngest sons, both barristers, of a man already mentioned, Charles Kendal Bushe, resided successively in No. 57. Thomas Bushe lived there from 1824 to 1835, before selling the house to his younger brother, Arthur Bushe, who lived there for 30 years. In 1814, the mother of Thomas and Arthur, Nancy Kendal Bushe, née Crompton, penned an unusual account of the attributes of her four sons, an account that survived in the family archives. It provides an insight into the characters of two future residents of No. 57 Fitzwilliam Square, when both were children:

> (Thomas, b. 1801) My third son – now in Dublin owes it to his beauty which is now (he is 12) certainly very considerable that we have always spoken of him for the Army and that he was selected to meet the Duchess of Richmond's kind offer to make him a Page, his services in which Character will entitle him to a commission.

> (Arthur, b. 1803) At present tho very sencible and even ingenious and with a disposition to inform himself, a taste for Poetry, or at least a relish for it, and a talent for drawing he has shewn less genius than any of my Boys, and as a scholar stands the lowest among them, his temper is the very sweetest and most accommodating that I have ever met with and his affections the warmest, he is particularly gallant and courageous.[22]

Nancy mentions Thomas's good looks and apparently he was considered the most handsome man in Dublin. From 1860, Arthur Bushe was Master of the Queen's Bench in Ireland. A stained-glass fanlight containing the Bushe family coat of arms remains to this day in No. 57 and must have been installed at this time.

Bushe Family Coat of Arms, detail of fanlight in No. 57

To continue a theme of prominent judicial fathers, two residents of No. 29 were sons of famous judges. David Plunket QC was son of William Plunket, the Lord Chancellor, and lived here from 1839 to around 1857. David's niece Katherine Plunket, a prolific botanical artist, died close to her 112th birthday, and as such was the oldest person in Irish history. Jones Pigot, son of chief baron of the Exchequer David Pigot (1796-1873), lived in No. 29 from 1902 to 1913. His father was evoked in *Recollections of Dublin Castle and Dublin Society*:

Then there was Chief Baron Pigot, whose rage for taking notes was a sort of mania. He must note everything down, but was a very slow writer; hence the evidence of a witness was a most extraordinary process. A few words were uttered, after which came a long pause, during which the judge was carefully writing. After a reasonable period the witness would begin again when he was violently interrupted – 'Stop! stop, sir! do you not see I am taking down your evidence? How can I do so if you talk? Keep your eye on the top of my pen, and when it stops, you may go on.' He was a truly upright and conscientious man, but a sore trial to counsel and suitors.[23]

Also in the 1840s we find the barristers Hamilton Geale (more noted as a travel writer) in No. 30; and Robert Tighe, long-term resident of No. 66. In 1889, the Royal Dublin Society received the Tighe Bequest of 222 volumes of classics, especially rare editions of Horace, from Robert Tighe's Fitzwilliam Square library.

The Young Irelanders

O'CONNELL'S 1844 HEARING WAS THE FIRST in a series of state trials that resulted from the political and social unrest of that terrible decade. The Young Irelanders were a romantic group that broke away from the Repeal Association, frustrated by O'Connell's increasing tendency towards compromise with federalists and the Whig party. They were initially led by Thomas Davis, Charles Gavan Duffy and John Blake Dillon (a Fitzwilliam Square resident, whom we shall examine in another chapter). As the movement progressed, the radical counsels of members such as John Mitchel gradually won over the more moderate opinions of leaders such as William Smith O'Brien and, as Foster wrote:

> ... by the mid 1840s the Young Irelanders were ... being pressed towards the realisation of their rhetoric. The catalyst was provided by the great natural disaster of the Famine.[24]

The rising in Ireland in July 1848 consisted of an incoherent conspiracy and botched rebellion reluctantly headed by Smith O'Brien. Mitchel had already been tried and convicted of treason-felony that

May. The rising ended in famous ignominy at the Widow McCormack's cabbage patch in Waterford in late July.

James Henry Monahan (John O'Connell's counsel in '44), later of No. 5 Fitzwilliam Square, was appointed Attorney General for Ireland in December 1847. As such he was responsible for the prosecutions that arose from Young Ireland activities in 1848 and, in general, he is remembered as having carried out his duties professionally and effectively. O.J. Burke wrote: 'The name of Monahan is inseparably connected with the suppression of the Irish Rebellion of 1848.'[25] The most controversial aspect of his work was the (well-founded) accusation of jury packing, that is, acquiescing in the removal of names of Roman Catholics from the jury lists.

Prior to Mitchel's trial in May, both Smith O'Brien and Thomas Meagher had been acquitted on charges of sedition, thanks to the dissenting voices of Catholic jurors. Clarendon, the Lord Lieutenant, was adamant that Mitchel, facing the same charge, should be convicted. The charges against him were changed from sedition to treason-felony, and it fell to Monahan to challenge each and every one of the 19 Catholics that appeared on the jury panel. Monahan, himself a Roman Catholic, later defended his actions by saying that only those who could not be relied upon to give an impartial verdict, regardless of their faith, were excluded, but there is no doubt he acted pragmatically and unjustly in order to secure a conviction. The irony of Monahan packing the jury, when he himself had assailed the same practice during O'Connell's trial in '44, was not lost on Gavan Duffy, who wrote that Monahan, 'clamoured against the omission of Catholics from the panel ... while he was still on his promotion'.[26]

A jury of twelve Protestants were chosen and the trial commenced in the Green Street courthouse (where, until recently, the Special Criminal Court sat) on 25 May 1848. Mitchel was found guilty on the second day of the trial and on the third, Judge Lefroy passed sentence of 14 years transportation. The scene in court on the morning of sentencing was described in *The Felon's Track*:

> The applause of the galleries was hushed by the crier's voice
> – 'Silence! take off your hats'; and on the right stalked in the

gaunt figure of James Henry Monahan. Triumph, animosity and fear marked his night-bird face. Even yet it was hoped the great opponent of his 'government,' whom by rascality alone he could convict, would strike his colours, and sue for mercy. Even yet it was feared that a rescue would be attempted.... As Monahan and his retainers entered, the red face of Lefroy oozed through the bench curtains, and followed by the pale Moore, 'the court was seated.' ... There was a dead silence. 'Jailor, put forward John Mitchel,' said the official. A grating of bolts – a rustling of chains, were heard behind. The low door-way at the back of the dock opened, and between turnkeys Mitchel entered.[27]

The trial of John Mitchel, 1848

Mitchel famously denounced the court after his sentence and had to be led away amid riotous scenes. His counsel, Robert Holmes, was accused by Lefroy of employing language almost as objectionable as the prisoner's, so Holmes challenged Monahan, as Attorney General, to proceed against him if indeed he had violated the law. Mitchel was taken from Green Street to the North Wall that very afternoon and left Ireland to begin his sentence.

Monahan's work prosecuting the Young Irelanders continued, including the conviction that September of William Smith O'Brien for high treason at a special commission in Clonmel. His was a thankless task. Naturally, he was attacked by those he sought to condemn and their associates, but he also received criticism when certain prosecutions failed to result in conviction. Gavan Duffy wrote:

> The breach in the indictment on my third arraignment greatly damaged the Attorney-General in public opinion. His management of the case was pronounced by a sarcastic critic to be an Iliad of blunders. He ought to have made the law formidable, it was said, and he only made it contemptible. He ought to have won public sympathy for the prosecution, and he only won it for the prisoner; but though he was a man of violent passions, it was admitted that he had shown coolness and courage under exasperating defeats and the harassing criticism of Mr. Butt [Isaac Butt appeared as counsel for many of the defendants].[28]

The 'violent passions', noted above, were alluded to in a somewhat more affectionate description of Monahan, given by his friend William O'Connor Morris:

> Monahan was talkative, rollicking, rather 'hail fellow, well met,' but the most good-hearted and simple of men. Impulsive, and perhaps rather thoughtless, he seasoned his conversation with oaths, like Wellington. I heard him tell a nobleman much too fond of the bottle, 'Damn you, I am as sober as a judge and you are as drunk as a lord;' ... and the Chief Justice by no means abstained from expletives of the kind on the Bench. 'Be off, you damned woman,' he once blurted out when he had ordered witnesses out of court in a very nasty trial.[29]

In October 1850, Monahan was appointed Chief Justice of the Court of Common Pleas. This was the year he moved into No. 5 Fitzwilliam Square. Edward Pennefather had died in 1847, following several severe bouts of gout, and the house had remained vacant since then. Monahan would reside there until his death in 1878.

The Infamous Case of *Thelwall v Yelverton*, 1861

Before moving on, we must look at Monahan's involvement in the sensational case of *Thelwall v Yelverton* that appeared in the Court of Common Pleas on 21 February 1861. Theresa Longworth, daughter of a Catholic Manchester manufacturer and Major William Charles Yelverton, Viscount Avonmore, an Irish Protestant, met on board a cross-channel steamer in 1852. They sat up on deck talking all night, and next day Charles escorted Theresa through London. They maintained contact over the next three years through a series of increasingly flirtatious letters. During the Crimean War (1854-56) they met near Constantinople.

Theresa Longworth

Yelverton was on active service; Longworth was working as a nurse with the French Sisters of Mercy in whose employ she had to wear the habit of a novice nun. Yelverton was so enchanted with her when they met (a vision of charm, charity and chastity) that soon after, according to Theresa, he proposed marriage. He wanted to marry in a Greek Orthodox church immediately, but she wished for a public Catholic marriage. They returned to England separately but maintained contact.

To set out in a few lines the convoluted series of meetings and supposed ceremonies hardly does the story justice, but in essence, the couple exchanged private vows in Edinburgh in April 1857, essentially constituting a 'Scotch marriage', and those vows were formalised in a Catholic church near Rostrevor, County Down, that August. Their relationship was kept secret from Yelverton's family at his insistence, though they lived in Edinburgh for the rest of the year as man and wife. Just before Christmas, Theresa revealed she was pregnant, so Yelverton took her to France so she could come to term abroad. He returned to Edinburgh and while they were separated Theresa miscarried.

When she returned to Scotland in June 1858, Yelverton came to her hotel to inform her that, in her absence, he had courted and proposed to Emily Ashworth Forbes, a general's daughter and the widow of a professor at Edinburgh University. Yelverton demanded that Theresa renounce her marital status and offered her money to emigrate to New Zealand and start a new life. Theresa refused and instituted proceedings in the Scottish courts to validate her rights as a spouse. The Dublin case was instituted by John Thelwall (a relation of Longworth's) to recover the cost of goods supplied to Theresa, for which Yelverton, if he was her husband, would be responsible.

In the course of the trial the salacious minutiae of the relationship was examined in detail, mostly in the forensic scrutiny of the couple's correspondence and testimony. In the public galleries all the sympathy was for Theresa, 'the wronged woman'. Yelverton, on the other hand, came across as unusually heartless, particularly as his defence rested on the assertion that his entire courtship of Theresa, which spanned years and continents, was expressly intended for her to become his mistress rather than his wife (not to mention his base abandonment of her following her miscarriage). The jury in the case had to answer whether the couple's Scotch marriage was valid and/or whether the Irish marriage was valid (the second question also required the jury to find that Yelverton was a Catholic, as at that time a Catholic priest could not perform a marriage ceremony for a Protestant or mixed faith couple).

In his summing up of the case for the jury, Judge Monahan of No. 5 Fitzwilliam Square could not conceal his sympathy for Theresa. O'Connor Morris light-heartedly suggested, though unfairly imputing Theresa's character, that the distinguished judge was perhaps smitten with Longworth:

> Chief Justice Monahan summed up the evidence with characteristic acuteness and skill, but I cannot say that he had not felt the influence of the blandishments of a dexterous siren, who had persistently made beaux yeux at him.[30]

In the course of his speech Monahan genuinely expressed abhorrence at Yelverton's actions, particularly the defendant's account of their meeting in Constantinople:

> It was superintended by a number of French Sisters of Charity, who wore a peculiar habit or robe. He says he spoke of love, but not of marriage; that he took off her bonnet and embraced her ... and that then for the first time he formed the idea in his own mind to dishonour her and make her his mistress. I am not surprised, much as I deprecate exhibitions of feeling in a court of justice, at the expression of indignation the avowal of this man must have excited in the breast of every person with a particle of honour or virtue in his composition. This girl, who underwent one of the most searching cross examinations I ever witnessed, and in whose conduct up to that moment there does not appear to have been anything to justify a person in imputing to her anything that would be discreditable or improper in any woman, excited the admiration, love and affection of this man, as he tells us. But, my God, should not the garb in which she appeared, and the work of charity in which she was engaged, have had some influence on this man, and driven from his mind the idea which, he says, he entertained that time! My God, gentlemen, all of us see in this city numbers of young and beautiful women who have engaged in this holy work of charity, and though men may entertain different opinions as to the prudence and propriety of a conventual life, there is not a man among us who would be capable of offering an insult to those young and devoted women as they go to and fro on their mission of charity, visiting the haunts of suffering and misery. That, gentlemen, is the account this man gives of himself, and the idea he entertained at that time. He says he loved and admired her but that she was not of gentle blood and that therefore he formed the idea or desire of obtaining possession of her person, not in an honourable manner, but by dishonouring her. That is his declaration. However gentlemen, whatever may be the feelings of indignation which such a declaration naturally excites in the mind, we must endeavour to get rid of them here, and consider the case, not as a matter

of feeling, but as one on which we have a duty to discharge according to the principles of law and justice.[31]

The reading of the verdict resulted in remarkable scenes, as set out below:

Chief Justice Monahan: How say you, gentlemen. Was there a Scotch marriage?

Foreman: Yes, my lord.

Chief Justice: And was there an Irish marriage?

Foreman: Yes, my lord.

Chief Justice: Then, you find the defendant was a Roman Catholic at the time of the marriage?

Foreman: So we believe, my lord.

Before the Foreman had spoken the last of his words, which gave the plaintiff an unqualified verdict, the universal joy and approval of all within hearing found expression in a most enthusiastic burst of cheering, again and again re-newed, accompanied by various other demonstrations of applause. Hats and handkerchiefs were waved, the members of the bar stood up and joined heartily in the public mani-festations of delight, many of them actually took off their wigs and waved them with energy.... The cheering in court for the verdict had been caught up by the multitude who thronged the hall, and vehemently reiterated by them. One of the greatest demonstrations of popular enthusiasm that perhaps ever was witnessed in the city of Dublin, took place as the Honourable Mrs. Yelverton proceeded from the Four Courts to the Gresham Hotel. It was one of those things that should be seen as it is impossible to be described. Over fifty thousand people frantic with joy proceeded to bid her welcome as she issued from the hall.... In anticipation of the arrival of the Hon. Mrs Yelverton, the space in front of the Gresham Hotel was crowded to such an extent that it was almost impossible for horses or vehicles to pass the street. The bases of Nelson's Pillar were fully occupied by persons who joined in the cheering of the thousands who were now approaching, who surrounded the carriage of a great and brave woman who had suffered much and had conquered in the end.... Cheer after cheer came from the hearts of the people, and mid a scene of perhaps unsurpassed excitement the carriage, which was rolled up the left-hand side of Sackville-street until it came in front of the hotel, crossed the street, and drew up at the centre entrance.... In compliance with the universal call of the vast multitude, numbering many thousand, she presented herself at one of the drawing-room windows. When the enthusiastic applause which her presence excited had subsided, she came forward on the balcony and said:

'My noble-hearted friends, you have made me this day an Irishwoman, by the verdict that I am the wife of an Irishman (vehement cheering).

I glory to belong to such a noble-hearted nation (great cheering). You will live in my heart for ever, as I have lived in your hearts this day (tremendous applause).

I am too weak to say all that my heart desires, but you will accept the gratitude of a heart that was made sad, and is now made glad (loud cheers).

Farewell for the present, but for ever I belong in heart and soul to the people of Dublin.'[32]

Some clues to the thoughts of Judge Monahan on the whole affair might be gleaned from William Fitzpatrick's description in his *History of the Dublin Catholic Cemeteries*:

Notwithstanding the apparent roughness of his nature, Monahan possessed a heart of exquisite tenderness. The sexton of [Glasnevin] Cemetery stated that every week the Chief Justice visited the grave of his wife; and within the little chapel which he raised over her remains, would pour forth his soul in lamentation and prayer.[33]

Trials of the Fenians, 1865

THE FINAL TWO STATE TRIALS WE SHALL examine are those of the Fenians in 1865 and Charles Stewart Parnell in 1880. In both cases, Charles Barry, later Lord Justice Barry of No. 3 Fitzwilliam Square, was prominent. Barry was recalled by F.J. Little in his capacity as Lord Chief Justice of Appeal:

> Then there was Lord Justice Barry, whose curious countenance made one wonder was he really a live man or an Egyptian mummy propped up for the occasion on the Bench, an effect which was heightened by his habit of keeping his eyes shut as if in a prolonged doze – a dangerous delusion for Counsel to entertain, as once was found in the Court of Appeal, by a Senior who was denouncing a scandalous attempt by the other side at joinder of diverse causes of action 'which,' he thundered, 'as your Lordships are well aware, is contrary to the tradition and practice of the Courts'; whereupon Barry half opened one eye and drawled out, 'When I was at the Bar I once drafted a plea of assault and battery, slander, and trover of a candlestick.'[34]

John Stephens, a veteran of the 1848 rising, established a revolutionary secret society in Dublin on St. Patrick's Day 1858, whose members in due course became known as the Fenians. The movement attracted Catholic Church hostility and concerted police investigations. On 16 September 1865, the office of the Fenian organ, *The Irish People*, was raided and prominent members Thomas Clarke Luby, Jeremiah O'Donovan Rossa and John O'Leary were arrested on charges of treason-felony. Stephens was also picked up, but he was sprung from Richmond prison within a week.

Chief Justice Charles Barry of No. 3

Charles Barry, who lived in No. 3 from 1861 until his death in 1897, was Crown Prosecutor at the time. Other Fitzwilliam Square residents were also involved in the Fenian prosecutions. The Crown Solicitor Matthew Anderson had been living in No. 63 Fitzwilliam Square since 1861 with his son and colleague Samuel Lee Anderson. They operated out of offices at No. 2 Inns Quay. It fell to Matthew and Samuel to prepare the cases against Luby, O'Leary, O'Donovan Rossa, et al. for the prosecutor Barry. They briefly recorded their activities in a solicitor's day book, now kept in the National Library [shorthand is expanded]:

Re: 'Irish People' & Fenian conspiracy

September 16 [1865]: Read letter from Attorney General [James A Lawson (1817-1887)] to attend him at once at the castle on important business. Went up at once (Samuel Lee Anderson; Matthew Anderson out of town). Received instructions to attend at the Head Police Court with Mr Barry and have the prisoners who were arrested last night remanded – Thomas Clarke Luby, O'Donovan Rossa & 20 others ...

At 2½ o'c with Attorney General, Solicitor General, and Law Adviser at Ryan's lower castle yard – received instructions as to reading & examining all the documents found - At 3 o'c at Head Police Court with Mr Barry when prisoners all brought up before Messrs Stronge and McDermott [Dublin police magistrates] & remanded for a week.

September 18: Monday (M.A. with S.L.A.) Attending at 11 o'c at Castle, Attorney General, Solicitor General and Law Adviser - and all day examining papers in their room...Received instructions from Attorney General to apply to Mr Stronge for an order to prevent all the prisoners having intercourse with any but professional men. Attending before Mr Stronge when he made such order – handed order to Mr Ryan to bring up to Redmond Bridewell ...

September 20: Wednesday – At Stamp Office got copy Declaration of Proprietor of 'Irish People'. Attending Castle as directed 12 o'c – again at 3 o'c when instructed to go through all the selected papers and make a list of them for the Attorney General. Set to work at once (SLA) in Mr Ryan's office – all afternoon ...

The cases prepared, on 1 October 1865 Crown Prosecutor Barry of No. 3 outlined the charges against the arrested Fenians before a police magistrate and the men were committed for trial. Reports of Barry's statement in the police office caused great controversy as he overtly linked the Fenian movement to socialism. He reportedly told the magistrate:

> But it has been deemed expedient, and I think wisely, that notwithstanding the unprepared state of the case, no time should be lost in laying the evidence before the public, so as to enable the public to judge, from the authentic source of evidence used in a court of justice, the real nature and extent of the Fenian conspiracy undiminished by incredulity and not exaggerated by panic. The design ... partook of the character of socialism in its most pernicious and most wicked phase. The lower classes were taught to believe that they might expect a re-distribution of the property, real and personal, of the country. They were taught to believe that the law by which any man possessed more property than another was unjust and wicked, and the plan of operation found to have been suggested was horrible to conceive. The operations of this revolution, as it is called, were to be commenced by an indiscriminate massacre – by the assassination of all those above the lower classes, including the Roman Catholic clergy, against whom their animosity appears, from their writings, to be especially directed.[35]

The Freeman's Journal remarked that 'a man of Mr Barry's antecedents and position' would hardly have made such a charge if it could not be backed by evidence, while Archbishop Cullen wrote in a pastoral letter:

> ... they are said to have proposed nothing less than to destroy the faith of our people by circulating works like those of the impious Voltaire, to preach up socialism, to seize the property of those who have any, and to exterminate both the gentry of the country and the Catholic clergy.[36]

The trials of the men by special commission in Green Street courthouse before judges Keogh and Fitzgerald, beginning 27 November

1865, resulted in inevitable convictions. In their speeches before sentencing, the Fenian prisoners specifically added the nature of Barry's charge to their list of usual grievances, which included the issues of packed juries and impartial judges. Luby stated:

> Now, with respect to [Mr Barry's] charges – in justice to my character – I must say that in this court, there is not a man more incapable of anything like massacre or assassination than I am. I really believe that the gentlemen who have shown so much ability in persecuting me, in the bottom of their hearts believe me incapable of an act of assassination or massacre.[37]

O'Leary's speech from the dock was more impassioned:

> Mr O'Leary: I have to say one word in reference to the foul charge upon which that miserable man, Barry, has made me responsible ...
>
> Mr. Justice Fitzgerald: We cannot allow that tone of observation.
>
> Mr O'Leary: That man has charged me – I need not defend myself or my friends from the charge. I shall merely denounce the moral assassin.[38]

Barry would continue to prosecute Fenians as he advanced in his career. He was successively solicitor general, attorney general, a justice of the Queen's Bench and finally, as mentioned, lord chief justice of appeal.

The Trial of Parnell and Others, 1880

THE FINAL STATE TRIAL TO INVOLVE A SLEW of Fitzwilliam Square inhabitants was that of *Queen v C.S. Parnell and others*, for conspiracy to incite tenants not to pay rents, that commenced in the Queen's bench division of the High Court on 28 December 1880. Residents of numbers 3, 9 and 13, all on the east side of the square, played prominent roles (they could have carriage-pooled to the Four Courts). Initially, the presiding judge was Lord Chief Justice, George Augustus Chichester May, who lived in No. 13 from 1863 until his death in 1892. Charles

Charles Stewart Parnell, MP – President of the Land League

Barry, subject of our previous sketch, of No. 3, was also a judge on the panel. In No. 9 lived the Attorney General, Hugh Law (1818-1883), a Fitzwilliam Square resident since 1873. In politics Law was a liberal; his appointment by the new Gladstone administration in 1880 was his second stint in the office of attorney general.

This was at the height of the Land War, just after the summer that saw the compact of the 'New Departure' between Devoy, Davitt and Parnell. In September, Parnell had made his famous Ennis speech, in which the methods of what became known as the boycott were outlined. On 23 October, Gladstone's cabinet decided to prosecute Parnell and his associates for conspiracy.

The most sensational aspect of the trial was Justice May's decision to step down on its first day. It had been suggested that in a previous application to postpone the trial, Justice May had made observations that seemed to impute guilt to the traversers. As he was stepping down he said:

> It appeared to me that the state of this country afforded a conclusive reason against granting the postponement ... and I gave a description of the disorder that prevailed ... it was my duty to speak the truth, and the whole truth upon that subject, and I adhere to everything I then stated.

However, he then admitted that on that previous occasion, he was too late in modifying his statement when he added, 'I mean those are the charges and accusations which the traversers have to meet', and that after taking advice, he decided to step down. At the end of his statement he referred to the vitriol and threat he felt that judges had to endure:

> [I] wish to promote the due administration of justice un-influenced either by public invective or secret menace ... I have experienced an ample share of both.[39]

The trial itself was something of a historical footnote. Chief counsel for the defendants, Francis McDonough QC, ensured that the jury contained a good proportion of Catholics and a prosecution was never likely. The collapse of the trial undoubtedly influenced the government in their bringing forward a coercion act in March 1881, which allowed for the suspension of habeas corpus. Parnell continued to foment opposition to the land acts and was summarily imprisoned in Kilmainham gaol in October, which led to the Kilmainham treaty the following year, and onwards – the inexorable march of history.

Conclusion

MARY BRYAN HAS NOTED THAT BETWEEN 1883 and 1922, the degree to which members of the legal profession outnumbered those of the medical profession on Fitzwilliam Square was practically reversed.[40] While extremely eminent lawyers continued to live in the square right up to the beginning of the Free State, we find less of their names connected with the major trials of their day. Other lawyers, such as Denis Henry of No. 25, John Atkinson of No. 68 and William Kenny of No. 69, were more noted for their political careers.

However, there are some residents we should note. Redmond J. Barry spent his final two years in No. 10 from 1911 to 1913. In those years he had attained the highest judicial post in the land: that of Lord Chancellor. Three other Fitzwilliam Square dwellers held this post: Hugh Law, noted above; Lord Ashbourne of No. 23 (whose name was Edward Gibson – his daughter Violet attempted to assassinate Mussolini in Rome in 1926); and Sir John Ross of No. 66, who was the incumbent when the office was abolished in 1922.

Richard Edmund Meredith, Master of the Rolls, lived in No. 31 from 1901 until his retirement in 1913. He is remembered for having eschewed party politics throughout his legal career. Stephen Ronan lived in No. 45 from 1892. In 1922, he was made Lord Chief Justice of Appeal. Sir Patrick Coll, Chief Crown Solicitor, lived in No. 54 from 1892 until his death in 1917.

Finally, a well known Dublin personality, Sir Thomas Lopdell O'Shaughnessy, lived in No. 64 from 1898 until his death in 1933. He was the Recorder of Dublin from 1905 and was appointed a member of the High Court in 1924. Moira Lysaght, in one of those sporadic lamentations for the loss of Dublin's characters, described him thus: 'Sir Tommie O'Shaughnessy – the Recorder – that top-hatted, cape clothed, tiny, arrogant personage'.[41]

Upon his death, *An Phoblacht* ran a piece entitled, 'Hangman's Friend Dead'.[42] His reputation in this regard was demonstrated by the trial of Felix McMullen, convicted of killing a civic guard in the course of a bank robbery and hung on 1 August 1924.

Throughout the troubled history of Ireland the principals of political movements, their leaders, visionaries, conspirators and agitators have invariably ended up in the dock. By following the legal inhabitants of Fitzwilliam Square into those courtrooms, we have been able to observe these set-piece trials through their eyes. Finding dispassionate descriptions of those eminent lawyers hasn't been easy; we've had to pick our way through the glowing sketches of legal eulogists and the hateful reminiscences of the convicted. Overall, the courts have provided a worthy stage for the eloquence of defence counsel; the Machiavellian zeal of prosecutors; the spat defiance of the accused; judges in their pomp handing out sentence, some with apparent relish, most with dispassion, perhaps a few with regret; not to mention the restless galleries and the heart-sore loneliness of the condemned. Whether courtrooms were filled with impassioned argument and uproar, or the incessant drone of procedure and dull speech, what a haven those Fitzwilliam Square homes must have been by comparison.

Let's follow Judge James Henry Monahan, escaping from the tumult of Inns Quay upon the conclusion of the Yelverton case in 1861. The dregs of a crowd still stream towards Sackville Street in pursuit of Miss Longworth's, rather Mrs. Yelverton's, carriage, but few pay him much heed. He glances through the notes of a brief while the carriage sways along the north quays. Turning right onto Carlisle Bridge he observes an extraordinary piece of street theatre from his window. A crowd throngs around the Gresham Hotel at the upper end of Sackville Street. Traffic is backed up on both sides and gawkers even clamber on to the base of Nelson's Pillar to hear Mrs. Yelverton's address. But his carriage trundles on. Rounding Trinity College he spies two sisters of mercy walking regally on College Green, habits billowing in the breeze, and he shakes his head recalling details of the trial. His carriage skirts the park of Merrion Square and approaches Fitzwilliam Square from the north. Home to No. 5 at last, he alights nimbly and goes briskly up the steps as the horseman continues on to the stable lane. In he strides without a backward glance, and the door closes.

View of Carlisle Bridge and Sackville Street

Endnotes

1. Morgan Llywelyn, *1916: A Novel of the Irish Rebellion*, p. 45; Beauchamp occupied No. 25 from 1880, though in reality he probably departed the house (if not his life) before 1911.

2. Louise Imogen Guiney, *James Clarence Mangan: His Selected Poems* (1897), pp. 5-6.

3. Ibid, pp. 10-11.

4. W.D. Ferguson, ed., *Early Sketches of Eminent Persons* by James Whiteside (1870), p. 252.

5. *The Eclectic Magazine*, September 1857, p. 56.

6. James Whiteside, *Early Sketches*, p. 244.

7. F.E. Ball, *The Judges in Ireland 1221-1921, Book VI*, p. 341.

8. Whiteside, *Early Sketches*, p. 248.

9. John Edward Walsh, *Ireland Sixty Years Ago*, pp. 21-22.

10. *The Correspondence of Daniel O'Connell, Vol III*, p. 328.

11. James Donnelly, *Irish Peasants, Violence and Political Unrest*, p. 136.

12. House of Lords, State of Ireland in Respect of Crime, Vol 19, pp. 716-717.

13. James O'Flanagan, *The Irish Bar*, p. 289.

14. James Wills, *The Irish Nation, Its History and Biography, Vol 3*, p. 700.

15. Ibid, p. 701.

16. Ibid, p. 704.

17. F.E. Ball, *The Judges in Ireland 1221-1921, Book VI*, p. 289.

18. William J. O'Neill Daunt, *Personal Recollections of Daniel O'Connell, Vol II*, p. 204.

19. Anthony Trollope, *The Kelly's and the O'Kelly's*, p. 11.

20. Ibid, p. 21.

21. *The Dublin University Magazine*, 1844, Vol. 23, p. 353.

22. Edith Somerville, *An Incorruptible Irishman*, p. 212.

23. *Recollections of Dublin Castle and Dublin Society*, p. 226.

24. R.F. Foster, *Modern Ireland 1600-1972*, p. 316.

25. Oliver Joseph Burke, *Anecdotes of the Connaught Circuit*, p. 311.

26. Charles Gavan Duffy, *Four Years of Irish History*, p. 710.

27. Michael Doheny, *The Felon's Track*, p. 143.

28. Charles Gavan Duffy, *Four Years of Irish History*, p. 739.

29. William O'Connor Morris, *Memories and Thoughts of a Life*, p. 160.

30. Ibid, p. 171.

31. Report of the trial in the case of *Thelwall v Yelverton*, p. 118.

32. Ibid., p. 130.

33. William Fitzpatrick, *History of the Dublin Catholic Cemeteries*, p. 146.

34. F.J. Little, *Dublin Historical Record*, Vol. 6, No. 1, pp. 14-15.

35. Edward William Cox, ed., *Report of Cases in Criminal Law, Vol X*, p. 185.

36. Ibid., p. 186.

37. T.D. Sullivan, *Speeches from the Dock*, pp. 159-160.

38. Ibid., p. 164.

39. Report of the Trial of the Queen against C.S. Parnell, pp. 1-2.

40. Mary Bryan, *The Georgian Squares of Dublin*, p. 107.

41. Moira Lysaght, *Dublin Historical Record*, Vol. 30, p. 134.

42. Uinseann MacEoin, *The IRA in the Twilight Years*, p. 238.

3

Scandals and Scoundrels

Perhaps it would be unfair (not to mention clichéd) to say that the graceful facades of Fitzwilliam Square have hid a multitude of sins; or that every house had its skeleton in the closet; every family its black sheep. But this was a residential square where from the outset the liberal professional classes were acutely aware of their place in the social hierarchy, where vestiges of landed gentry kept their class consciousness honed. So there were bound to be some breaches of etiquette, slips in decorum and occasionally a full-blown scandal that failed to remain behind closed doors. Also, some of the square's fellows (or their sons and brothers) at times fell short of the chivalric Victorian ideal of gentlemanly conduct, and these cads could boldly take their place beside Major William Yelverton in our own rogue's gallery. Some of the stories we touch upon in this chapter will take us from southern Sudan (the same time and events that inspired Conrad's *Heart of Darkness*) to one of the great unsolved murder mysteries of Hollywood. But our first scandal takes us back to the early years of the square, in fact the year of its completion: 1828.

A Very Public Affair: Lady Branden and Lord Melbourne

Richard Knight, master carpenter, took a few steps back on to the road and looked with satisfaction at the result of his labours. The newly completed house on the north east corner of Fitzwilliam Square was the last to be built and its presence, like a cap-stone or jig-saw piece, set off the whole square splendidly. Looking left along the north side where he stood, and then over his right shoulder at the extent of the east side, he allowed himself a moment's pride at the elegance of the buildings and the cosiness of their setting. Behind him, the garden was enclosed and coming along nicely; the granite paving stones were well cut and even, an ornament for the city. Already he had the first tenant for this newest house lined up: a William Burton Newesham, or William Barton Newenham, something like that. Anyway, he seemed a decent sort – as long as he paid promptly.

As he turned to go a carriage entered the square from Fitzwilliam Street and rattled to a halt outside No. 3 on the east side, just over the road adjacent. The footman sprang down and opened the carriage door for two well dressed ladies, a mother and daughter, and they ascended the steps to Lady Branden's house. The mother was giving her charge some last minute instructions and despite himself, Knight tried to overhear. Lady Branden's salon had gained a reputation for being the most sparkling and civilised in the city and Knight was pleased. Just the reputation the square needs, he thought, as he walked away. Attract the best people, the most moneyed, the most fashionable – then paused to wonder why he had yet to receive an invitation to one of her gatherings.

Lady Elizabeth Branden was the daughter of Colonel David La Touche, of the well established Huguenot banking family, and Cecilia La Touche née Leeson. On 3 May 1815, she married the Rev. William Crosbie, many years her senior, rector of Castle Island, County Kerry. That October he succeeded to the title of fourth Baron Branden on the death of his first cousin. They spent much of their marriage apart with Lord Branden at first taking care of his pastoral duties in the west, then taking extended vacations in England and the south of France. Elizabeth spent her time in No. 3 Fitzwilliam Square, a house bought for her by her father around 1821. It was undoubtedly a loveless marriage and it only produced children in its first two years. Maurice Crosbie died an infant in 1816. Elizabeth Cecilia Crosbie, named for her mother and grandmother, was born a year later. Philip Ziegler wrote of Lord Branden:

Within ten years of his marriage he was crippled by debts and gout, to the first of which disabilities his wife had undoubtedly contributed and which together rendered him unfit to meet her financial and sexual expectations.

He went on to describe Lady Elizabeth:

She was without doubt beautiful and educated above the usual level of women of that age. She was intelligent, perceptive and shrewd, and her vivacity served as an acceptable substitute for wit. She had spontaneous gaiety and the gift of communicating it to others; many people in Dublin had better cooks, more numerous servants, grander houses, but no one had created a salon in which it was more agreeable to pass an hour or two.[1]

William Lamb, who would later become Lord Melbourne, Queen Victoria's first prime minister, was a Whig politician appointed Chief Secretary of Ireland (second in command to the Lord Lieutenant, the chief governor of Ireland) in the summer of 1827. It was a time of political uncertainty in Britain with a government formed of a tenuous coalition of Whigs and moderate Tories. This was also the year before O'Connell's triumph in the Clare by-election which hastened the passing of the Catholic Relief Act 1829, that is, Catholic Emancipation. Lamb resided in the Chief Secretary's Lodge in the Phoenix Park, now known as the Deerfield residence (home of the U.S. ambassador). He met Lady Branden a few weeks after arriving in Dublin and soon after was visiting

William Lamb, 2nd Viscount Melbourne

Fitzwilliam Square on an almost daily basis. They attended parties and plays as companions with 'striking indiscretion', and Elizabeth seemed to relish in the stir caused by their very public liaison.

Lamb had been married to Lady Caroline Ponsonby since 1805. It had been a tempestuous union and they had formally separated in 1825. Caroline previously had a notorious affair with the poet Lord Byron; it was she who confided to her diary that he was 'mad, bad and dangerous to know'. Her physical and mental health declined throughout the 1820s, and although the marriage was an incessant emotional drain, the Lambs maintained cordial contact during Caroline's final years, the years of their separation. We can imagine that for William Lamb, the society of Lady Branden offered a lifestyle that had been sorely absent from his married life: the dashing couple who were the talk of the town, the solace of intelligent conversation and a kind of domestic companionship, and of course the thrill of sexual tension and perhaps conquest. It remains unknown if Lamb and Lady Branden ever consummated their relationship, though it was generally assumed by friends and acquaintances that they had. Although there is no conclusive proof either way in their correspondence, there are references to a relationship that was stormy and physical. Elizabeth wrote to Lamb in an undated letter:

> Pray come this evening. I will not do anything to annoy you such as biting hitting and so forth – but you must do something more to quiet me than looking stern and cunning. This is all a most unsatisfactory way of spending an evening, designed for better purposes.... One might as well be in company with an old woman as with you.... I had no idea that I could have felt so strong an aversion and almost thirst for revenge as I did after you left me the night you nearly broke my arm ... this morning I love you as much as ever.[2]

Ziegler suggested that it was Lamb's 'failure to respond to her sexual or other demands which caused Elizabeth Branden the deepest upset'.

Despite such episodes, Lamb and Branden took great pleasure in their companionship and correspondence during his time in Dublin. In January 1828 he was recalled to London because of political and personal reasons – his wife Caroline was gravely ill and had weeks to live. He wrote to Elizabeth on 28 January:

The six months we have just passed seem to me as if they
were the last sunshine that would gleam upon my life.

The voyage to England was perilous, tossed by a 'heavy gale of
wind right against us.... Never was a worse scene on this side of the
infernal regions'. A melancholy situation awaited him; his wife was
in her final agonies. Ziegler noted: 'To write to your mistress from the
deathbed of your wife is an exercise difficult to carry off with grace or
even decorum. Lamb made a good shot at it':

> I am afraid you will think me negligent but you do not know
> the melancholy here, which I have come to witness. She is
> dying, dying rapidly, and that with a perfect knowledge of
> it and the greatest composure.[3]

Lamb's grief for the death of his estranged wife was sharp but brief.
He was soon preoccupied once more with politics and his Irish mis-
tress, with whom he kept a loving correspondence while in London.
Five months later his father died and Lamb succeeded to the title of
Viscount, Lord Melbourne.

At the same time, a darker element began to enter his letters to
Elizabeth, when he revealed a preoccupation with flagellation, more
particularly for discipline, but with definite erotic undertones. It started with a recommendation of flogging to deal with the misdeeds of
Elizabeth's daughter Cecilia. Melbourne had been disciplined in this
manner as a child and had also punished his own ward Susan (how
wonderfully Dickensian) in the same fashion. However in future letters he began to imagine taking a birch rod to Elizabeth's maid, and
in time to Elizabeth herself. The following description he gave of the
practice is anything but wholesome:

> It is difficult with the most violent blows to produce much
> effect upon the thick skin of a dog covered with hair. But
> a few twigs of birch applied to the naked skin of a young
> lady produce with very little effort a very considerable
> sensation.[4]

When recalling one of the Fitzwilliam Square maids, he wrote:

> I shall mention first what interests me the most and that
> is the reference in your last letter to your being left alone
> with that troublesome woman. I never think of her without
> wishing intently that I had the power to order her a birch
> application upon that large and extensive field of derrière,
> which is so well calculated to receive it.[5]

Picture the maid collecting that very letter in the post one morning
in No. 3. She leafs through the various missives until she spots a familiar hand and mischievously brings that letter to the front of the pile.
Then, breathlessly ascending the stairs to the drawing room, she finds
Elizabeth by her writing desk and places the letters at her side, with
an insolent glance at her mistress. Elizabeth does not allow her eye to
flicker towards them until the maid has been gone a full minute; but
imagine the poor woman's indignation if she knew of its content!

Elizabeth was not to be spared in these reveries:

> Why do you not write? You cannot be terribly ill – otherwise
> I should hear of it. If I did not think that you were too angry
> to be jested with, I should say that I would certainly get a rod
> for you and apply it smartly the first time I see you.

However, it would be stretching credulity to suggest that they in-
dulged in such practices while secluded in No. 3 during the candle-lit
nights of winter, 1827. This is borne out by a letter from Melbourne to
Elizabeth in 1831 in which he said:

> So you are duller and fractious, are you? I wish I were with
> you. I would administer promptly what is necessary upon
> such occasions, which I have always lamented I did not do
> two or three times when you were in Dublin.[6]

But what of Lord Branden? He seems to have turned a blind eye to
his wife's activity while Lamb was still Chief Secretary, hoping her influence could further his advancement. When Lamb returned to London
early in 1828 he called upon Lord Branden, who was residing there at
the time, and apparently Branden welcomed the visit as courteous and
honourable. However, when Branden realised he would gain nothing

from the affair, he laid his hands on some of his wife's correspondence and at first tried to blackmail Lamb, then instituted proceedings against him for the now archaic claim of criminal conversation. The motives of Lord Branden's actions seem to have become common knowledge, as demonstrated by an entry in *The Creevey Papers* for 17 June 1828:

> Talking of Secretaries for Ireland, do you know of Wm. Lamb's crim. con. case? The facts are these. Lord Brandon, who is a divine as well as a peer, got possession of a correspondence between his lady and Mr. Secretary Lamb, which left no doubt to him or any one else as to the nature of the connection between these young people. So he writes a letter to the lady announcing his discovery, as well as the conclusion he naturally draws from it; but he adds, if she will exert her interest with Mr. Lamb to procure him a bishopric, he will overlook her offence and restore her the letters. To which my lady replies, she shall neither degrade herself nor Mr. Lamb by making any such application; but that she is very grateful to my lord for the letter he has written her, which she shall put immediately into Mr. Lamb's possession.[7]

The case was dismissed due to the paucity of evidence presented by Lord Branden, which led every observer to suspect that a deal had been struck. Indeed, this was the case. A go-between hired by Lamb reported:

> Our friend Lord B. has had a fit of delicacy which in him was truly ridiculous. He did not wish for the money to be paid to him, or to affix his signature to any receipt. This is straining at gnats after swallowing a camel. To obviate all difficulties I went myself to Snow's Bank and presented your draft and got from them two one thousand pound notes, which I have this instant paid into Farquhar's Bank.[8]

Lord Melbourne had escaped without a permanent stain on his character, but, as is often the case, the reputation of the woman was more vulnerable. Branden pursued his wife over the custody of their daughter and Elizabeth had to bring Cecilia to London, then Paris, and for a time lived under an assumed name. Lord Branden died in Nice in 1831; his hatred for his wife apparent in his will:

> As for my most vile and vicious wife, whose infidelity in my eyes was the least of her crimes, I donate and bequeath the sum of one shilling.[9]

Also in his will he urged his daughter not to marry unless she was willing to be faithful to her husband, and to abandon all other men.

Melbourne and Lady Branden maintained their close correspondence, though the ardour inevitably cooled. She went to live in Geneva, their ongoing friendship attested to by the fact that Melbourne packed off his ward Susan to live with her in order to find a husband. Melbourne was keen to do right by Elizabeth and paid her an annuity of £1,000 a year after the death of her husband, a payment that continued in the fourteen years that Elizabeth survived Melbourne's death. His interest in Elizabeth waned as he became consumed by his political career and other affairs, not to mention the almost paternal bond he formed with the young Queen Victoria. There's no doubt that Elizabeth lived comfortably in her remaining years, but she longed for the love and excitement that attended her salon in Fitzwilliam Square. In 1844, she wrote to Melbourne, reproaching him for the late payment of the annuity:

> Oh dearest Ld M just consider the painful position I am placed in and pray, pray I beseech you do not add to it. I have suffered enough in various ways God knows! I have nothing to look back to with pleasure or to look forward to with hope.[10]

Fitzwilliam Square would not see another relationship like it.

Before we move on we should recall Lord Branden's posthumous advice to his daughter, Cecilia, and consider the tragic end of her own marriage. In 1837, she married a man with a name not to be trifled with: Henry Galgacus Redhead Yorke, member of parliament for the city of York. *The Gentleman's Magazine* for July 1848 described his death:

> This gentleman died by his own hand. The agent chosen to effect his rash purpose was prussic acid, which he swal-

lowed in the Regent's Park. He was observed by several persons shortly before twelve o'clock, walking upon the gravel path leading from the entrance-gate into the park, and one of the number ... saw him raise both hands suddenly to his temples, and immediately afterwards stagger and fall on the grass. She called out for assistance, and two men who were near the spot hastened towards the unfortunate man, whom they found in the agonies of death....The coroner remarked that he had personally known Mr Yorke ... [and that] the whole of the unfortunate gentleman's manners led to a strong belief that he was not in his right mind.[11]

The widowed Cecilia was left to raise three children.

Abduction of an Heiress, 'From Motives of Lucre'

IN 1830, WE FIND WILLIAM BURTON NEWENHAM, Richard Knight's erstwhile tenant, still residing in No. 68 Fitzwilliam Square. He was born on 2 June 1806 and left little mark on the city of Dublin. Leaving the city in 1831, his name would not surface in historical journals or chronicles for the next several years. This changed in March 1844 when he was taken into custody in England and, two months later, sentenced to two years' imprisonment for unlawfully abducting a girl under the age of sixteen out of the possession and against the will of her mother. In law reports Newenham was described as 'a person of no fortune or property whatsoever, either in possession or expectancy'.[12] In the course of the trial it became clear that he had inveigled his way into the confidence of the widowed mother in order to take possession of the teenage daughter and her inheritance.

Frances Louisa Wortham was born on Christmas eve 1828, the only daughter of Francis and Jane Wortham of Connington in the county of Cambridge. Mr Wortham was due to inherit some 400 acres in the Cambridgeshire countryside because of the terms of a complex series of indentures dated August 1828. However, by June 1840 he still could not take possession of the land and the family lived in rather straitened circumstances. To make some extra money, he took a lodger into the family home, William Burton Newenham – formerly of Fitzwilliam Square. The father had invited his daughter's eventual abductor into the home. Newenham learned of the overdue bequest that was likely to descend to Frances and who knows when he first drew his designs against her during the two years he spent in the homestead. On Mr. Wortham's deathbed in January 1843, William promised the dying man he would befriend his wife and daughter.

Frances was at boarding school at the time and William, with false counsel, told Jane he would take copies of the deeds to a solicitor he knew in Furnivall's Inn to see about her daughter's inheritance. He also spoke to an old friend George Dann, a solicitor's clerk, saying he had been appointed guardian of an infant girl, between twelve and thirteen, who was entitled to a considerable property. He began writing letters to Frances at her school, 'bearing on Love Letters',[13] which Frances immediately destroyed for fear of their discovery. In midsummer, Frances returned home to her mother, now living in Islington. On the morning of 13 October 1843, she quarrelled with her mother because she did not wish to return to boarding school where she was continually ill. William was present in the house at the time. Later that day, Jane announced she was going into town on business but would return for tea. In her absence, William suggested that Frances accompany him on a walk to Furnivall's Inn to see the solicitor. 'My mamma will be displeased,' she said; but William said he would leave a note: 'My dearest Jane, we are going to Furnival's Inn. Yours affectionately, dear Jane, William.'[14]

Frances asked why he had written in so familiar a style but he told her not to mind. She left the house with only the dress she was wearing. William engaged a cabman, beyond Frances's earshot, then told her to get in. During the cab journey William stopped at a house and returned with a black square luggage box with brass nails. The cab continued.

Frances didn't know the way to Furnivall's Inn so was not unduly alarmed until they arrived at Euston Station. Newenham brought her to a first class carriage and told her to sit in the far end. She later told a police magistrate that she was frightened. They went by train (Frances's first ever train journey) to Birmingham where William said he intended to marry her and that they would contact her mother in a day or two. They continued their journey to Gretna Green and a 'Scotch marriage' ceremony was performed. Upon returning to London, William once again spoke with George Dann.

> He said he was married, and that he had returned from Gretna the preceding Friday; that he had carried off, or went off with, a girl who had some money and he was anxious to ascertain whether she was a ward.
>
> I said to him, 'Surely it is not that little girl you spoke to me about?' And he said, 'Yes, it is.'[15]

Jane returned to her house that evening and found the note. Immediately alarmed, she went to her daughter's room but found that no articles were missing from her wardrobe or toilet box. No doubt every mother could imagine that frantic search. Of course, her worst fears were realised when Frances failed to return and she would not see her daughter until the following March. In that time William and Frances lived in a one-roomed flat at the top of a house in Reading where Frances carried out the menial tasks. She was soon with child. Her mother meanwhile had placed advertisements describing them both and offering a reward for information on their whereabouts. On 28 March 1844, Inspector William Penny called to their lodgings and arrested William. According to Inspector Penny, while he was in the apartment to make the arrest, Frances told him that she was William's lawful wife. On 6 May, William was committed to Newgate gaol for two years upon a charge of felony: for abducting the plaintiff away from motives of lucre. Frances gave birth to their daughter while he was incarcerated. In 1846, Jane Wortham had to petition the House of Lords to have her daughter's Scotch marriage dissolved, so that she could be allowed to marry again.

The Loftus Sisters of No. 34

IN EARLY 1838, THE TALK OF FITZWILLIAM SQUARE undoubtedly centred on the strange goings-on in No. 34. This time there was no scandal, just the terribly sad tale of two spinster sisters and the decline of their mental health. The circumstances were described in the Annual Register under the heading, 'Extraordinary Case of Insanity – Dublin':

[Martha Matilda Loftus] was seventy-eight years old, an unwedded daughter of the late T Loftus Esq., Killyon, county Meath, and was left 3,500l. with 3,000l. charged for her on the family estates by her father's will. From the details of her eccentric habits it appeared, that she would not sleep on a bed in her house, in Fitzwilliam-square; that she lived in her drawing room, converting it into a kitchen as well as sleeping-room, frequently appearing naked at the windows, or scarcely clothed at all when going into the street, or driving about town in a jaunting car; she caused a number of red pocket handkerchiefs to be stitched into a gown; her sister, Jane Loftus, was also deranged. Her parrot dined off the same plate with her; and fancying that a musical instrument had been invented on which parrots could play, she importuned the music sellers to procure it for her favourite polly. In boxes, kept near the large fires always burning in her chamber – a very dirty one – large sums of money were found.... Coins, plate, gold watches, and other valuable property, thrust between rags, book-leaves, and concealed amidst dirty vessels, clothes, &c. about the apartment. She always appeared very ill dressed, unwashed, and squalid.[16]

But of course it is unfair to merely recall these unfortunate women in the years of their decline, when during the course of their lives they were most likely a source of love and companionship for many.

An Ill-judged Prosecution

THROUGHOUT THE TIME OF OUR FIRST THREE tales there lived in No. 49 Fitzwilliam Square Lady Catherine Frankfort, widow of Viscount Frankfort de Montmerency. She moved there a few years after the death of her husband, Lodge Evans de Montmerency, a well-known eighteenth century Irish politician, in 1822 and remained until her own passing on 12 November 1851. It's likely she never knew W.B. Newenham while he lived on the square, or heard of his subsequent dastardly exploits. She may have looked with sorrow or exasperation at the piteous Loftus sisters that lived around the corner at No. 34. And who can say what she thought of Lady Branden's affair? Perhaps she was scandalised or amused, indifferent or even sympathetic. After all, she herself had married a man much advanced in years, though there is nothing to suggest their union wasn't a happy one. However, in 1842, her own family became the subject of gossip and unflattering newspapers articles, thanks to a case pursued in London by her son, Lodge Reymond, second Viscount Frankfort.

The viscount lived in Southwick Terrace, Paddington, and late on the evening of 26 May 1841 two women came to his house. One was an acquaintance, an actress named Miss Mitchell. Frankfort had never before seen her companion, the 18-year-old Alice Lowe. Miss Mitchell wished Frankfort to circulate some benefit tickets for a certain theatre and they conversed for some minutes in the hallway; all the other lights in the house had been put out. Frankfort testified that on that first night he did not exchange a single word with Miss Lowe nor asked about her: 'I don't inquire who comes to my house.'[17] With their business complete, Mitchell and her friend withdrew.

Two nights later, Alice returned to Frankfort's house quite alone, according to his testimony. Frankfort was already in bed but was called down to see her. She waited in the darkened drawing room, only illuminated by a light in the hallway. Frankfort testified that he attempted to persuade her to leave, saying her friends would be alarmed at her absence.

> Lord Frankfort: I kept the cab waiting till nearly one o'clock, and then, when I saw that she was determined to stop, I sent it away.
>
> Mr Bodkin (prosecutor): How long did she remain with you?
>
> Lord Frankfort: Till the 22nd of July.

Quite a stop. The cause of the prosecution was the alleged theft by Miss Lowe of certain articles (gold-framed miniatures, snuff boxes and other items with a combined worth of several hundred pounds) from Frankfort's bedroom when she eventually left the house. Alice was defended by a Mr. Adolphus. In early exchanges both sides tried to impute the character of the plaintiff and defendant. The former, a man who would seduce a young girl and then prosecute her; the latter, a femme fatale who brazenly entered a man's house to satisfy her sexual desires and kleptomania. Another prosecutor, Mr. Clarkson, attempted to read a statement respecting Miss Lowe's previous character, but the judge ruled it was irrelevant.

> Mr. Clarkson persisted in stating that the prisoner had been 'a gay woman' [a prostitute]. Mr. Adolphus rose to object, and at the same moment Alice Lowe, who had from the first looked ill and wept much, fell from her chair in a hysterical fit.

Frankfort testified that he kept the objects in question in a bedroom drawer that Alice would have had access to, though he always kept it locked when he was not in the room. He said he had given the accused several gifts, but not these items. Also, 'when she came she did not bring any clothes with her, but I had plenty of clothes supplied for her'. Alice's lawyer questioned the viscount:

> Mr Adolphus: Were not some of the prisoner's clothes kept in the same drawer?
>
> Lord Frankfort: No.
>
> Mr Adolphus: Are you sure of that?
>
> Lord Frankfort: There were no clothes of hers in the drawer except a hair-brush.
>
> Mr Adolphus: Was the drawer kept locked?
>
> Lord Frankfort: It was always locked when I went out.
>
> Mr Adolphus: Do you mean to say that you locked up her hairbrushes?
>
> Lord Frankfort: Oh, yes.

It then emerged that Alice was not quite at liberty to leave the house during the time that she stayed.

> Mr Adolphus: Was there any agreement as to what the prisoner was to have or receive from you?

Lord Frankfort: No; I merely told her that I was not going to keep her to run about the streets; and if she left my house at all she was to keep away altogether. I told her, she was welcome to go out, but if she did so, she must stay out ... [Then referring to her clothes] ... I ordered the Mantua-makers and milliners to come to the house to measure the prisoner and I paid for the things.

An unfortunate use of the word prisoner in the context of his answer. Before the jury Mr. Adolphus was adamant that the items had been gifted to Alice and that Frankfort only wished them returned after she had left his clutches.

Could any one doubt that he was determined to get back the jewels, which he repented having given to her?

Casting Frankfort as the villain, he said. 'It has been proved, that for two whole months this young creature was kept almost a prisoner from the light of heaven,' and he put it to the common sense of the jury whether she would have endured such a condition unless his Lordship had given her some equivalent. After the summing up, the jury consulted for ten minutes, without retiring, and returned a 'not guilty' verdict. The outcome was met with scenes that echo those of another trial we have examined:

The verdict was received with shouts of applause in the court, echoed by the crowd without; and for several minutes order could not be restored. A second indictment was withdrawn; and Alice Lowe was discharged. She left the court in a cab; her appearance outside being greeted by loud shouts, and several well-dressed persons pressing forward to shake hands with her.[18]

It is remarkable that in both this trial and in the Yelverton case, the sympathy in the public galleries was so firmly behind the ill-treated woman. It's striking that in both cases the public felt that a woman had been wronged by a man in a higher social class, both of whom had revealed a callous indifference to the women in question. There seemed to be a fatal blind spot in the characters of both Yelverton and Frankfort, perhaps common then to men of their background; a lack of insight into how their frank testimony would be received by the public at large: Yelverton's admission that he pursued Longworth so that she would be his mistress rather than his wife; Frankfort's casual confession that he had refused to allow his lover leave the house. Frankfort obviously felt he had every right to treat Alice in this fashion, but reports of the case could not have elicited much maternal pride in Lady Catherine Frankfort, of No. 49 Fitzwilliam Square.

Cannibalism in Central Africa

IN 1890, A FITZWILLIAM SQUARE RESIDENT was once more exercised by the need to protect the reputation of a family member. Andrew Jameson, of the whiskey distilling family, was born in Scotland in 1855. He moved into No. 9 Fitzwilliam Square in 1886 and remained there for

Jameson family crest in chimney-piece of No. 9

a decade. It was Jameson who commissioned the distinctive interior redecoration of No. 9, including dark oak panelling and a carved chimney-piece containing the Jameson family crest, the same crest which is displayed on every whiskey bottle. At the same time in London plans were in motion for a high profile expedition to Africa called the Emin Pasha Relief Expedition. Emin Pasha, whose real name was Eduard Schnitzer, was a German governor of Equatoria (southern Sudan), then an Egyptian outpost. When the Egyptian administration of Sudan was overthrown by followers of Mohammed Ahmed Al Mahdi (Mahdists) in 1885, Emin Pasha and the families of his Egyptian employees were left isolated. The notion of a rescue effort undertaken right through the heart of Africa proved hugely popular in Britain, and the first gathering of the relief committee met in December 1886. It eventually raised £32,000 and received hundreds of applications to enlist. The plan was to approach Equatoria from the west, sail up the Congo river and a further tributary, and make a final push through unexplored territory overland. Emin Pasha could then escape back over this newly forged route. The expedition was led by Henry Morton Stanley, the famous African explorer who went in search of Dr. Livingstone.

Andrew Jameson's younger brother, James Sligo Jameson, was an artist, naturalist and big game hunter (if the latter two are not a contradiction) and he paid £1,000 to the relief committee in order to join the expedition, primarily in his capacity as naturalist. However, the whole mission was something of a debacle. At an early stage Stanley divided his force into the advanced column and the rear column. The former continued on towards Equatoria. The latter encamped in order to gather supplies

James Sligo Jameson

and carriers, left under the command of Major Edmund Barttelot and James S. Jameson. It took Stanley almost another year to reach Emin Pasha through the Congo jungle. Meanwhile, the rear column was paralysed by inaction, illness and the sadistic leadership of Barttelot. On 19 July 1888, he was shot dead by a member of the Maniema people. Jameson, completely out of his depth, decided to journey back down the Congo river to a point where communication was possible with England. He left the camp on 8 August, contracted a chill two days later which developed into fever, and died on 17 August 1888.

On the same day, Stanley returned to the base camp and was disgusted to find the rear column in such a shambles. Eventually, in September 1889, Stanley led his remaining force, including Emin Pasha, to Bagamoyo, the capital of German East Africa. To compound an ill-fated expedition, during a banquet held in his honour, Emin stepped out of a second storey window believing there to be a balcony, and was severely injured. As such, Stanley had to return to London without the man he was sent to rescue. At first he was lauded for ostensibly completing his mission. However, criticisms were soon levelled at the human cost endured and the tales of brutality carried out against the indigenous populations. Stanley countered by laying the blame squarely on the incompetence of the rear column and the men in command: Barttelot and Jameson. There were many examples of the former's appalling behaviour. However, it was a tale involving Jameson that particularly horrified public opinion – a charge which to this day has lent his name a certain infamy.

Tippu-Tib, African slave trader

In May 1888, Jameson visited a local chief and slave trader called Tippu-Tib to try to arrange some supplies and additional men for the camp. While at the chief's house he witnessed some native dances and Tippu told him 'that the festivities usually concluded with a banquet of human flesh'.[19] From this point the tale grew in the telling. According to Stanley, Jameson was fascinated by the practice of cannibalism and so purchased a young slave girl, handed her over to the revellers and made sketches in his notebook while she was butchered and eaten. This was a story first related by an expedition interpreter who was present at the scene, but this man had a deep personal dislike of Jameson and he later retracted this version of events.

However, when Stanley retold the tale on his return to Britain, it was taken by the public as proof that even the most civilised of men could lose their humanity in that dark continent. Of course, Jameson was no longer alive to answer the claim and so it fell to his widow and brother Andrew to rescue his reputation. While in Fitzwilliam Square, Andrew Jameson would occasionally receive letters from James in the Congo. They were addressed to 'My dear Andy', and told of the struggles in the rear column in the absence of Stanley. We can picture Andrew Jameson opening these exotic letters, stained, battered and well-travelled; breaking the wax seal and unfolding the outer page that acted as envelope; his joy at hearing from his younger brother tempered by the contents. For Andrew, it was heartbreaking not only to read of the terrible hardship, then death of his brother, but also to have his memory tarnished with Stanley's incredible claim. He helped his sister-in-law edit together James's diaries and letters into a volume called *The Story of the Rear Column* in order to clear his name. Andrew wrote a preface from his house at No. 9, decrying those who had accused his brother of such barbarism, especially Stanley:

> The dream of [James's] early life was to add his name to the long roll of those who have striven for some good and useful object. At length the occasion offered itself, as he believed, in the Expedition in which he lost his life; to join it he sacrificed his wealth, his home, his family joys and comfort, to live 'laborious days', and find some scope for the pent-up energies within him.... What is his reward? He is sought to be made the scapegoat of his Commander's ill-judgment and neglect! Charges of disobedience, disloyalty, forgetfulness of promises, desertion, cruelty, cowardice, and murder are brought against him, on the authority of discredited liars....The charges are brought against Jameson when he is in his grave, when the common usage of humanity suggests silence, and when a man of a noble and honourable cast of nature would altogether prefer to lie under an unjust suspicion rather than asperse and defame the voiceless dead. This, however, is not the course which Mr. Stanley has followed.[20]

However, when we come to James's own diary entry for the cannibal incident at Tippu-Tib's house, we can see that although he certainly did not intend for a murder to take place, he was guilty of a serious lack of judgement, one that had horrific consequences for an innocent child, which are upsetting even to read:

> Tippu-Tib, who came in before it was over, told me that they usually kill several people, and have a grand feast, for the Wacusu are terrible cannibals.... I told him that people at home generally believed that these were only 'travellers' tales', as they are called in our country, or, in other words, lies. He then said something to an Arab called Ali, seated

next him, who turned round to me and said, 'Give me a bit of cloth, and see.' I sent my boy for six handkerchiefs, thinking it was all a joke, and that they were not in earnest, but presently a man appeared, leading a young girl of about ten years old by the hand, and I then witnessed the most horribly sickening sight I am ever likely to see in my life. He plunged a knife quickly into her breast twice, and she fell on her face, turning over on her side. Three men then ran forward, and began to cut up the body of the girl; finally her head was cut off, and not a particle remained, each man taking his piece away down to the river to wash it. The most extraordinary thing was that the girl never uttered a sound, nor struggled, until she fell. Until the last moment, I could not believe that they were in earnest. I have heard many stories of this kind since I have been in this country, but never could believe them, and I never would have been such a beast as to witness this, but I could not bring myself to believe that it was anything save a ruse to get money out of me, until the last moment.

The girl was a slave captured from a village close to this town, and the cannibals were Wacusu slaves, and natives of this place. When I went home I tried to make some small sketches of the scene while still fresh in my memory, not that it is ever likely to fade from it. No one here seemed to be in the least astonished at it.[21]

The publication of Jameson's diaries did manage to clear him of the most serious charge: that of intentionally buying a slave girl in order to sketch her death as it occurred. However, though not his intention, that was the result, and if he did not callously sketch the scene while the gruesome assault was taking place he did draw it from memory later. The diaries of Jameson as a whole reveal a man who was unable to deal with the realities of imperialist exploration. He joined the expedition in search of adventure, scientific pursuit and big game hunting. Instead he experienced the monotony of river travel, encampment and the casual brutality of overseeing slave workers. He was entirely incapable of organising the rear column into an effective force to follow after Stanley, was paralysed by inaction and eventually died of fever while attempting to contact home. Andrew's efforts to rescue James's reputation were not wholly in vain, but it necessitated revealing his adventurer brother to be a rather tragic and pathetic figure. Andrew Jameson moved out of No. 9 Fitzwilliam Square when he was appointed governor of the Bank of Ireland in 1896.

Murder in Hollywood

MOVING INTO A NEW CENTURY, JUST AFTER the conclusion of the second Boer War, we come upon our final tale, that of William Cunningham Deane Tanner – murdered in Hollywood in 1922, a yarn worthy of the most lurid pulp fiction.

The widow, Jane Deane-Tanner, busied herself in the drawing room of No. 27 Fitzwilliam Square. Despite the time of year, it was unseasonably cool and she stoked the fire she had ordered set that morning. She thought this new house suffered terribly from draughts compared to her previous home in Fitzwilliam Street. She had moved only recently after the death of her husband Thomas. Not three months ago he was in full health. The most innocuous scratch of an exposed nail poisoned his blood, and Jane could not continue to live in the house in which he died.

In the room also were two of her surviving three children. Jane sat down again and resumed her chat with Ellen, her eldest daughter, most beautiful and also best trusted of her family. Three years earlier her second daughter, Lizzie, had died at the age of 25. She was the most sweet-natured girl, everyone's favourite, and was sorely missed on occasions like these when she always endeavoured to keep the conversation light-hearted. Jane's youngest son, Denis, sat apart. He had just returned from active service in the Boer War and was given to episodes of introspection, but Jane felt that he had always possessed an odd disposition.

They had gathered together because William, the absent family member, was due to arrive that afternoon on a visit from New York, with his new American wife in tow. William had left for America in 1890. As a young man he wished to pursue a career in acting and he often quarrelled with his parents who thought he should follow his father into the military. He had found some theatre work in America but by now was running an antiques shop on Fifth Avenue and had recently married Ethel (Effie) Hamilton, a chorus girl on Broadway.

A commotion on the street brought Denis to the window. 'It's Willie', he said, as he watched his brother help the cabman take a luggage trunk up the steps. He noticed the young woman standing to the side, her thick black curls and large eyes and thought he should return with William to New York and find a wife of his own. Ellen joined him at the window. 'Would you look at him; he looks so handsome. Oh, and his wife is tiny, the poor thing.' Down below William paid the cabbie, and as he looked up at the new family home, spied his siblings at the window and beamed up at them. As he was raising his hand in greeting the front door must have opened for his attention was drawn forward and he offered his wife his arm to bring her into the house. Jane got up from her seat, smoothed her black dress and said, 'Come, we'll go down to greet him'.

After William's demise, Ethel (then remarried to an Edward Robins) recalled the visit for a New York reporter:

> Mrs. Robins said last night that shortly after their marriage she and Tanner visited his folks in Ireland. They were entertained royally and she realised for the first time that the young blood she had married off Broadway was a veritable sportsman in Ireland. His family entertained her at their home in Fitzwilliam Square and afterward they paid a visit to Cork, where the old family seat was located.
>
> 'They were the Deane Tanners,' Mrs. Robins explained, 'to differentiate them from the other Tanners. The name is rather a familiar one in Ireland, and in England I think it is rather derogatorily applied to some small coin, a six-pence, I think. His father had been a member of Parliament; his uncle was a justice of the peace. Altogether the family was quite to the front.'[22]

When the trip was over they returned to their apartment at 40 Washington Square. Within a year Ethel had given birth to a daughter and in 1903 Denis joined his brother in America. However, all was not well with William. His marriage was not a happy one; his upbringing of upper-class reserve was incompatible with Ethel's tendency to descend into tears and tantrums. He also ran up a series of debts, especially after the Wall Street financial panic of 1907. But he gave no clue as to what he was about to do.

At around noon on 23 October 1908, William left his antiques shop on Fifth Avenue to go to lunch but didn't return. Nor did he go home and no one of the name William Deane Tanner was ever heard of again. No credible motive could be found for his desertion of his wife and daughter. In 1912, she got a decree of divorce and was granted full custody of her child. Quite bizarrely, in the same year Denis followed his brother into oblivion. He had, since his arrival, married an American girl called Ada who had borne him two children. On the morning of 24 August 1912, he played with his two kids as normal, kissed them both fondly, left for work in good spirits and was never seen again. It was rumoured that he had made contact with his lost brother and had gone to join him.

Ethel remarried an Edward Robbins in August 1914 and it would be five years before she discovered, in the most extraordinary fashion, that her former husband was still living. The circumstances were described in *The New York Herald*:

> With her daughter Mrs Robins went to a motion picture theatre in this city one night. They chose the theatre without knowing what picture it was featuring. For several hundred feet of film it was just a new picture as far as they were concerned, but suddenly the hero appeared. Mrs. Robins sank back in her seat too startled to speak. Her daughter stood up.
>
> For the laughing face on the screen was that of the long missing [William] Deane-Tanner a little changed – somewhat older looking they decided when they finally settled back to wait for the hero's next entry. They sat through the picture and then saw it again and learned that the man whose face they knew was acting and directing movies under the name of William Desmond Taylor.[23]

Four years after leaving New York, William Deane Tanner arrived in California, changed his name to William Desmond Taylor and found his true calling in the new motion picture industry. He acted in several

William Desmond Taylor, signed photo to Mary Miles Minter

films but made his name as a director and became president of the Motion Picture Directors Association.

Taylor worked with many of the early Hollywood starlets and was the subject of infatuation for more than one. The two women with whom he was most closely associated were Mabel Normand and Mary Miles Minter. Normand was a popular comedic actress, one of Taylor's closest friends and perhaps a former lover. Minter was a beautiful young actress who was passionately in love with Taylor. She claimed that they had been engaged but in fact Taylor seemed intent on spurning her advances, partly because of the difference in their ages, partly because of the threatening attitude of Minter's archetypal stage mother Charlotte Shelby, who was obsessively protective of her daughter.

On 1 February 1922, Mabel Normand visited Taylor in his Alvarado street bungalow to borrow a book that he had recommended. She was driven there by her chauffeur William Davis and she told him she would be out directly. While he waited Davis cleaned the limousine and spoke briefly with Henry Peavey, Taylor's personal assistant, who was leaving the house for the day. After about half an hour Normand and Taylor emerged from his bungalow. Taylor escorted her back to her car, the borrowed book tucked under her arm. He greeted the chauffeur in a familiar fashion and blew a kiss to Normand as the car pulled away. She was the last person to see him alive, apart from his killer.

For when Taylor retuned to his house an intruder, who had either been hidden in the house for some time or slipped in while he escorted Normand outside, emerged in his living room and fired a single bullet, killing him instantly. His neighbour, Faith MacLean, heard the shot but assumed it to be a car backfiring. Still, she went to her front door and witnessed a figure dressed in a long dark coat and wearing a muffler exit

Taylor's house walking backwards. This person turned, saw MacLean and flashed a smile, then casually re-entered the house as if having forgotten something. A moment later the figure re-emerged, closed the door and walked unhurriedly away. The killer's actions were so nonchalant that MacLean assumed nothing was amiss and only realised her error when Taylor's body was discovered the next morning by his assistant Peavey. In later testimony, MacLean said she thought the murderer 'looked funny', as those who wear costumes on a film set, and could not swear that it was not a woman dressed as a man.

Mary Miles Minter

The murder caused a sensation in Hollywood. Newspapers trawled through a list of suspects that included some of the most famous names in the industry. The police investigation was so poorly handled that a huge amount of evidence from the crime scene was lost and the murder remained unsolved. As such, it has provided fertile ground for amateur sleuths to comb

Mabel Normand

through the evidence and present theories of their own. Among the most popular is that Taylor was killed by Charlotte Shelby, incensed by his relationship with her daughter, and a woman with a history of unstable and violent behaviour. The most outlandish claim is that Taylor was killed by his missing brother Denis Tanner, though this is really only suggested because of the romance of the story rather than any shred of proof. The most humdrum explanation is that Taylor was gunned down by a professional hit-man because of his interference with the selling of drugs within the movie studios. MacLean's description of the killer's dispassion would lend credence to this view.

However, in 1999 a man named Raphael Long wrote of going in his youth to the assistance of an elderly reclusive neighbour, 'a kindly little old lady', who was suffering a heart attack in October 1964. He wrote:

> Meanwhile, our neighbour was highly agitated and obvious-ly in a great deal of pain. Apparently, she had just converted to Roman Catholicism and was deeply concerned with the consequences of the hereafter. She wanted a priest, which was impossible, and she wanted to confess her 'sins'. She then went on to explain that she had been a silent screen actress. She further stated that she had shot and killed a man by the name of William Desmond Taylor. And she continued by saying that they nearly caught her and that she had to flee the country. There were several other claims that she made which I simply don't recall. Our only con-cern at the moment was in getting her immediate medical attention. And besides, none of this made one bit of sense. This wasn't the woman we knew for fifteen years. The idea that this kindly woman could take a gun and shoot another human being was preposterous. The statement about being an actress was equally unbelievable. It was obvious to me that she was suffering under some pain-inspired delirium. At the time, I must confess my total ignorance of the name William Desmond Taylor.[24]

The woman, whom they knew as Pat Lewis, died before medical help arrived. When later cleaning out her house they discovered trunks of old correspondence and promotional photographs. Across one was scrawled the name Patricia Palmer, one of the eight names used by the silent movie actress Ella Margaret Gibson. Gibson had appeared in several movies with Taylor but was never a formal suspect in his mur-der investigation. She had earlier been arrested separately on charges of vagrancy and opium dealing, and she was also charged with being part of a blackmail and extortion ring in 1923. It seems to me unlikely that Long concocted the story of Gibson's deathbed confession, but whether she was speaking from 'some pain-inspired delirium', or was in fact telling the truth, we'll probably never know.

The twenty years that followed William Deane Tanner's
final meeting with the living
members of his family, in the salon of No. 27 Fitzwilliam Square
in 1902, were truly remarkable
– 'a biography few screen writers
would have the temerity to palm
off as fiction'.[25] It demonstrates
that even the uniform houses of
a peaceful residential square can
contain lives less ordinary; that occasionally people, especially those
of a privileged social background,

Margaret Gibson

find themselves unexpectedly in the most astonishing situations, with
the result that their actions and motives are weighed by the public at
large, and their reputations are forever coloured by that verdict.

IN THIS BRIEF COLLECTION OF SORDID tales the most bona fide Fitzwilliam Square scandal was Lady Branden's affair with William Lamb in
the late 1820s, which kept Dublin's salons abuzz with innuendo and
hearsay, resulted in court cases, a failed marriage and effectively the
exile of the lovelorn lady. When considering scoundrels we need look
no further that William Burton Newenham, resident here only briefly,
but later guilty of a base and duplicitous seduction of a modest heiress. We've also looked at residents who had the reputations of family
members belittled in the national press: Lady Frankfort's son for his
ill-judged prosecution of a waifish young lover; and Andrew Jameson,
whose deceased brother was condemned for an apparent merciless act
of savagery. Fitzwilliam Square only acted as a staging post in the remarkable life of William Deane Tanner; a point where two (of his three)
lives met, a mingling of the old Irish and new American worlds. Back
then there were the welcomes and hopeful conversations of a reunited
family as he introduced his wife to his grieving mother, elder sister
and a brother who would later replicate William's immersion in, then
desertion of American family life. Only later would Tanner abandon

his betrothed, lead a remarkable double life, achieve fame and fortune, only to be killed by a mystery assailant.

Endnotes

1. Philip Ziegler, *Melbourne: A Biography of William Lamb*, pp. 101-102.

2. Ibid., p. 103.

3. Ibid., p. 104.

4. Melbourne to Lady Branden, 21 Feb 1831. H. Montgomery Hyde, *A Tangled Web: Sex Scandals in British Politics and Society*, p. 66.

5. Melbourne to Lady Branden, 30 Aug. 1830, Ibid., p. 65.

6. Melbourne to Lady Branden, 19 May; 18 Jan. 1831. Ibid., p. 67.

7. Thomas Creevey, *The Creevey Papers*, ed. Herbert Maxwell (1904), Vol. 2, p. 160.

8. Ziegler, *Melbourne*, p. 108.

9. Ibid. (translated from French), p. 109.

10. Lady Branden to Lord Melbourne, 26 Dec 1844, Ibid., p. 110.

11. *The Gentleman's Magazine*, Vol. 184, p. 96.

12. *The Jurist*, 1848, Vol. 1, Part 4, p. 1071.

13. Testimony of Frances Louisa Wortham, 23 April 1844. *Sessional Papers of the House of Lords*, 1846, Vol. XIX, p. 293.

14. Testimony of Jane Wortham, 22 April 1844, Ibid., p. 292.

15. Testimony of George Dann, 22 April 1844. Ibid., p. 292.

16. *Annual Register,* Vol. 80, pp, 65-66.

17. This and subsequent testimony taken from *Annual Register* Vol. 84, pp. 171-174.

18. *Annual Register*, Vol. 84, p. 174.

19. *Dictionary of National Biography*, Vol. 29, p. 233.

20. Andrew Jameson, preface to *The Story of the Rear Column*, ed. Mrs James Jameson, pp. xv-xvi.

21. James Sligo Jameson, *The Story of the Rear Column*, p. 291.

22. *New York Daily News*, 6 February 1922. Most of the subsequent material is taken from various issues of *Taylorology*, a newsletter edited by Bruce Long dealing with the mysterious death of William Desmond Taylor.

23. *New York Herald*, 5 Feb. 1922.

24. Raphael Long, *Taylorology*, Issue 84, December 1999.

25. *The Milwaukee Sentinel*, 26 October 1952.

4

Writers

Consider the written output of sixty-nine houses in 120 years: notes and correspondence, business reports and diary entries, drafts of poetry, prose and memoirs – enough to fill an archive. The incessant scrape of pen on paper; quills, nibs and fountain pens; ink pots and blotters. We can picture some of them: a gentleman deep in study in the first floor return, surrounded by tomes and parchments; a lady corresponding from her writing desk, winter sunshine streaming through a parlour window; a young governess in the cold dark of her third-floor bedroom, confiding in her diary by the light of a single candle while rain drops beat and boards creak. In this chapter we shall examine the literary output of Fitzwilliam Square, in particular the lives of the writers who lived and worked there. We shall also look at some novels that used the square as a setting and will meet certain residents who provided the inspiration for characters in works of fiction.

The drawn out construction of Fitzwilliam Square – first laid out in a survey map of 1789 and finally completed in 1828 – corresponds to the Romantic period of English literature, dominated by the older generation of Romantic poets: Blake, Coleridge and Wordsworth; and the newer: Byron, Shelley and Keats. It was not a golden age for original drama but the novel was flourishing with the work of Radcliffe, Scott and Austen. Romantic literature was a reaction against eighteenth century rationalism and classicism, a philosophy represented in the uniform architecture of the emerging Fitzwilliam Square. Later we will be concerned with the arrival of national ballads and poetry, the Irish literary revival and in particular the themes of the Anglo-Irish 'big house' novel, a genre that reflected the anxieties and uncertainties of the Protestant landowning classes as their power ebbed and they came increasingly under attack from nationalist forces.

The Honourable Mrs. Price Blackwood

IT MUST BE SAID THAT THE SQUARE'S earliest connection to literature is rather oblique. In the first chapter we studied an 1822 estate map by John Roe which named some of the early speculators in Fitzwilliam Square. Among them was Price Blackwood, who had acquired up to six properties on the east side. The Blackwoods were wine merchants

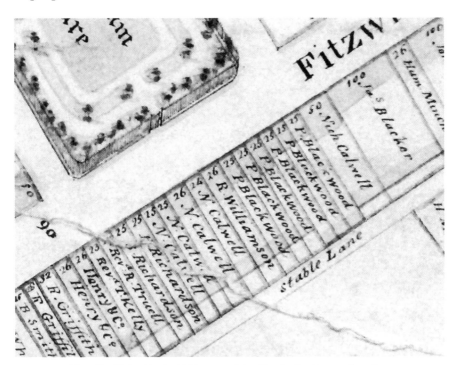

*Detail of John Roe's 1822 map of the Pembroke Estate showing
Price Blackwood's holdings on the east side of the square*

of Harcourt Street and Barons of Dufferin and Claneboye (a peerage created in July 1800, no doubt to reward support for the Act of Union). The 1813 Act to enclose and improve the central garden of Fitzwilliam Square also named Price Blackwood as one of fourteen commissioners. Blackwood served in the British Navy and by 1825 he was living in London. There he married Helen Selina Sheridan, granddaughter of the famous Irish playwright Richard Brinsley Sheridan. She was the elder sister of Caroline Norton who was married in 1827. (In 1836, George Norton sued then Prime Minister Lord Melbourne, accusing him of having an affair with Caroline – a tale with distinct echoes of the Lady Branden case of the previous chapter.) Both sisters were poets and composers. Helen Blackwood is best remembered for her ballads 'The Charming Woman' and 'The Irish Emigrant'.

Helen Blackwood

The former, a popular song of 1835, was a tongue-in-cheek warning for sensible men not to marry 'charming women' as they tended to be well-read, too thin, eclectic in taste, wilful and penniless.

> Yes, she's really a charming woman!
> But, I thought, I observed, by the bye,
> A something that's rather uncommon,
> In the flash of that very bright eye?
> It may be a mere fancy of mine,
> Though her voice has a very sharp tone,
> But I'm told that these charming women
> Are inclined to have wills of their own!

'Lament of the Irish Emigrant' was written around 1848, a sentimental ballad dealing with a young Irishman bidding farewell at the graveside of his wife and child before leaving for America. Aimed at the British middle-classes, it is a sanitised depiction of the Famine, though Blackwood successfully displayed an empathy for people from whom she was socially removed:

'Tis but a step down yonder lane,
And the little church stands near-
The church where we were wed, Mary,
I see the spire from here;
But the grave-yard lies between, Mary,
And my step might break your rest,
For I've laid you, darling, down to sleep,
With your baby on your breast.

Another Fitzwilliam Square resident, Alfred Perceval Graves (more anon), was fulsome in his praise of the lament:

> Living a happy domestic life amid Irish surroundings, her warm heart beats in such close sympathy with her peasant neighbours that ... she writes as is if she were one of themselves.[1]

Price Blackwood succeeded his father Hans as fourth Baron Dufferin in 1839. He died two years later aboard the Reindeer steamer between Liverpool and Belfast, from an accidental overdose of morphine. Helen, then Lady Dufferin, died in 1867.

The Poet James Henry of No. 6

As MENTIONED ELSEWHERE, THE POET James Clarence Mangan was employed as a scrivener in the Fitzwilliam Square office of the solicitor Thomas Leland from 1829. While Mangan worked in Fitzwilliam Square his verse began to appear frequently in journals such as the *Comet*, the *Dublin Penny Journal*, the *Dublin University Magazine* and later in the *Nation* and the *United Irishman*. He died in poverty in 1849 during the cholera epidemic that swept Ireland following the Famine. In 1837, the clerks, solicitors and other employees of Thomas Leland's offices vacated No. 6 Fitzwilliam Square West. At the same time, the medical doctor, classical scholar and poet James Henry (1798-1876) moved into the house directly opposite, No. 6 east. Henry took up residence there with his wife, Anne Jane née Patton, and their four-year-old daughter, Katherine Olivia. He was born in College Green on 13 September 1798 to Robert Henry, a wealthy Protestant woollen-draper. His early education at Unitarian schools left unhappy memories and inspired in him a religious scepticism that would remain throughout his life. He attended Trinity College and graduated with the gold medal in classics in 1819. He then turned his attentions to medical study, completing an MD thesis on Malaria in 1832 and carrying on an extensive practice (he was also vice-president of the Royal College of Physicians in Ireland). Henry described his early practice in an autobiographical poem of 1853:

James Henry, poet of No. 6

> Five years, long years, I visited
> Early and late the poor man's bed,
> Lived midst contagion, filth and groans,
> Pored over dead men's mouldering bones.[2]

In character he possessed contrary qualities of austerity and tenderness common among medical practitioners in the nineteenth century (and perhaps today still). J.P. Mahaffy, writing his obituary, described him thus:

> There was a curious combination of rudeness and kindness, of truculence and gentleness, of severity and softness in him, which made him different from other men.[3]

Describing his practice, Mahaffy wrote that:

> ... his sceptical and independent ways of thinking estranged him from the religious and commonplace practitioners around him.... He even advanced to the shocking heresy that no doctor's opinion was worth a guinea, and accordingly set the example of charging five-shilling fees, an unheard of thing in Dublin in that day.

Henry's views on this subject were expressed in an epigram published in *Kottabos – A College Miscellany*:

> Sickness takes but your life; the doctor worse
> Than any sickness, takes both life and purse.
>
> J.H.[4]

His successful practice meant he lived comfortably in Fitzwilliam Square and was able to devote his leisure time to literary pursuits. He gained a reputation as a poet and satiric pamphleteer; Valentine Cunningham describes him as a 'wonderfully cranky, witty, scathing versifier'.[5] He published five collections of poetry in his lifetime but they were of quite a low standard and soon faded from public memory. He was rediscovered recently by Christopher Hicks, who edited the *Selected Poems of James Henry* in 2002. Henry's eccentric use of rhyme, metre and stress (as can be noted in the first couplet quoted above – the rhyme of 'visited' and 'bed') can be quite jarring. He has been mentioned in the same breath as the Scottish poet William McGonagall (an infamous writer of doggerel), but such comparisons are quite unfair. Henry's verse is infused with great energy and good humour and many of his later poems, particularly those following the death of his wife in 1849, are contemplative and poignant.

Two comical poems written from No. 6 Fitzwilliam Square in March 1841 are good examples of his early style. Both are dedicated to a Miss Sheridan. The first eulogises her for the quality of her coffee; the second excoriates the quality of her griddle cake. It seems clear that the poet and lady were good friends and that Henry knew Miss Sheridan would treat the exaggeration of the paean and the lampoon with the same good humour.

To Miss Sheridan, on her having made coffee for the author the preceding evening; composed the following morning while breakfasting alone.

> Your coffee it was very strong, bright-eyed Miss Sheridan,
> And like a subtle spirit through all my veins it ran,
> Making me feel more like a god than a mortal man,
> As I sat on the sofa beside you, bright-eyed Miss Sheridan.

Your coffee it was very sweet, silken-haired Miss Sheridan,
Far sweeter than the famous honey that once flowed in
  Canaan,
Or the nectar quaffed of yore in celestial divan,
And no wonder, for it was you made it, silken-haired
  Miss Sheridan ...

The coffee I have this morning, lily-armed Miss Sheridan,
Is as different from last night's as Drogheda from Japan,
Or the coarsest sole-leather from the finest cordovan,
Just because you are not here to make it, lily-armed
  Miss Sheridan,

My toast is burnt to a cinder, rosy-fingered Miss Sheridan,
My butter is only fit to be put into the frying-pan,
And my milk would water the garden, if it were
  poured through the watering-can-
How could it be otherwise, when you are far away from me,
  rosy-fingered Miss Sheridan...

(Fitzwilliam-square, Dublin, March 14, 1841.)

Two days later he changed his tune:

To Miss Sheridan, on her having presented the author with a piece of griddle-cake.

The cake you sent me was detestable
And perfectly indigestible;
I never tasted anything so abominable;
Its smell was intolerable,
And its very look was horrible.
It was as hard as a piece of maple,
As tough as a ship's cable,
As black as a muff of sable,
As old as the Tower of Babel,
And as ugly and sharp-cornered as the gable
Of Mr Pennefather's stable ...

Ever since I tasted your cake I have been miserable,
With appetite inconsiderable,
Sick, giddy and irritable,

Shivering, quivering, and to stand unable,
Desponding, inconsolable,
With head-ache uncontrollable,
And stomach-ache deplorable,
My condition's unendurable,
My life's uninsurable,
And, what's worse, I'm incurable...

But then to meet my death from such a belle,
So graceful and agreeable -
It's utterly inconceivable,
And the whole story, from beginning to end,
    never-believe-a-belle.[6]

(Fitzwilliam Square, Dublin, March 16, 1841.)

In 1845, Henry inherited a large bequest and was able to give up his medical practice to pursue the great passion of his life: a minute study of, and commentary on, Virgil's *Aeneid*. With his wife and daughter in tow, he left Fitzwilliam Square to pursue his studies in the great libraries of Europe. The intrepid party traipsed the continent (mostly on foot) tracking down battered manuscripts, rare editions and obscure commentaries of the great work. This happy existence was marred by the death of Henry's wife Anne in 1849, leaving, as John Richmond wrote:

> ... a permanent undertone of gloom in his work: his wife died after a short illness of ten days on March 5th, in Arco in the valley of Riva.... He was not allowed to bury his wife (as a heretic) in the churchyard of Arco, so for two months he and his daughter visited a temporary tomb by the side of the River Sarca, and then (no doubt illegally) he had his wife exhumed and cremated by night in the presence of his friend Ottenthal in a tile burner's kiln on the hill of Ceole.[7]

Henry gathered the ashes and kept them with him always. He described the events of her death and burial in a poem called 'Dirge'. Here he describes the refusal of Arco's wardens to allow her burial in the churchyard:

Within the sound of Sarca's wave
We laid her in her lonely grave,
Till bigotry should cease to rave;
For Arco's bigots, to the shame
Of all who bear the Christian's name,
Against her closed their churchyard gate;
Ah! if thou hadst but heard them prate
Of faith, and creed, and heresy,
And how no corpse should buried be
In faithful corpses' company,
That had not, ere it died, confessed
To the same credence as the rest.

He goes on to describe her clandestine cremation:

We came with spades at dead of night,
And with the lantern's flickering light,
And corpse and coffin from the clay
Rise silently, and bear away
To where on lonely Ceole's hill
Gaped the tile burner's blazing kiln.
Two hours before the rising sun,
The heat intense its work has done,
And with the relics in the urn,
Safe to our lodgings we return.[8]

James and Katherine continued their erudite work over the next twenty years, walking from library to library; in the course of their studies they crossed the Alps seventeen times.

As we have noted, Henry had no faith in the Protestant church (or any other) but politically he was a keen defender of the Protestant ascendancy in Ireland. In verse and pamphlets he ridiculed attempts at Repeal of the Union and Catholic relief efforts. The Irish poor law of 1838 created a nationwide system of poor relief on the back of poor rates paid by Irish landowners. Henry railed against the system in a satirical poem called 'The Poor Law Guardian's Song', written in Fitzwilliam Square in 1841.

Says Poor-law Guardian Robbery
To Poor-law Guardian Charity:-
'What if you and I should agree
To rob our neighbour Industry,
And divide his ill-gotten property,
Among our dear children three,
Improvidence, Sloth, and Beggary?'... [9]

Such sentiments display little empathy with the suffering in Ireland in that decade, particularly considering that Henry must have come into contact with impoverished Dubliners during his early years as a doctor.

In 1861, he wrote a pamphlet concerning the Yelverton case, with which we are already familiar (see Chapter 2 for a refresher), and once again went against the grain of public opinion to criticise Miss Theresa Longworth and her priest. His response to the affair was in the form of a letter entitled 'Letter from an Irish Protestant Conservative in Naples to his correspondent in Dublin. The Late Yelverton Case', dated 18 March 1861 and signed 'You Know Who'. He began by wondering at the acclaim Theresa received upon the conclusion of the case in Dublin:

> ... a city in which Miss Longworth has received, not from the men only, but from the women, such an ovation as no woman ever before received in Dublin, in Ireland, in England – anywhere in the world!

He suggests that Longworth and the Rostrevor priest conspired so that they could take corporeal and spiritual possession of William Yelverton:

> You know what hopes Miss Longworth had in a far less promising case, how she expected, with the help of the priest and the ceremony and the certificate, to bring the stray sheep into the fold, and that, anxious as she was to have the dashing fellow bodily for herself, she was not less anxious that Christ should have him spiritually.... It was he (the priest), I say, should have been drawn home in triumph.... A man's soul saved, a child's soul saved, a lady's character cleared, a sensitive, punctilious, half maidenly,

half matronly conscience soothed and quieted forever ... a pillar subtracted from under the Protestant Church of Ireland, and placed under the Roman Catholic.

He re-imagined Theresa's procession to the Gresham hotel, this time with the priest at her side:

> The priest hoisted into the carriage, beside the lady, and both drawn home together. I think I see them – the whole procession vivid before my eyes. The priest and the lady side by side in an open phaeton ... the phaeton seems to be drawn by ladies. They were the ladies who were obliged to leave the gallery without hearing the cream of the defendant's evidence.... It is like a vision. The lady is dressed as a sister of charity.

Henry's biographer Richmond was surprised that the old poet would have so little sympathy for Theresa, but suggests that Yelverton's father had been a friend of the Henrys and this friendship had coloured his commentary.

Following their European studies, Henry and his daughter Katherine returned to live in Dalkey Lodge in County Dublin. There, they collated and prepared for publication the results of their mammoth labours. Mahaffy described the result:

> It is like the work of a sixteenth-century scholar, of a man who studied and thought and wrote without hurry or care, who loved his subject and scorned the applause of the vulgar crowd. As such, and as the fullest and best exegesis ever attempted of Vergil, Dr Henry's commentary cannot fail to take a permanent and unapproachable place.

In 1872, he suffered terribly from the sudden death of Katherine, 'the support of his age, and the hope of his future fame'. He died four years later.

> He never ceased thinking and talking of her, and looked with calmness and even with satisfaction upon his approaching death, though it afforded him no hope of meeting her again.[10]

Henry was interred with his daughter, along with the ashes of his wife Anne. An epitaph suggested by the poet in 1855 was not used on his gravestone, but it read:

Underneath this mouldering heap
Lies some poor clay
That once like thee could laugh and weep,
And had its day.

If by the world thou art despised,
A while here stay;
If pampered by the world and prized,
Away! Away![11]

Recalling Henry's opinion of the Irish poor laws, we note that Alfred Power, chief Poor Law Commissioner, moved into the house next door, No. 7 Fitzwilliam Square, a few years after Henry left for Europe. Power was an Englishman who had worked to establish the workhouse system in the industrial counties of northern England. In 1843 he came to Ireland where the poor laws and system of workhouses would soon prove wholly inadequate to deal with the catastrophe of the Great Famine.

During his school days in Repton, Derbyshire, Power showed himself to be something of an aspiring dramatist by writing prologues and epilogues for school productions of *Macbeth* in June 1821 and the tragedy *Virginius* by James Sheridan Knowles in July 1822. The young Power recited his work during the performances and also 'sustained the part of Macbeth'. His efforts were recorded in a miscellany of Repton and demonstrate that he engaged his task with youthful relish. For example, he describes Lady Macbeth's famous sleepwalking scene (in which, guilt-racked, she imagines her hand blood-stained):

Lo! guilty conscience, with her busy train
Of fear-wrought fantasies invades the brain,
Leads her wan victim from the couch of night,
Tranc'd in wild dreams of horror and afright.
See the pale sleeper, all unconscious stand,
As darkly muttering, from her stainless hand
She rubs – with phrensied eye and frantic glare,
The blood-red spot her fancy painted there.[12]

Of course, Power may well have blushed to have his juvenilia re-called but we do so now kind-heartedly. In subsequent years he would meet with much hardship in his career and family life. Just before he moved into No. 7 in 1848 a tragedy befell his young family. *The Worcester Chronicle* described the incident in November 1847:

> *Distressing Accident.* – A son of Mr Alfred Power, late the Assistant Poor Law Commissioner for this district, and now commissioner in Dublin, shot his sister dead last week. An attempt having been made to break into the house, Mr Power loaded a brace of pistols in case of further attack, and put them in what he considered an 'out of the way place.' His little son found them, and having no idea that they were loaded, called out to his sister, 'Mind your eye, or I will shoot you,' drew the trigger, and the ball went through her heart.[13]

Power continued to live in No. 7 east (one of the six previously owned by Price Blackwood) until 1864.

All of those noted thus far in this chapter have been connected to the east side of the square and there we remain. Michael Powell, previously of Merrion Square, moved into No. 13 Fitzwilliam Square in 1846. His only daughter Margaret married a Michael James Sweetman and they took up residence in No. 13. Three of the Sweetman daughters – Agnes, Elinor and Mary – all had written work published. The poetry of Elinor Sweetman was featured in *Irish Monthly* between 1889 and 1894. She also had collections of poetry published such as *Footsteps of the Gods* in 1893 and *The Wild Orchard* in 1911. Agnes Sweetman and her husband Egerton Castle were co-authors of several novels. The most famous Sweetman daughter was Mary. She was born in Killiney Park in 1859 and was educated in County Laois and then in Belgium. Mary married Francis Blundell, an English Catholic gentleman from Lancashire in 1879 (a union opposed by her mother). Francis died suddenly in 1884 and Mary never remarried. Her books appeared under the pseudonym M.E. Francis, or her married name Mrs. Blundell, and she wrote prolifically for thirty-five years. Her entry in *Ireland in Fiction* reads:

> All Mrs Blundell's writings are noted for their delicacy of sentiment, deftness of touch, pleasantness of atmosphere.

They are saved from excessive idealism by close observation of character and manners. Her Irish stories show sympathy, and even admiration for the peasantry.[14]

Her work was quite well received by contemporary critics but receives little modern attention. Tom Keegan wrote:

The most recently published edition of any of her novels was a 1971 reprint of The Pastorals of Dorset. It is both surprising and disappointing to see an arguably feminist novelist, who wrote astride the century and facilitated a transition out of the sentimental nineteenth century and into the nationalism and religious fervour of the twentieth, fall so easily out of print.[15]

Mary Sweetman's father had died when she was young and the Sweetmans left No. 13 Fitzwilliam Square in 1863 (replaced by George Augustus Chichester May – noted in Chapter 2).

Butchers and Graves

IF WE TURN FROM THE DOORWAY OF No. 13 Fitzwilliam Square and cross the road, a little to our right is the eastern gateway to the railed garden. Entering it now we crunch along the gravel path and skirt the central lawn. The top storey windows of the south and north sides peek at us over the tree-tops until we emerge from the western gate. Now, this time a little to our left are No.'s 40 and 41 on the west side of the square. In 1849, there were two reverend neighbours in these abodes, namely Charles Graves and Samuel Butcher. Graves had grown up in No. 41, the son of original owner John Crosbie Graves, chief police magistrate for Dublin [another son raised in No. 41, Robert Perceval Graves (1810-1893), was curate in Windermere, England and a good friend of the poet William Wordsworth]. Charles graduated from Trinity College in 1835 with the gold medal in mathematics and he became Professor of Mathematics in 1843 – we shall meet him again in Chapter 7. Samuel Butcher was also a scholar of Trinity College and he would become Professor of Ecclesiastical History in 1850 and Regius Professor of Divinity in 1852. Both men had large families that grew up together in the adjoining houses and played together in the enclosed garden. Graves's youngest daughter Ida (born 1859) later described the Butcher children in her book *An Admiral's Wife in the Making*:

> I was six years old when my father became Bishop of Limerick, and on the same day his close friend, Dr. Butcher, was consecrated Bishop of Meath. The wits made merry over the names Butcher and Graves, saying the Crown had given the Protestants of Ireland a Butcher in Meath to kill them and Graves in Limerick to bury them. I have no recollection of the Butchers in Dublin, though the sons and eldest daughter were the chosen companions of my elder brothers and sisters when they lived next door to one another in Fitzwilliam Square. They were a most remarkable family of brilliant mental endowments and great originality. Two only of the six are now living – J.G. Butcher, Unionist member for York, and Mrs George Prothero [Margaret Frances Butcher]. All four sisters were fine musicians – Lady Monteagle, Mrs Prothero, Mrs Crawley, and Eleanor, the youngest, who died unmarried but not unsought. The elder son Henry was for some years Professor of Greek at Edinburgh.[16]

Eleanor Butcher died shortly after her engagement to the artist Charles Furse. In 1883 she was in Venice and modelled for Henry Holiday's painting 'Dante and Beatrice', now in the Walker Art Gallery, Liverpool. Holiday himself recalled, 'Beatrice was painted from a beautiful girl, Miss Eleanor Butcher, no longer living'.[17] William Rothenstein wrote:

> Furse at this time was engaged to Miss Eleanor Butcher. She and her sisters, Mrs Crawley and Mrs (afterwards Lady) Prothero, were three enchanting ladies, spirited, enlightened and vivacious talkers.... Such natures as Eleanor Butcher's made life seem more worth living; to have her friendship, and that of others like her, was, I felt, a privilege. Alas! she who so loved life was to lose it soon.[18]

Margaret Frances Butcher, known as Fanny (one of the daughters in No. 40), married George Prothero, a lecturer in history at King's College, Cambridge in June 1882. C.W. Crawley wrote:

Prothero was fortunate in his marriage, for his wife's lively and almost elfin temperament were complementary to his grave and reserved manner ... her own talent lay in drawing individuals out of their shells. She was bored by people who had such thick skins that they needed no shells.[19]

'Dante and Beatrice' by Henry Holiday (1883). Eleanor Butcher, who was raised in No. 40, was the model for Beatrice, the central female figure.

George was the editor of the *Quarterly Review*, the London literary and political periodical, and had a wide circle of lettered friends. Both George and Fanny were close friends and correspondents of the American novelist Henry James (George was one of four sponsors for James's naturalisation as a British subject in 1915 – Prime Minister Asquith was one of the other three). Fanny, in particular, was a confidant of James and he called their relationship 'a perfect tangle of intimacy'. James described Fanny as:

> ... a little Irish lady ... the minutest scrap of a little delicate black Celt that ever was – full of humour and humanity & curiosity & interrogation – too much interrogation.

Elsewhere he affectionately described one of Fanny's character traits he found mildly irritating (the description might almost be of a character in one of his novels):

Portrait of Henry James by John Singer Sargent (1913)

> She has a tiresome little Irish habit (it gives at last on one's nerves) of putting all her responses (equally,) at first, in the form of interrogative surprise, so that one at 1st thinks one must repeat & insist on what one has said. But one soon discovers that one needn't in the least notice the habit – but go straight on with one's remark or statement & the whole annoyance drops. It is her only vice!

The tone of his letters to Fanny tended to be playful and warm, his prevailing mood of cheeriness or gloom conveyed with exaggerated flourishes. The following also conveys the mischievous, conspiratorial air of a gossip:

> Dear distant Neighbour! ...
> The Revel at the House of Hanover [Sir George Lewis] abounded in everything but particular reasons for its taking place. You would have been – for me! – a reason, but it abounded alas only in your absence. It abounded, however, in the presence of Mrs Crack [anthorpe], who abounded, in turn, in white satin, crimson trimmings, silvery hair and liquid eyes, & who sat opposite to me in full panoply of the same.[20]

Henry James suffered a stroke in December 1915, the first in a debilitating series, and died a few months later. His description of the first attack to Fanny contained what is now a famous fatalistic quote.

He is said to have told his old friend Lady Prothero, when she saw him after the first stroke, that in the very act of falling (he was dressing at the time) he heard in the room a voice which was distinctly, it seemed, not his own, saying: 'So here it is at last, the distinguished thing!' The phrase is too beautifully characteristic not to be recorded. He saw the distinguished thing coming, faced it, and received it with words worthy of all his dealings with life.[21]

George Prothero died in 1922 at the age of 73. Fanny Prothero, née Butcher, died in 1934.

Caricature of A.P. Graves by V. L. O'Connor (1916)

But if we return to Fanny's childhood years in Fitzwilliam Square we can look again at the lives of her neighbours: the Graves family. Several of the Graves children were writers but the most noteworthy was the second son, Alfred Perceval Graves (1846-1931). A.P. Graves was a poet and songwriter and was the father of the Great War poet and novelist Robert Graves. In 1930 he wrote an autobiography entitled *To Return to All That*, partly in response to his son's book *Goodbye to All That*. Alfred's recollection of his early life in Fitzwilliam Square is one of the few first-hand accounts of a childhood in one of those Georgian houses. His book begins in the nursery of No. 41:

My earliest recollection is falling at the age of one and a half with the back of my head on the bars of the nursery fire, and being dragged out of the fire-place by my brave little sister Helen, aged three. Our cries were heard below, and my parents and Dr. Robert Graves the physician, who was most providentially dining with them, rushed upstairs, put out the flames, and attended my burns. I still bear the scars.... When I was naughty the servants threatened to hand me over to the coal man, who would carry me away in his empty sack. This was a real terror that seemed always impending, for the great, grimy fellow bending under the weight of coal often came staggering up the staircase to pitch his load with a thundering crash into the wooden bin outside the nursery door.

He went on to describe No. 41:

My grandfather's [John Crosbie Graves] house was a literary and musical centre in the twenties and thirties of [the 19th] century, and when it passed to my father [Charles] and Uncle James the old musical tradition was kept up. As a very young child I used to lie awake listening to the singing. My nursery was four flights up, at the head of a deep and dangerous well-staircase, through which one could look sheer down into the hall below. My grandfather, a cautious man, who had tried in vain to prevent his four boys from sliding down the formidable banisters, caused stout nets to be fixed across the gulf at each landing. They were none of them ever enmeshed, but one day rushing forth from his study on hearing a heavy fall accompanied by loud outcries, he discovered their tutor floundering in the bottom net. Having saved the young man's life, he dispensed with his services on the spot, regarding him as an unstable guide for his sons. This seems to have had a chastening effect on young Pollock, who from this downfall rose to be a conspicuous figure on the Irish Bench.

Alfred finished his book by commenting on the career of his son Robert. It is clear that bad blood had developed between them and some of Alfred's remarks are rather ungenerous.

[M]y fourth son Robert has lately been much before the public ... chiefly with Goodbye to All That, an autobiography written at the age of thirty-three.... In writing of him I must point out that there is much in his autobiography that

I do not accept as accurate. For the change in his outlook I hold the war and recent experiences responsible. To these I impute the bitter and hasty criticism of people who never wished him harm.... Goodbye to All That calls for many more corrections than I can here enumerate, having been written largely from memory, sometimes from hearsay, and often long after the events described.... He gives me no credit for the interest I always felt and showed in his poetry. During the war I offered poems of his to editor after editor.... Finally, I may say that his estimate of his Grandfather Graves, founded on Limerick gossip, gathered while he was soldiering there, is an unfair one.[22]

The Graves family left No. 41 Fitzwilliam Square in 1863.

Some Fitzwilliam Square Characters

BEFORE MOVING ON TO LOOK AT WRITERS who lived in Fitzwilliam Square in the twenteith century we should first note some of the square's residents, two in particular, who appear as characters in works of fiction and also three books that were set in the square.

If we turn our attention to the north side of the square, in 1873 Sir Richard Bolton McCausland bought No. 61, spending his retirement there until his death in 1900. He had been called to the bar in 1841 and also lectured at Queen's Inns, Dublin. In 1856 he was appointed recorder of Singapore, upon which occasion he was knighted. He held that position for ten years. Walter Makepeace wrote of him in *One Hundred Years of Singapore* in 1921:

> Sir Richard McCausland sat on the Bench in the Straits for ten years, retiring on pension in 1866, and living for many years afterward in Ireland.... He was a very kind-hearted and genial Irishman, a sound and experienced lawyer, and a thoroughly courteous gentleman on the Bench. In private life he was immensely popular and in particular his services were in great request as an after dinner speaker, for he possessed the true Irishman's wit and capacity for the right word in its right place at the right time.[23]

Margaret Landon was the author of the 1944 book *Anna and the King of Siam*, which was adapted into the 1956 movie *The King and I.* Landon based her fictional work on the memoir of Anna Leonowens, *The English Governess in the Siamese Court* (1870), in which Leonowens detailed her position as governess and teacher to the children of King Mongkut from 1862 to 1867. Although Leonowens makes no mention of McCausland in her memoir, Landon introduces him as a character in her fictional adap-

King Mongkut of Siam

tation. She had some licence to do this however as McCausland was a correspondent of King Mongkut and met him at least once. Mongkut himself referred to Sir Richard in a collection of his letters entitled *A King of Siam Speaks*:

> McCausland, who was then Recorder of Singapore, had said that if he was free at the time he would take passage, as he would welcome an opportunity to meet me in person. Sir Richard Bolton McCausland is a friend of mine. We have been keeping correspondence and he has been giving me from time to time confidential information.[24]

Sir Richard and his sister appear in an episode of *Anna and the King of Siam*, almost certainly invented by Landon, concerning a banquet for the king's birthday in 1863:

> Among the guests were two strangers – Sir Richard Mc-Causland, Recorder of Singapore, and his sister. The Honourable Miss McCausland was in full evening dress of the very latest fashion, with low neck and short sleeves. The other ladies looked dowdy beside her.... The King himself

entered with a bottle of rose-water in each hand to sprinkle the guests, as was the pleasant Siamese custom.... Then he stopped suddenly. The unexpected vision of the beautiful Irish girl dumbfounded him...When he could move he said to her, 'Wherefore have you decorated yourself more than all the rest? Shall it be for my observation?'

The King, unconscious that he was breaking the rules of English etiquette, trotted around the embarrassed girl, chuckling and ejaculating, 'She is very fine! She is very fine indeed!' Suddenly he halted and asked, 'Are you an anecdote?'... Anna felt she must interpose herself between the impulsiveness of the King, who might not realise how preposterous it would seem to a man like Sir Richard that his sister be invited to join a harem. But before she could come to the rescue the King continued, 'I mean are you an unmarried woman?' [There followed an argument between Anna and the King regarding the definitions of anecdote and unmarried.]

Then, as if to settle the argument, he took his two bottles of rose-water and with a swift motion deluged the pretty girl before him from top to toe – hair, shoulders and gorgeous dress – with the entire contents of both bottles. 'There!' he said with satisfaction. 'Now, sit down everyone!' And smiling triumphantly he turned away to someone else.[25]

Of course, Leonowens' and Landon's depictions of Mongkut have been a source of great controversy in Thailand where he was considered a particularly cultured man and progressive king. It could be said aspersion was also cast on Sir Richard, whom Landon would have us believe sat silently throughout his sister's ordeal. Following Sir Richard Bolton McCausland's death in 1900 members of his family continued to live in No. 61 Fitzwilliam Square until 1914.

In the year of McCausland's death, 1900, *Thom's Directory* notes that Surgeon General Alexander Francis Preston (1842-1907) was living next door in No. 62 Fitzwilliam Square. He did not remain in the square for very long and is absent from the 1901 census – the only occupant recorded for No. 62 being Private Alfred Charles Toomer of the Royal Army Medical Corps (who perhaps was a military aide to Preston).

Alexander Preston was a graduate of Trinity College and entered the Army Medical Service in 1863. He served in China and India and was present at the battle of Maiwand in Afghanistan in 1880 during the second Anglo-Afghan War. Preston suffered serious injuries as described by the *British Medical Journal*:

> Surgeon-Major Preston was in medical charge of the 66th Regiment of Berkshires at the battle of Maiwand, and was very severely wounded (shot through both loins and left forearm) while attending to a wounded man of his regiment in the front line of fire, and was mentioned in despatches.[26]

Preston survived the ordeal and advanced through the ranks, becoming surgeon-general on 6 July 1896. He was Principal Medical Officer of the Army Medical Department in Dublin between 1896 and 1902.

It is generally believed that Arthur Conan Doyle, author of the Sherlock Holmes novels, based the army and medical background of his character and narrator Dr. John Watson on the experiences of Alexander Francis Preston. In the first Holmes novel, *A Study in Scarlet*, Watson's description of his own Afghan service closely resembles that of Preston. He says that upon becoming a doctor he completed a course prescribed for surgeons in the army and was attached to a regiment:

> The regiment was stationed in India at the time, and before I could join it, the second Afghan war had broken out.... The campaign brought honours and promotion to many, but for me it had nothing but misfortune and disaster. I was removed from my brigade and attached to the Berkshires, with whom I served at the fatal battle of Maiwand. There I was struck on the shoulder by a Jezail bullet, which shattered the bone and grazed the subclavian artery. I should have fallen into the hands of the murderous Ghazis had it not been for the devotion and courage shown by Murray, my orderly, who threw me across a pack-horse, and succeeded in bringing me safely to the British lines.

Dr Watson returns to England an invalid and, short on funds, determines to find shared accommodation. He is introduced to Sherlock

Illustration by Sidney Paget of Dr John Watson (l)
with Sherlock Holmes (1893)

Holmes by a mutual friend who knows that Holmes wishes to find a flatmate to go halves on some rooms he had discovered at 221B Baker street. Holmes famously greets Watson:

> 'Dr. Watson, Mr. Sherlock Holmes,' said Stamford, introducing us.

> 'How are you?' he said cordially, gripping my hand with a strength for which I should hardly have given him credit. 'You have been in Afghanistan, I perceive.'

They agree to share rooms and it is some weeks before Holmes explains his powers of perception.

> 'Observation with me is second nature. You appeared to be surprised when I told you, on our first meeting, that you had come from Afghanistan.'

'You were told, no doubt.'

'Nothing of the sort. I knew you came from Afghanistan. From long habit the train of thoughts ran so swiftly through my mind, that I arrived at the conclusion without being conscious of intermediate steps. There were such steps, however. The train of reasoning ran, 'Here is a gentleman of a medical type, but with the air of a military man. Clearly an army doctor, then. He has just come from the tropics, for his face is dark, and that is not the natural tint of his skin, for his wrists are fair. He has undergone hardship and sickness, as his haggard face says clearly. His left arm has been injured. He holds it in a stiff and unnatural manner. Where in the tropics could an English army doctor have seen much hardship and got his arm wounded? Clearly in Afghanistan.' The whole train of thought did not occupy a second. I then remarked that you came from Afghanistan, and you were astonished.'

As mentioned, Surgeon-General A.F. Preston's time in No. 62 Fitzwilliam Square was brief. In 1902, he retired from the Army Medical Service and was replaced in the house by Robert Blake McVittie.

Fitzwilliam Square as Setting

THERE ARE THREE BOOKS THAT ARE SET against the backdrop of Fitzwilliam Square during the time of the Great War and the 1916 Rising, the War of Independence, the Civil War and first years of the Irish Free State. The first is a children's book called *Wisp: A Girl of Dublin* by Katharine Adams, published around 1922. It is set mostly in an imagined No. 50 Fitzwilliam Square and tells of a group of middle-class cousins that are sent to live together in Dublin while their parents are involved in the war effort. They befriend a spirited young girl from the Cuffe Street tenements, who saves the oldest cousin Keith from arrest by insurgent forces around St Stephen's Green on Easter Sunday 1916.

We Are Besieged by Barbara Fitzgerald is a 'big house' novel that begins with the burning of Butler's Hill, the manor house of Archie Butler and his wife Moira. They flee to the Fitzwilliam Square home of Moira's sister, Helen Adair and her two daughters Caroline and Isabel, where Helen's zeal and siege mentality in the face of the new political reality leads to conflict within the family.

The Truth About my Fathers is a modern memoir by Australian writer Gaby Naher. Naher interweaves narratives of her own life story and search for her biological father, with an imagined reconstruction of the lives of her grandparents, Ernst and Emma Naher. They moved from Switzerland to Dublin in 1923 and founded the Swiss Private Hotel in No. 34 Fitzwilliam Square. The hotel was the childhood home of her adoptive father George Naher, and the tales he told his daughters form the basis of Naher's reconstruction.

Front piece of Wisp: A Girl of Dublin, *1922*

Wisp: A Girl of Dublin is an idyllic children's story in which the looming threats of world war and national revolution are hardly allowed impinge. The story focuses on two American sisters Christine and Beryl Langsley who move to temporary lodgings in Dublin in late 1915 with their governess Miss Peck. They soon learn that their cousins that live in India are to join them and that they will live together in the vacant house of another uncle, James Mortimer Langsley of No. 50 Fitzwilliam Square, while their parents are engaged in the war effort.

> An old empty house filled with big, gloomy rooms! Could anything be more delightful? All of them there together.

They visit the house before their cousins' arrival:

> They left the governess to look about at her leisure, and began their tour of investigation. Up and down, in and out they looked and discovered and exclaimed. It was really a

delightful house! There were so many unexpected corners and turns and cubby-holes!

In the course of their search they discover a small attic-like room at the top of a disused stairwell and decide to make it their secret room.

They had already met Wisp, an orphan girl who lived in the garret of a Cuffe Street tenement house, while walking in St Stephen's Green. She was described with her friends playing as faeries:

> 'Step up and out this way!' As she spoke she floated, or so it seemed, along the path. She was so very thin, and she moved so lightly, that it seemed as though she might blow away with the leaves that danced along the path.

Wisp befriends the Langsley cousins; they mingle with the Cuffe Street children without argument and interact with an affable array of Dublin characters. There seems to be greater scope for quarrel within No. 50 between the newly introduced cousins. For instance, while Christine and Beryl discuss one of the cousins late at night in their bedroom they turn to discover she is standing in the doorway. However, ruffled feathers are soon smoothed and they become fast friends. Even the eldest cousin, Keith, whose late arrival is heralded with an ominous *Turn of the Screw*-like letter, turns out to be a fairly normal young man, if a little taciturn.

The secret room in the attic is eventually used by the cousins to give surreptitious school-lessons to Wisp, who in turn was teaching the young children of Cuffe Street. However, Keith discovers the room and forbids the lessons. The book ends as the 1916 Rising is breaking out and Keith is caught out while travelling through the city. Wisp rushes to rescue him despite the wrong he had done her. Her confrontation with the rebel soldiers on Dawson Street and her twee colloquial speech demonstrates the far-fetched and poorly judged nature of the book.

> Wisp seemed to appear in their midst all of a sudden.... As usual she wore no hat and her hair flew wildly about her dusty, eager little face.... 'Ain't ye Tod Gaffery what has been friend to Foggy Moyne? Shure, I know ye well and Foggy's me best friend. Can't ye believe me when I tell ye straight that [Keith]'s our friend too?'... She seemed sud-

denly to hold the whole situation in her hands.... Whoever
the boy might be, the little girl was one of their own people,
speaking their own way.

The characters in *Wisp: A Girl of Dublin* seem to have been completely invented by Adams. No Langsley ever lived in No. 50 Fitzwilliam Square. The surgeon William Doolin was living in the house in
1916.

We Are Besieged by Barbrara Fitzgerald is a more serious reflection
on the conflict in Ireland during the War of Independence and beyond,
told from the point of view of Protestant landowners as the old social orders change irrevocably. Once more the book is let down by the
phonetic accents of non-Protestant characters and the unrealistic vehe-
mence of certain others. For example, the opening scene is the arson
attack on Butler's Hill by IRA volunteers. Their commander addresses
Archie Butler:

> In the name of the Irish Republican Army we have ordhers
> to burn down the house. Ye have ten minyits to clear out
> and save what stuff ye can. Open the door!

Archie's wife Moira joins her sister Helen Adair in her Fitzwilliam
Square drawing room, telling her of the ordeal and fears that the Black
and Tans will carry out reprisals on their behalf. Helen's response is
emphatic:

> I hope they catch them and burn them. Shooting's too good
> for the Sinn Feiners!... Isn't it just like them to bite the hand
> that fed them.

Moira tells Helen that a British withdrawal from Ireland is inevitable and she replies:

> The British would exterminate the Irish, after what's hap-
> pening now, rather than leave us in their power.

Moira, by far the more philosophical of the two, ends the conversation with what is almost a soliloquy, encapsulating the concerns at the
heart of all 'big house' novels:

'... in a few years it'll be we, Protestants and Unionists, who will be against the Government.' She went on, as if she were speaking in a dream: 'We're fighting against something that is stronger than we are, stronger than the British and that you cannot fight with arms and men. The country is losing something today that it will not recover in a life-time or in a hundred years: I mean the happy relationship between gentry and people. A loyalty that we have not understood and to which we could not subscribe has made us strangers to them in a night. The land has risen up and possessed the people and they have turned against us, whose loyalty is outside the land. So the country that we had foolishly come to think our own has rejected us for the people and there is no striving against it. We go back to an England that has lost all knowledge of us and that can never be our home, or we remain, as aliens besieged, in a land that has lost its welcomes.'

Elsewhere the book contains good imagined descriptions of the interior of the Fitzwilliam Square house or, as in the following, the central garden:

The high red houses of Fitzwilliam Square were lit up by the westerning sun; they glowed tranquilly in the warm light and upper windows threw back a fiery gleam.... Children shuffled noisily along, scattering showers of gold as they went and their shouts rang out in the still air. Inside the dusty railings, evergreens, jaded after the long summer, showed grimy and dishevelled. Nursemaids and governesses were stirring and calling to the children to come home to tea; perambulators were making for the gates; old gentlemen rose stiffly, nodded to the children and clanged the gates behind them; soon the place would be deserted, lights would spring up behind drawn blinds and the Square would be submerged in that translucent city twilight, so stringently blue that streets and houses seemed to belong to a motionless submarine world of dark shapes and blue light.

Ernst and Emma Naher and their young son George arrived in Dublin in June, 1923, the immediate aftermath of the Irish civil war. They had been restaurateurs in Switzerland and felt there were opportunities for a better life in Ireland where they could afford to run their own hotel. They

George Naher sitting at the rear of No. 34. c. 1925

purchased the leasehold of No. 34 Fitzwilliam Square in August and founded the Swiss Private Hotel. The family emigrated to Australia in 1927 where they continued to be hoteliers. There, George grew up, eventually adopting two daughters, Jackie and Gaby. Gaby Naher's memoir, *The Truth About My Fathers,* examines her own paternity partly by looking back at the relationship of Ernst and George, reconstructing their early family life in Dublin and Australia. She describes the hotel and living arrangements at No. 34:

Emma, Ernst and George all slept downstairs in the basement; Emma and Ernst were in the room traditionally occupied by the housekeeper and George in the narrow pantry that lay between their room and the kitchen. George's room was dark and crowded with great earthenware jars of food, and dead rabbits, chickens and pheasants hanging from the ceiling.... On the ground floor was the main reception hall with a cloak rail, a bevelled-glass oil lamp hanging from the ceiling and great doors opening into the guests' dining room and sitting room. Higher up, on the first, second and third floors, were the guests' bedrooms, some of which were large enough to accommodate a couple of armchairs, a writing table and a small dining table at which a guest might elect to dine in private.

George would later tell his daughters that the house had formerly belonged to Count George Plunkett and thrilled them with stories about the ghost of Joseph Mary Plunkett (the count's son – executed in 1916) who roamed the house.

When Emma and Ernst finally opened the Swiss Private Hotel, the ghost of Count Plunkett's eldest son – as the story goes – still wandered the house's high-ceilinged rooms. The ghost, apparently, had his likes, dislikes and habits. He took an interest in the very young, in the children and babies who slept in what had once been his childhood home. Daddo [George Naher] says he clearly remembers the ghostly form of a soldier leaning over him when he was in his bed. On the occasions Emma babysat for her guests she'd regularly enter the room of a crying baby to find the same figure of the soldier bending over the baby's crib. The ghost would also appear to priests who stayed at the hotel, and liked to extinguish their candles when they read the Bible in their rooms at night.

The house contained other chilling clues to a violent history:

There were bloodstains on one of the walls that Emma scrubbed for days but that reappeared when the weather changed. In the cellar below the house they found shackles.... Had the chains been used to confine [Joseph], or other members of the family?

In another strand of her memoir, Gaby Naher describes a visit to Dublin to research her family history. She discovers that Count George Plunkett and his family had not lived in 34 Fitzwilliam Square at all, but rather 26 Fitzwilliam Street.

One of the underlying truths of my family – the tale of its brush with history in Dublin – is, quite simply, untrue.

However, she is not disappointed. Instead she feels a renewed connection with her adoptive father:

If anything, I am delighted. Daddo was pulling our legs all along. Daddo was a storyteller, just like me.

Naher comes to believe that her grandfather Ernst 'is the true family ghost'. She describes his destructive presence in the family: undermining the confidence of his son and the hard work of his heroic wife; his drinking and gambling; his association with political subversives who would hole up in the derelict mews of No. 34. Naher mixes fact and fiction to construct a scene that explains the disparate elements of her family story: the ghostly figure of the soldier, the bloodstained wall, her grandfather's ill-judged involvement with Republican dissidents; and the family's hasty emigration to Australia.

Free State soldiers come to No. 34, 'in the darkest, coldest hour of the morning', and Ernst slips away into the night. Emma leaves George in his small room to take the stairs to the ground floor and allow five soldiers gain entry. As they search the hotel Emma returns to her son.

> The room Emma shares with her husband has already been ransacked. Emma stops short at the entrance to the pantry, she is still as a fallen bird. A soldier stands over her boy, holding his gun as though anticipating ambush. He has pulled back George's covers and is eyeing the bed and the boy suspiciously. The man looks up to Emma. Is the boy dead? Emma shakes her head, tells the soldier that her son is afraid. She begs that her son be left alone.
>
> A rifle sounds upstairs and the echo of its explosion rings in the stairwell. George's eyes fly open. Emma dares not even take a breath and the soldier pushes past her. George flies from his bed, into his mother's arms, and the two stand together, waiting.... Silence settles over the house above her. After a time Emma imagines the building sighing, relaxing into the silence.

Emma goes through the house to reassure her guests; one family offers to mind George for the rest of the night. At first she tries not to notice the dark stain on the landing wall. Creeping out to the stables she finds evidence there that men had been hiding-out. Back in the house:

> ... she goes with water and rags to the ground-floor landing. She doesn't need to see the colour of the dark wet stain to know that it's blood. The smell has been in her nostrils since she first passed the stain with her son.... Emma places a tall-backed chair on the landing, right up against the wall, where she can still see the faint tracing of the stain.

Naher's memoir brings No. 34 Fitzwilliam Square to life but of course it's up to the reader to decide which elements of the ghost stories, bloodstains and midnight raids are fact and which are fable. It's certainly true that Ernst, Emma and George left Fitzwilliam Square in 1927 for Sydney. Ernst's unhappy life ended on the banks of the Brisbane river on 5 March 1938 when he slit his own throat. He left a suicide note for the Queensland coroner:

> I will shortly kill myself with my razor. Reason, lack of everything. If suitable you can use my body for anatomy researches. All my assets and debts go to my wife.

He finished:

> I'm very sorry for the trouble.
> – Ernst Naher.

THE TALES OF THE SWISS PRIVATE HOTEL have already brought us beyond the time-frame of this book and I am mindful of going further. To track down the names of a brood of impoverished writers that might have stopped in the increasingly flat-riddled Fitzwilliam Square between the wars and beyond, would be a daunting task. However, in the same year the Naher family left Ireland there were a number of writers living in the square. The novelist and poet Winifred Mary Letts had married William Verschoyle of No. 19 in 1926. Letts is best remembered for her Great War poetry and in particular the poems 'The Spires of Oxford' and 'The Deserter'.

In the top two-storey flat of No. 26 (then in the possession of Brian Crichton) lived the Dutch students Hilda and Willem van Stockum. Hilda wrote and illustrated her first children's book in 1934 and she would go on to publish dozens more in a prolific career. Her brother Willem was studying mathematics in Trinity College and would later make important contributions in the field of general relativity. He had hoped to study under Einstein at Princeton University but his career was cut short by World War II. Willem became an RAF bomber pilot and was shot down over Laval, France on 10 June 1944, a few days after the invasion of Normandy.

Across the square in a flat in No. 67 lived the writer Francis Stuart and his wife Iseult, the daughter of Maud Gonne. Stuart became a prolific novelist but his career was overshadowed by the time he spent in Nazi Germany where he broadcast German propaganda aimed at Ireland. Iseult famously received a marriage proposal from W.B. Yeats in 1916 and he referred to her marriage to Stuart in his poem 'Why Should Not Old Men Be Mad' (1936):

> A girl that knew all Dante once
> Live to bear children to a dunce.

W.B. Yeats of No. 42

And of course Yeats himself moved to No. 42 Fitzwilliam Square in 1928 after selling his old townhouse at No. 82 Merrion Square. No. 42 belonged to the gynaecologist Bethel Solomons and Yeats lived in two upper floors with his wife, George Hyde Lees. Yeats briefly described the new flat, and George's efforts at redecoration, in a letter to Augusta Gregory:

George has made our flat at 42 Fitzwilliam Square charming.... My study is about as big as the old & looks out over the square – blue walls & ceiling & gold coloured curtains. Her dining room I have not yet seen, but Lennox [Robinson] saw it & was loud in its praise.[27]

George apparently also painted the sitting room black, 'as an aid to inspiration'.

Yeats moved into No. 42 a full century after James Clarence Mangan began work in the offices of Thomas Leland a few doors up in

No. 47. Yeats said of Mangan in 1891, in an essay entitled 'Clarence Mangan's Love Affair': 'To the soul of Clarence Mangan was tied the burning ribbon of genius'.[28] If you go to Fitzwilliam Square and find shelter from the drizzle beneath a tree overhanging the western railing, you can look up at the upper stories of numbers 42 and 47 in one glance. The gulf of time means little now so we can imagine these two national poets walking along Fitzwilliam Square west almost side by side. Mangan reaches his workplace first, shuffling into the stifling air of the scriveners' office; while Yeats, the arch-poet, continues on towards his charming flat and grand study. Hardly separated in space, but in time by the span of a century – perhaps Willem van Stockum could express it better.

Endnotes

1. A.P. Graves, *The Cambridge History of English Literature*, Vol. 14, Part 2, p. 342.

2. James Henry, *My Book* (1853), p. viii.

3. J.P. Mahaffy, *Selected Poems of James Henry*, ed. Christopher Ricks (2002), p. 15.

4. James Henry, Kottabos, *A College Miscellany, First Series* (1874), p. 216.

5 Valentine Cunningham, *The Victorians: An Anthology of Poetry and Poetics*, p. 55.

6. James Henry, *My Book*, pp. cl - cliii.

7. John Richmond, *James Henry of Dublin*, p. 25.

8. Henry, *My Book*, p. lxxii.

9. Ibid., p. clvi.

10. J.P. Mahaffy, *Selected Poems of James Henry*, pp. 14-15.

11. John Richmond, *James Henry of Dublin*, p. 59.

12. Alfred Power, *Historical and Topographical Description of Repton* (1854), ed. Robert Bigsby, p. 318.

13. *The Cottager's monthly visitor* (1847), p. 396.

14. Stephen J. Brown, ed., *Ireland in Fiction* (1970), p. 110.

15. Tom Keegan, *Irish Women Writers: An A-to-Z Guide*, ed. Alexander Gonzalez, p. 125.

16. Ida Poore, *An Admiral's Wife in the Making*, pp. 18-19.

17. *Famous Paintings selected from the world's great galleries and reproduced in colour* (1913), p. 2.

18. William Rothenstein, *Men and Memories: A History of the Arts 1872-1922*, p. 206.

19. C.W. Crawley, 'Sir George Prothero and His Circle: The Prothero Lecture' (1969), *Transactions of the Royal Historical Society*, Fifth Series, Vol. 20, pp. 106-107.

20. Henry James, *Dear Munificent Friends: Henry James's Letters to Four Women*, ed. Susan Gunter, pp. 192, 193, 196.

21. Edith Wharton, *A Backward Glance*, p. 185.

22. A.P. Graves, *To Return to All That*, pp. 11, 15, 318-334.

23. Walter Makepeace, *One Hundred Years of Singapore*, Vol. 1, p. 191.

24. King Mongkut, *A King of Siam Speaks*, p. 166.

25. Margaret Landon, *Anna and the King of Siam*, pp. 215-217.

26. *British Medical Journal*, 1 April 1884, p. 481.

27. Ann Saddlemyer, *Becoming George: The Life of Mrs W.B. Yeats*, p. 402.

28. W.B. Yeats, *The Collected Works of W.B. Yeats – Volume IX*, ed. John Frayne and Madeleine Marchaterre, p. 135.

5

Artists

S PARE A THOUGHT FOR THE COMPILER OF a commonplace book of life in a Georgian square about to hold forth on an area with which he is not all that familiar, namely, Irish art history. Picture him thumbing through spineless street directories or tottering under the weight of memorial books in the registry of deeds, searching out the names of Fitzwilliam Square artists, not at all confident he will recognise them from their artless neighbours. But the square's most famous resident was an artist, Jack B. Yeats of No. 18, on the south corner with Fitzwilliam Place (though he took up residence well after 1922, the supposed cut-off date of this history, seemingly more honoured in the breach). It is certainly true that the square has a strong connection with Irish art, as the birthplace and home of many distinguished painters, not to mention important patrons and critics. It will also become clear that the square is notable for its number of women artists, and looking at their contributions will make a refreshing change to the male-centric worlds of legal and military history. The square itself provided a fine setting for art, not only the space for artist studios and salons, but also inspiration in the beauty of the buildings, enclosed garden and the Dublin mountains visible beyond. Many a description of the square notes the effects of the changing light on the red brickwork, the sash windows, railings and foliage. A good description of this shifting light was given by the surrealist painter Ithell Colquhoun in her book *The Crying of the Wind: Ireland*:

As often here, rain overtook a fine morning at midday; in Fitzwilliam Square the air, almost warm, was burdened with the scent of laburnum, red may, pink may, lilac. This is a city with little feeling of claustrophobia, for the Dublin Mountains are always visible beyond; and from the square they seem, in some lights, tantalisingly near. Low clouds part, and the clearness of the air suddenly reveals them, strong purple; then a shadow, a veil of rain sweeps across and nothing is left of them but mist. A few minutes later the veil thins and they appear beyond it, obscurely blue; or a sudden shaft of sunlight tears it open, and the lower slopes come forward in their native green, their bracken grown sides seeming, at this distance, like a bank of moss. They change colour and texture with all the weather's freaks.[1]

But casting back to the early years of the nineteenth century, the first artistic resident of the square was not a whiskered old portraitist, or young lady water-colourist, but an amateur etcher named Willcocks Huband.

Willcocks Huband of No. 63

MR. SAMUELS, THE BUTLER OF No. 63 Fitzwilliam Square, clutching a visiting card and message, goes looking for Mr. Huband in a back room on the second floor. The room had been converted into an etcher's studio and print room and there he knocks and awaits a call to enter. Pushing the door gingerly (more than once he had incurred displeasure for knocking over misplaced inkpots, acid bottles and glass plates) he enters a room of ordered clutter.

The large window is screened by a sheet of architect's tracing paper stretched across a wooden frame. The effect is a pleasantly diffused light; gleams of any kind are unwelcome when working with polished copper plates. Beneath the window is a workbench upon which sits a jigger: a smooth wooden box with rounded edges. Atop that are two wax-covered copper plates – works in progress. Beside the jigger is a gas ring-heater and the bench is otherwise filled with cylinders of wax, a cup holding various etching points, scrapers and gravers, rolls of muslin, sheets of glass and a short-lipped tray brimming with an ominous liquid: the mordant bath.

Shelves and cubby-holes line the walls containing tins of ink powders, jars of turpentine, oils and other solvents, unused plates of copper and zinc, mushroom shaped horsehair-filled leather dabbers, sheets of blotting paper and acid bottles carefully labelled and stopped. The centre of the room is dominated by a star-wheeled printing press, over which two figures are hunched. Willcocks Huband and his thirteen-year-old boy George carefully examine a sheet of paper on the travelling-bed of the press. George checks the sharpness of each line with youthful earnest, for this is a print of his own etching and he is eager for his father's approval. Willcocks murmurs kindly:

'It shows real promise. We'll print and bind your whole series – and send a copy to the Society's library. Won't it be grand – your name will accompany mine in the catalogues'.

Then without turning Willcocks asks who had called. 'It's Mr Goodbody of Dawson street again,' said the butler.

'What's he offering this time?'

Samuels consulted a scrap of paper. 'A crate of champagne from Charente via Marseilles, a pipe of port from Douro, some Staffordshire porcelain decorated by Donovan's of Poolbeg street and a parrot.'

'A parrot?'

'Yes sir. And he says that's his final offer.'

'Thank heavens. Send him away.'

Willcocks Huband was born in Dublin in 1776, the son of Joseph Huband, a wealthy barrister. He entered Trinity College in 1792 and studied law under William Magee, later archbishop of Dublin. While studying he also received his first lessons in drawing the human form from a Milanese student named Orsato. Huband also found inspiration in illustrated treatises on etching to be found in the old college library. He continued his legal studies in the Inner Temple in London. He may have been compelled to study outside of Ireland because of sympathies with the cause of the United Irishmen in 1798. The name Wilcox Huband is listed on a plaque in the Four Courts commemorating the 'members of the legal profession who in 1798 sacrificed their lives or their careers in the pursuit of the vision of a Free Ireland Uniting Protestant Catholic and Dissenter'. Also a King's Inns Bencher's minute book notes that 'Willcox Huband', a law student, had his name erased at a meeting held in the Chancery Chamber on 15 November 1798.[2]

Etching c. 1810 by Willcocks Huband of No. 63

While in London he received further instruction on etching from the Abbe Racine, an emigrant from France. In 1800, his previous indiscretions must have been overlooked for he was called to the Irish bar, where the demands of his new profession temporarily curtailed his artistic development. In 1802, he toured Europe, particularly Paris and the Low Countries, and it has been noted that his work was influenced far more by Dutch rather than Italian masters. Returning to Dublin in 1803,

he began printing his own treatises on language, artistic taste and etching technique. To do this he acquired a set of type, cast-off by a printer, and an old bellows press of a kind used by travelling players to print their playbills. One of his earlier self-printed books was a curious reference book entitled *An Orthographical Vocabulary, Showing Where the Final Consonant Should Be Repeated in Spelling the Past Tense and the Participles of English Verbs* printed in 1809; a simple list of those words such as abetted for abet, abhorred for abhor, abutted for abut.

The work that brought him a certain amount of fame was self-produced in 1810 and entitled *Critical and Familiar Notices on the Art of Etching upon Copper: Through which are Interspersed Some Prints, Etched by an Amateur*. A biographer described the volume and the curious effect it had on bibliophiles and bibliopoles:

Mr. Huband took off the impressions of the plates himself, and printed but twenty copies of this unique production, which he also bound with his own hands. We are not to be surprised, if so great a rarity in the history of printing became an object of eager desire and curiosity, in proportion to the difficulty of obtaining a copy. The Rev. Thomas F. Dibdin, in his capital work, The Bibliographical Decameron, vol. iii., thus makes conspicuous mention of Mr. Huband and this coveted volume: 'Mr. Huband is a very distinguished book-man, for I am told that he wrote a book on engraving; that he printed it with his own hands, and engraved the plates: so that he beats the curate of Lustleigh, in the county of Devon, immortalized in Nicholson's 'Anecdotes'. Lord Spencer possesses the only copy I have seen in England of this curious performance. It was presented to him by the author.' When the bibliomania was at its height some years ago, Mr. Huband was regularly assailed by post-letters and visitors from a great distance, anxious to obtain a copy, by valuable gifts, solicitation, and courtesy. Offers were made to him of rare and costly books, wines, horses, and elegant articles of furniture, in lieu of the envied treasure; but these offers he uniformly refused. The few which he printed off were presented to his esteemed friends only. When it was ascertained that no temptations nor entreaty could induce the author to grant a copy, excepting to his selected favourites, the competition began around those who were known to have received the book from him. I have been assured by credible authority, that one gentleman (after Dibdin's notice of the volume had made it a rage among bibliopolists) refused a hogshead of wine, and another a carriage, for his copy. I state these freaks of an ungovernable appetite for typographical rarities exactly as they were told to me, and I have never heard them doubted.[3]

One copy was presented to the library of the Royal Dublin Society, which extolled 'the varied genius it displays in the originality of its design, the critical elegance of its composition and the masterly execution of its plates'.

Huband began his treatise humbly:

If it were indispensable that the writer who treats upon an art should himself be adept at it, I at once acknowledge my incompetence for the task I am undertaking; but when we reflect ... that Professor Saunderson, of Cambridge, who delivered such admirable discourses in the properties of light, was totally blind, perhaps I may be somewhat pardoned for my seeming presumption.

Elsewhere in the book more repugnant sentiments are casually expressed. When discussing the value of the first few prints of a famous etching he wrote:

In London, these early impressions are frequently purchased by the Jews, who, it is unnecessary to add, require an exorbitant advance of price for them.

Huband moved into No. 63 Fitzwilliam Square in 1820 and remained until his death in 1834. In 1822, his son George produced a small book of etched comic sketches for which the Dublin Society presented him with a silver medal. Willcocks Huband later noted that George 'discontinued the practice of drawing, from an apprehension that its allurements might possibly seduce him from more important studies'.[4] He eventually joined the British army and became a captain in the 8th Hussars. In that same year, 1822, Willcocks lost a young daughter named Anna. Another short run of his most famous work was re-printed in 1823, no doubt leading to another unseemly scrabble for copies from rare-book collectors.

The Hone Family of No. 1

WHILE MR. HUBAND MAY HAVE MASTERED the techniques of his discipline, his is not a name that would be readily associated with Irish art history. For that we must scour the names of Fitzwilliam Square residents in earnest. But we may be in luck, for a quick perusal of the deeds of No.1 shows that on 28 April 1831 the house was leased by Nathaniel Calwell (the original owner) to the spinster sisters Eliza and Ellen Hone. The name Hone is very much associated with Irish art, particularly Nathaniel Hone the Elder (1718-1784). He was born in Dublin, the son of a Dutch merchant. As a young man he moved to England and gained a reputation as a portrait painter and miniaturist. In 1768, he was elected one of the founder members of the Royal Academy and several of his famous paintings now hang in the National Gallery of Ireland and the National Portrait Gallery in London. But how to connect Nathaniel Hone the Elder to Eliza and Ellen? An auction catalogue entry from Adam's fine art auctioneers provides some clues. The lot in question was a watercolour miniature painted on ivory by Horace Hone (1756-1825), son of Nathaniel the Elder. It's entitled 'Miniature portrait of Joseph Hone in military uniform (1775-1857)' and dated 1797.

Miniature of Joseph Hone by Horace Hone

Horace Hone came to Ireland in 1782 and worked almost exclusively in Dorset Street, Dublin (it's good to mention the northside for once) until he removed to England a few years after the Act of Union. While in Dublin Horace often painted his Hone cousins whose tendency to intermarry has left a complicated family tree. Adam's auction notes on the sitter of this particular miniature read as follows:

> Joseph Hone was a merchant of Mountjoy Square and 47 Harcourt Street and Rockfield, County Dublin and was J.P. for the City of Dublin, County Tipperary and King's County.... On the death of his first wife he married Mary Crosthwaite the daughter of Leland Crosthwaite of Dollymount, Clontarf, who was the Governor of the Bank of Ireland from 1808-10. They had five sons and four daughters. Their eldest son (also Joseph) lived at 1 Fitzwilliam Square and at Saint Doulough's Park, Raheny.

So, we're making progress. The reverse of that miniature contained locks of the sitter's hair and was inscribed with a label:

> Joseph Hone 1775-1857 m. Mary Crosthwait, his son Nathaniel built Doulaghs. His daughter Ann married Brindley Hone (1796-1862) and their son was Nathaniel Hone RHA.[5]

In other words, the Joseph Hone of the picture was father of a Joseph Hone who lived in No. 1 Fitzwilliam Square (perhaps a brother of Eliza and Ellen) who was the uncle of the latter named Nathaniel Hone the Younger RHA (1831-1917).

Hone the Younger (the great-grand-nephew of Nathaniel Hone the Elder) studied engineering in Trinity College and upon graduating in 1850 worked as an engineer on the Midland Great Railway for three years. In 1853, he began seventeen years of life in France. During his first years in Paris he studied under Adolphe Yvon (1817-1893) and Thomas Couture (1815-1879) and practised painting by copying the pictures of the old masters in the Louvre. In 1857, he travelled to Barbizon to study landscape painting and encountered other artists such as Millet, Corot and Harpignies. The outbreak of the Franco-Prussian war in 1870 prompted first a move to Italy and then a return to Ireland in 1872, in which year he married Magdalen Jameson of the whiskey distilling family. In 1876, Hone began exhibiting his paintings at the Royal Hibernian Academy and he would continue to do so for the remainder of his life. He became a full member of the RHA in 1879 and in later years would move to St. Doulough's in Raheny, the house built by his uncle. He died in 1917. John Crampton Walker quotes Thomas Bodkin's description of his work:

> Thomas Bodkin in his admirable book on 'Four Irish Landscape Painters,' devotes many pages to this artist, and aptly sums up with this appreciation of his art: - 'To his deep feeling for the colour of a landscape, and his marvellous power to reproduce it, he joined a talent for bold design, a breadth of vision, and a vigour of execution that combined to lift him to a foremost place among the landscape painters of his age, no matter what their country.'[6]

Perhaps we can find a connection between Nathaniel Hone the Younger and No. 1 Fitzwilliam Square. Looking at *Thom's Directory* we see that the name Nathaniel Hone replaces the name Miss E. Hone after 1848, when Nathaniel would have been studying at Trinity College. But that name continues until 1856, three years after Nathaniel the Younger had left for France. In fact, the Nathaniel referred to in *Thom's* was the artist's uncle and we can recall this Nathaniel was mentioned on the reverse of the miniature examined above. He was the son of the sitter Joseph Hone and the builder of the house at St. Doulough's. He was also a director of the Bank of Ireland, High Sherriff of Dublin county in 1870 and a Freeman of the City of Dublin. He died on 13 February 1880. After 1856, No. 1 was in the possession of Thomas Hone. He was also a director of the Bank of Ireland and died at Yapton, Monkstown, County Dublin in 1875. By deed dated 20 August 1860, Thomas sold No. 1 Fitzwilliam Square to the master brewer Matthew Peter D'Arcy.

The Townscape Painter Rose Barton

By happy coincidence another No. 1 dweller provides a neat segue to the sketch of our next artist. An 1835 subscription list for the British Association for the Advancement of Science notes an Augustine Barton living in No. 1 Fitzwilliam Square. Indeed, this is the Augustine Barton described in our opening chapter, the young man of Rochestown, County Tipperary, who would squander a small fortune on real estate in Australia. He later returned to Dublin and married the widow Emily McCalmont. Perhaps he lodged in No. 1 briefly, but it is odd, for we know the family townhouse was at No. 23 on the south side of the square. Indeed, Augustine's father and brother, Dunbar and Samuel Barton respectively, were living in No. 23 in 1835. We may recall that Augustine and Emily, after their respective adventures, took up residence in the house soon after their marriage in October 1853. Augustine was then settled as a solicitor in Dublin and registrar in various divisions of the Four Courts. Emily already had two sons from her first marriage and she would have two daughters, Alma and Rose, with Augustine. The second daughter, Rose Barton, born on 21 April 1856, was a famous Victorian water-colourist and townscape painter. Some sources say she was born in Dublin, others say Rochestown. If the former is true then No. 23 is a likely candidate for her birthplace, but in any case her early years were divided between the Rochestown countryside and the Fitzwilliam Square townhouse.

Raymond Brooke, a son of Alma Barton, described their upbringing:

> These two ... were strictly brought up by their mother, to the extent that Aunt Rose was always relieved if she got past the door of the drawing room in the house in Fitzwilliam Square, without her mother hearing her and calling her in. It must not be thought from this that she was not fond of her mother – she was indeed extremely fond – but Mrs B. immediately observed any lapse in the way her daughters were turned out.... She had what might nowadays be thought somewhat odd views on diet and always made her baby daughters drink Guinness's stout – saying it was good for the complexion.... Later they had a German Governess, were taught drawing, and both played piano creditably.

Rose, a cousin of the novelist Edith Somerville, began exhibiting with the Watercolour Society of Ireland at the age of sixteen. Augustine Barton died in 1874 and the following year Rose and her sister were brought by their mother to Brussels to receive further lessons in drawing and painting. In 1877, Barton exhibited her first painting at the Royal Hibernian Academy, a work entitled 'Dead Game'. Her sister Alma married in April 1881.

> Not long afterwards, Aunt Rose had an unfortunate love affair. The young man had got heavily into debt and his family said that before any arrangements could be made he must go overseas and remain away until he had righted his finances. Aunt Rose, however, never saw him again, for in less than six months he had contracted some type of fever and died.[7]

Barton then decided to make art her profession and studied at the studio of the French artist Henri Gervex and in London under Paul Jacob Naftel. Her watercolours are noted for the ambient effects of weather, particularly the fog and rain of London streets. Anne Crookshank wrote:

Rose had a real feeling for weather, especially the foggy atmosphere of London with its glimmering street lamps, rain-washed streets and busy thoroughfares.[8]

Her work became better known in Dublin and London thanks to her illustration of two books: *Picturesque Dublin Old and New*, written by Geraldine Fitzgerald in 1898, and her own book, *Familiar London*, 1904. In that book Barton described how she was inspired by the shifting moods of London's streets.

> I often wonder how many there are in London who see it as it really is. Not long ago, I happened to be in Westminster on a December afternoon. It had been raining heavily all day, and the sky, which had just cleared, was flooded with a golden light. The towers of the Abbey stood up against it in misty blue. A string of hansom cabs coming along, reflected in the wet streets, looked like a procession of black gondolas. It was a striking effect. I gazed at it entranced, and then walked home feeling as if I had had a glimpse of fairyland. I was met with the remark, 'Did you ever see a more odious day? I am splashed with mud from head to foot!'

> Men talk rapturously about 'mountain distances' and 'air perspectives'; but what can be more striking than the blue-grey fog that turns the end of a London street, as you look down it, into mystery and beauty that give to the present a tinge of the uncertainty of the future, and throw a halo of poetry over the most commonplace homes?[9]

According to her biographical entry, Barton was a broad-minded social observer with a fondness for betting on horseracing. She died in Knightsbridge, London on 10 October 1929. Raymond Brooke, as her executor, had to settle a bet with a London bookie for £3 on the Monday after her death.

William Dargan and the Foundation of the National Gallery of Ireland

ON 11 FEBRUARY 1867, FITZWILLIAM SQUARE saw its largest funeral procession when the body of William Dargan, the railway engineer, was conveyed from No. 2 to Glasnevin cemetery. James Scannell described the sombre march:

> The arrangements were placed in the hands of Messrs Gerty and Rorke, Undertakers, of Baggot St ... for one of the largest public funerals seen in Dublin for a number of years. Well before 9 a.m. on Monday, February 11 those wishing to pay their last public respects to this great man began to line the streets of Dublin, while some went to Fitzwilliam Square East where the undertaker's staff had the task of marshalling all those in their carriages who wished to join the cortege and placing them into assigned positions. At 9 a.m. the remains of William Dargan in a coffin of highly polished oak, bearing gilt mountings and a burnished shield ... [were] carried from his last residence to a waiting hearse outside, which was drawn by 4 horses. The cortege was led by 700 railwaymen....The hearse was followed by three mourning coaches, each drawn by two horses. Then came the Lord Mayor's State Coach containing Sir John Gray, M.P., Lord Mayor of Dublin ... followed in turn by between 200 and 250 carriages containing a wide spectrum of people with whom Dargan had been associated during his lifetime.... On arrival at the cemetery in Glasnevin the remains were carried to the Mortuary Chapel on the shoulders of railway employees ... followed by a large crowd through the cemetery to the O'Connell Circle where the coffin was placed in a vault, its final resting place.[10]

Imagine some 250 horse-drawn carriages stretching from the east side of Fitzwilliam Square back along the length of Fitzwilliam Place towards Leeson Street, and the spectacle of such a procession through Dublin's streets. The civil engineer William Le Fanu (brother of the gothic author Joseph Sheridan) knew Dargan well and described him in his *Seventy Years of Irish Life*. Since William Le Fanu was also a resident of Fitzwilliam Square (No. 59 from 1853 to 1877), we will quote his sketch of Dargan's career and character:

> Dargan was the son of a tenant farmer, in the county of Carlow. At a school near his house he received a sound elementary education, and from early years showed special

144

aptitude for figures. After leaving school he obtained a subordinate appointment – that of timekeeper, if I remember rightly – on the great Holyhead Road, under Telford, the engineer. His intelligence, and the trust which he inspired, so pleased Telford that a few years later, when the new mail-coach road was about to be made from Dublin to Howth Harbour, from whence the packets carrying the mails for London were to start, he entrusted to Dargan the superintendence of the work. So satisfactory was his performance of his duties that, on the completion of the road, the Treasury granted him a gratuity of £300 in addition to his salary. This was the capital upon which he commenced his career as a contractor.... His first large undertaking was the construction of the railway from Dublin to Kingstown, which was begun in 1831, and was the first passenger railway made in Ireland, and the second in the Three Kingdoms ... I have settled as engineer for different companies many of his accounts, involving many hundred thousand pounds. His thorough honesty, his willingness to yield a disputed point, and his wonderful rapidity of decision, rendered it a pleasure, instead of a trouble, as it generally is, to settle these accounts; indeed, in my life I have never met a man more quick in intelligence, more clear sighted, and more thoroughly honourable ...

Dargan's next project for his country's good was a thoroughly successful one. It was the great Industrial Exhibition in Dublin in the year 1853, all expenses in connection with which, including the erection of the building itself, were defrayed by him. It was opened by her Majesty the Queen and the Prince Consort, who came to Ireland expressly for the purpose. They did Dargan the honour of visiting him and Mrs. Dargan at his beautiful residence, Mount Anville, a few miles from Dublin. Her Majesty wished him to accept a baronetcy, which he declined, at the same time expressing his gratitude for this mark of her Majesty's approval. The Queen then announced to him her intention to present him with a bust of herself and also one of the Prince Consort; and, with her usual thoughtful kindness, desired that he should select the sculptor by whom they were to be executed. He, from his friendship for the man, selected Johnny Jones, of whom I have already said much.

His next project was the establishment of a great thread factory at Chapelizod, near Dublin, where he purchased, and added to large mill premises, and, at great expense, fitted them with all the necessary machinery. It may have been that the demand for thread was sufficiently supplied by the English manufacturers; but whether it was from this or from other causes, the undertaking completely failed.

After this Dargan, unfortunately for himself, threw all his energies into the Dublin, Wicklow, and Wexford Railway, in which he invested nearly his whole fortune, and of which he became chairman. In connection with this line he spent large sums on the improvement of Bray, the now well-known watering-place on the coast about midway between Dublin and Wicklow. He built the Turkish baths (now the assembly rooms) at a cost of £8,000, and also a handsome terrace. He made the esplanade, which has since been secured by a sea-wall and much improved by the energetic town commissioners. He also aided largely in providing first-rate hotel accommodation there. This expenditure, though large, would not have seriously impaired his means had the railway proved as successful as he hoped it would have done; but the great depression in railway property, which began about that time, so lowered the value of all his investments that they for a time became of little worth; and this remarkable man (for a remarkable man he was) a few years later died comparatively poor, and, to use his own words, 'of a broken heart'.

I had almost forgotten to mention two of his favourite maxims. These were 'A spoonful of honey will catch more flies than a gallon of vinegar', and 'Never show your teeth unless you can bite'. On these, as he himself often told me, he had acted from early years, and it was to them that he attributed much of his success in life.[11]

It is Dargan's involvement with the Dublin Exhibition of 1853 that concerns us in this chapter. The exhibition had so direct an effect on the artistic heritage of the city that a statue of Dargan stands outside the Merrion Square entrance of the National Gallery of Ireland. In June 1852, Dargan approached the Dublin Society with plans for a spectacular exhibition on Leinster Lawn, in imitation of the London exhibition of 1851. Dargan felt that Ireland needed to enhance its image after the harrowing effects of the Famine and planned a showcase of Irish industry and fine arts. The Sligo-born architect John Benson was commissioned to construct an exhibition hall in imitation of Joseph Paxton's Crystal Palace

William Dargan of No. 2

in London. The result was a series of glass domes, wrought iron and fluted glass with a frontage of 300 feet onto Merrion Square.

The exhibition opened on 12 May 1853 and Somerville-Large described the reception of its principal sponsor:

> The hero of the hour was not the Lord Lieutenant, nor any of the Knights of St Patrick present in their regalia, nor the municipal officials, but plain honest, modest Mr Dargan. The author of the Exhibition's catalogue, John Sproule, described how 'the Chairman then formally introduced Mr Dargan to His Excellency. This was the signal for the most cordial demonstration on the part of the assembled thousands that has ever been witnessed. The position of Mr Dargan at that moment was one that even a sovereign might envy; surrounded by the wealth and intelligence of his native land, in the Temple dedicated to Industry, erected solely at his expense, all joining the enthusiastic acclamations of respect, which were again and again repeated'.[12]

Queen Victoria visited the exhibition in late August and, as Le Fanu noted, visited Dargan and his wife at their home at Mount Anville, near Blackrock. The *London Illustrated News* noted that the visit was the first that had been paid by a British sovereign to a 'commoner' in modern times.

What set the Dublin exhibition apart was Dargan's insistence that one-third of the exhibition space should be devoted to displays of the fine arts, mostly lent from the private collections of Irish peers.

> The decision must have seemed quixotic. The great mass of the population of Ireland was still suffering the after effects of the Famine and looking for food to put in their mouths. Surely an emphasis on agriculture and industrial development was more relevant in a country slowly recovering from disaster than wall-to-wall paintings arranged right up to the curve of Benson's roof? But Dargan shared the Victorian conviction that art fulfilled an important social need ...

> The vindication of Dargan's intention to make art the most prominent aspect of his Exhibition was the popularity of the Painting and Sculpture Hall. The surprise this aroused was expressed in *The Journal of Industrial Progress*: 'It is a remarkable fact that when the Great Exhibition was opened to the working classes at sixpence, they displayed in the attention to which they daily examined the wonders of Art before them, an amount of reverence as well as good taste ... no really high Work of Art graced the Exhibition Halls that did not ever command its circle of attentive admirers, whose earnest and often reverential countenance showed, that while they did not always perfectly understand, they could at least respectfully look up to what was above them and what they felt contained something of the Spiritual, the Divine'.

Earlier, in 1853, a Dargan Testimonial Committee had formed to honour Ireland's foremost philanthropist and raise a subscription for scholarships and industrial instruction of 'young men of genius whose humble birth or limited means might offer a barrier to advancement'. Although £5,000 was raised, the management of the committee was rather haphazard and unfocussed. Meanwhile, another more disciplined group styling themselves the Irish Institution determined to establish a permanent building to house a National Gallery for Ireland. Somerville-Large notes that:

... at this stage the Dargan Committee had to be included in the enterprise, persuaded literally by peer pressure that paintings and art should reflect Dargan's achievements rather than industry.... Plans for training intelligent working-class boys were thrown to the winds.

The £5,000 was set aside for the construction of the gallery building. On 30 March 1864, the National Gallery of Ireland was opened and a statue of Dargan by Thomas Farrell was unveiled. Dargan was not present for the unveiling but the Lord Lieutenant paid him tribute:

But we raise his Statue because he supplies a memorable instance of how a simple, earnest, honest man, without any help from birth or fortune, by the energetic exercise of the faculties which God has given him, may not only raise himself to a commanding level beyond his own original position, but may also confer signal benefits upon the men of his day, and upon the country which has learned to be proud of him, and thus prides to show it. And we place his Statue here, because on this very ground before us it was that the patient zeal, the strong faith, the disinterested liberality of Mr Dargan brought to a successful issue that great Dublin Exhibition which gave a fresh impulse to the undertakings of art and science, of which we see the imposing monuments before us.[13]

Perhaps Dargan was absent because of his mounting financial embarrassments which compelled him to move from Mount Anville to No. 2 Fitzwilliam Square in the same year as the Gallery's opening. In 1866, he fell from his horse and suffered serious injury. This blow seemed to break his spirit and he lost interest in his increasingly fraught financial concerns. He died in No. 2 on the 7 February 1867.

The Benson Sisters of No. 42

IN THE YEAR BEFORE THE NATIONAL GALLERY's opening the renowned surgeon Charles Benson moved into No. 42 Fitzwilliam Square. While at least two of his sons followed him into the medical profession, his daughters Mary Kate (1842-1921) and Charlotte (1846-1893) became artists. Mary Kate Benson was the better known and from 1874 to 1887 she was secretary of the Dublin Amateur Artist's Society. During periods living abroad she studied under the artists Hubert von Herkomer and P.H. Calderon, and exhibited paintings in the RHA from 1873 to 1906. In 1916, she organised an exhibition of her work in aid of the Dublin Fusiliers' prisoners of war fund. She suffered badly from arthritis in later years and died in Howth in March 1921. No. 42 remained in the Benson family until 1917 when Bethel Solomons moved into the house with his family.

Sir Walter Armstrong and the Ghost of Hugh Lane

FITZWILLIAM SQUARE CONNECTIONS WITH ART in the nineteenth century are completed by the art critic and writer Sir Walter Armstrong (1850-1918) who lived in No. 41 from 1893 to 1900. He had been appointed director of the National Gallery in 1892, a post he held for twenty years. His obituary in *The Times* on 9 August 1918 briefly described his career:

> Many friends, and all British and Irish students of the history of art will greatly regret to learn that Sir Walter Armstrong, the late Director of the National Gallery of Ireland, died yesterday at his residence in Carlisle-mansions, Westminster. They will hardly by surprised, for his health had been rapidly failing for some months; but none the less his death removes one of the keenest and most learned of our critics of painting, and one who had been for many years a very useful public servant.

He was born in 1850, was educated at Harrow and Exeter College, Oxford, and for some 10 years after 1880 was art critic to several newspapers, such as the *Pall Mall Gazette*, the *Manchester Guardian* and the old *Manchester Examiner*. He soon made his mark in the art world, and was consulted by students and collectors, becoming an authority especially on Dutch seventeenth century and English eighteenth century painting. In 1892, he succeeded the late Henry Doyle as Director of the Dublin Gallery, which his predecessor had reorganised and developed; and in this post Armstrong remained for over 20 years, his services recognized by a knighthood in 1899.

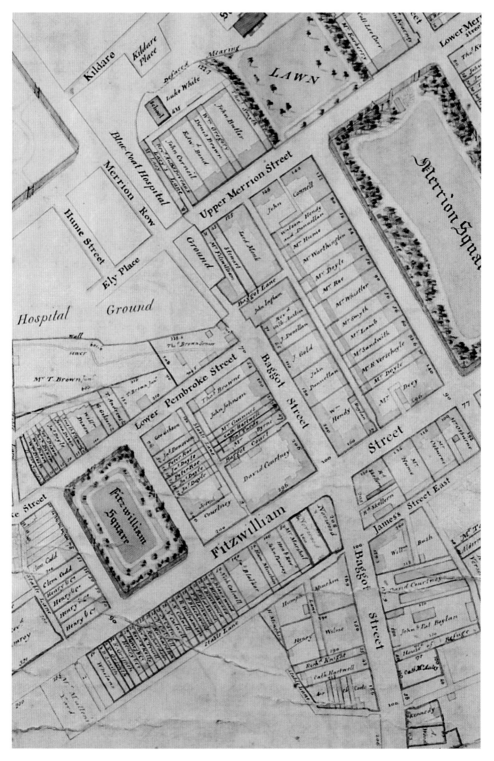

Detail, a map of part of the estate of the Earl of Pembroke (John Roe, 1822)

The O'Gorman Mahon of No. 64

Lord Ashbourne of No. 23

Chief Justice Charles Barry of No. 3

J.G. Butcher of No. 40

'Going to the Levée at Dublin Castle' by Rose Barton, originally of No. 23

Interior of the Dublin Exhibition, 1853

'Nursery Tea' by Mainie Jellet, painted in No. 36 in 1918

'Decoration' by Mainie Jellett, 1923

*Two views of the same scene at Poulaphouca by Dermod O'Brien of No. 65, –
dated c. 1922 and 1939, showing the evolution of his style*

'Fitzwilliam Square in May' by Kitty Wilmer O'Brien of No. 65 – a view across
the square towards Jack B. Yeats's house at No. 18

'Fitzwilliam Square' by Charles Ginner

While in Dublin he found time to write many books, among which his stately volumes on Sir Joshua Reynolds, Gainsborough, and Raeburn were the chief; these still hold a position of authority.

One of Armstrong's successors as director of the National Gallery was Hugh Lane, now better known for establishing Dublin's Municipal Gallery of Modern Art in 1908, the world's first modern art gallery. He was aboard the *RMS Lusitania* on 7 May 1915 and drowned when the ship was torpedoed by a German u-boat. At the same

Portrait of Sir Hugh Lane by John Singer Sargent, 1906

time, Hester Travers-Smith was a well known medium who held twice-weekly séances in No. 61 Fitzwilliam Square. The playwright Lennox Robinson was a regular sitter at Hester's gatherings and would eventually marry her daughter, Dolly. In her book *Voices from the Void*, Travers-Smith describes a séance held at No. 61 in May 1915 just after the sinking of the *Lusitania*:

> About five o'clock on the day we heard of the loss of the Lusitania I saw posters on my way home, saying: 'Lusitania reported sinking'. I did not buy a paper, and had no personal interest in the sinking ship, as I knew of no one on board. Sir Hugh Lane's name did not occur to me, probably because he had been in America such a very short time....The Rev Hicks recorded in silence, while Mr Lennox Robinson and I sat blindfolded and talked to each other while the message was being spelled out by our hands. After a couple of minutes Mr Hicks said: 'Would you like to know who is speaking? It is Sir Hugh Lane, and he says he has been drowned, and was on board the Lusitania'. We were terribly shocked – we both knew Sir Hugh – and

asked Mr Hicks to read the message to us. It ran as follows: 'Pray for Hugh Lane'. Then, on being asked who was
speaking, 'I am Hugh Lane; all is dark', came through. At
this moment a stop press edition of the evening paper was
called in the street, and Mr Robinson ran down and bought
one. When he came up to me he pointed to the name of Sir
Hugh Lane among the passengers. We were both distressed,
but continued our sitting. Sir Hugh Lane described the scene
on board the Lusitania. 'Panic, then boats lowered – Women
went first,' he said. He stated that he was last in an over-
crowded boat, fell over, and lost all memory until he 'saw a
light' at our sitting.[14]

Travers-Smith grew disillusioned with Dublin's increasingly militant
nationalism and moved from No. 61 Fitzwilliam Square to London in
1919. She maintained contacts with Dublin's literary circle, particularly
W.B. Yeats and Lennox Robinson. She exerted an unhealthy power over
Robinson and was furious when he married her daughter in 1931. Yeats's
wife George in particular reviled Hester. She wrote of her:

> ... the unbending hard essence of everything I loathe men-
> tally, emotionally and temperamentally, she makes me
> think of lumpy beds, Russian fleas and ipechuana wine.[15]

Mainie Jellett of No. 36

IN THE EARLY TWENTIETH CENTURY TWO young neighbours on the west side
of Fitzwilliam Square would go on to have artistic careers, one more
distinguished than the other. The older was John Crampton Walker
who moved with his family into No. 38 around 1902 when he was 12
years of age. He was a landscape painter educated at Trinity College
and the Dublin Metropolitan School of Art. In 1914, he displayed his
first work at the Royal Hibernian Academy and would show 132 works
there throughout his career. Apart from his painting, Walker is remembered for a 1926 publication entitled *Irish Life and Landscape,* a collection
of 67 reproductions of the work of twentieth century Irish artists with
short commentaries on each. He included one of his own paintings in
the volume: 'Looking towards Glenbeigh, Co. Kerry'.

Two doors up in No. 36 Fitzwilliam Square, on the very corner with Pembroke Street Upper, lived the Jellett family. William Morgan Jellett, a Dublin-born barrister, married Janet Stokes and moved into the house in 1895. Their first daughter, Mary Harriet, was born there on 29 April 1897, and they would have three other girls besides: Dorothea Janet, Rosamund and Elizabeth. All four daughters were known by their pet-names: Mainie, Bay, Babbin and Betty. Michael Purser, a son of Betty Jellett, described the characters in the house in his book, *Seven Generations, Four Families*. Of William Jellett he wrote:

> William Jellett (1857-1936) was of course a barrister, and the front room on the ground-floor level was where he worked on his briefs. In the morning he would walk down to the Four Courts, leaving his brief case to be carried in the 'Legal Express' (an antediluvian horse-drawn vehicle, fitted out with hooks inside on which to hang the cases, and pulled by a somnambulant bag of bones and dust); and in the evening he would return, calling in at the University Club on the Green, or the Masonic Hall in Molesworth Street, to meet his cronies. But later he would work in this front room, lights on, no curtains drawn. As a prominent Unionist he was a sitting target, and indeed he received several death threats. 'I defy the cowards' he would say – and he was never shot at.[16]

Mainie Jellett's early childhood in No. 36 was nurturing and contented. An early indication of an independence of spirit in the artist as a young girl came in a letter from William to a vacationing Janet in June 1898:

> All well here. Datooska is gradually establishing a right to walk in the Square and has twice declined to leave at request of the gardener.[17]

The early pet name was indicative of Janet's upbringing in India. Mainie's mother was an accomplished musician and left the minding and education of her children in the hands of a series of governesses. Arnold wrote:

These teachers were chosen for their unorthodox views. Mrs Jellett sought women 'with imagination' ... and this resulted in some strange additions to the family circle. One of them was a Miss Chenevix, whose fiercely republican views were very much at variance with the equally fierce unionism of William Morgan Jellett. Another was a German girl, Fraulein Schuster, who is remembered because she used to pounce on the girls from behind curtains.[18]

A mainstay of the house would be Nannie Annie Skerritt, who stayed with the family for forty-seven years. Purser described Nannie Skerritt's style of supervision in the central garden in which:

> ... there were plenty of children. Rows of nannies sat on the benches in the square keeping an eye on them – and gossiping. Their own Nannie didn't: 'I couldn't be bothered with all them ould wans.' When her charges were to come home from playing out there, Nannie leant out of the top window and screeched for them. The Jellett children were considered lucky by their Protestant friends, because they were allowed to play with Catholics.

Purser also noted:

> Nannie had a brother, home from the South African War, who made the girls a dolls' house, called it 'Ladysmith Hall' and painted a massive Union Jack on the roof. But this partisan enthusiasm was too much even for the Jelletts and William over-thatched it with straw that had wrapped champagne bottles, so as not to offend the sensibilities of visiting nationalist children.[19]

The Jellett children each received lessons in music and painting. The latter instruction came from Elizabeth Yeats, the poet's sister, who visited No. 36 once a week to give lessons in the dining room. Other children from the neighbourhood attended these lessons, including the writer Elizabeth Bowen:

> I first knew Mainie Jellett when we were both little girls: her mother and mine were friends, and neighbours in Dublin, and Mainie and I must have first met and looked

at each other solemnly before we were either of us able to speak. The little Jelletts and I used to meet on our school-room walks through the streets and squares, and were often in and out of each other's homes. And I was one of the children who went to the painting classes, which, held by Miss Elizabeth Yeats in the Jelletts' Fitzwilliam Square dining-room, saw the opening of Mainie's life as an artist. I remem-ber the excitement of that free brushwork – the children's heads bent, all round the big table, over crocuses springing alive,

Photo of Mainie Jellett, aged 16

with each stroke, on the different pieces of white paper.... I have never lost the proud sense of being at least a contem-porary of Mainie's, and a friend in the sense that distance and separation do not damage. To have worked with her must surely have been a great thing.[20]

Jellett entered the Dublin Metropolitan School of Art in 1914. Wil-liam Orpen was still teaching there but he would soon leave to become a war-artist in France. In 1917, Jellett began studying at the Westminster Technical Institute under Walter Sickert, the first of three particularly influential tutors. In 1921, she went to study in the Andre Lhote acad-emy in Paris. Soon after, Jellett and her friend Evie Hone (a relation of the nineteenth century Hone family of No. 1) boldly turned up at the studio of Albert Gleizes outside Paris, importuning him to become his students. An obituary for Jellett later noted:

Albert Gleizes was one of the most distinguished modern artists in Paris, but he had never thought of teaching till two unknown and very serious young Irish girls introduced themselves and announced diffidently that they had studied his exhibited work and wished him to be their teacher! But he took them on, and, in both cases, Ireland has occasion to be gratified at the results of her children's daring.[21]

The influence of these three teachers marked what Jellett described as 'major revolutions' in her development as an artist. Elizabeth Bowen wrote:

She speaks of having gone through three major revolutions in her work, style and ideas and of after each of these starting more or less afresh. The first came with study with Walter Sickert – revolution in composition and use of line, realism, new understanding of the Old Masters. Sickert, being in the direct line of French Impressionist painting, was the stepping stone towards the next revolution – Paris and Lhote's studio, with its work on modified cubist theories. 'With Lhote, I learned how to use natural forms as a starting point towards the pure creation of form for its own sake ... and to produce work based on a knowledge of rhythmical form and organic colour groping towards a conception of a picture being a creative organic whole, but still based on realistic form.' Lhote was, in his turn, to be a stepping stone to the third revolution; as a student of Albert Gleizes. With him: 'I went right back to the beginning, and was put to the severest type of exercises in pure form and colour ... I now felt I had come to essentials and thought the type of work I had embarked upon, would mean years of misunderstandings and walls of prejudice to break though, yet I felt I was on the right track.' So it happened that Mainie Jellett brought back to her native city a dynamicism that at first, as she had expected, was found unfriendly, destructive, even repellent.[22]

The difficult critical reception for Jellett's modernist, non-representational art was highlighted by George Russell's hyperbolic description of her 1923 work 'Decoration'.

We turn from Clarke's pictures and find Miss Jellett a late victim to Cubism in some Sub-section of this malaria....We hope the visitors will not be led away ... (by) the sub-human art of Miss Jellett.[23]

By no means were these the first modernist images to be displayed in Dublin, but the controversy surrounding Jellett's work led to re-newed public debate about modernism in Irish art. This is the sub-ject of Bruce Arnold's book, *Mainie Jellett and the Modern Movement in Ireland*. During the 1930s, Jellett's work became slightly less abstract as she experimented with figurative religious imagery. She also gave lessons, lectures and wrote books on art theory and technique. In 1943, she was elected chairwoman of the Irish Exhibition of Living Art but was too ill to attend its opening. Jellett was diagnosed with cancer and ended her life in a nursing home on lower Leeson Street on 16 February 1944. Elizabeth Bowen, who knew the artist from her earliest years, described her in her final months:

I saw her last, in October, 1943, in the quiet back room of the Leeson Street nursing home, where she lay with her bed pulled out under the window. A fire burned in the grate, and brick buildings in October sunshine reflected bright-ness into the room. The eager generous little girl of my first memories was now a thin woman, in whom the fatigue of illness, mingling with that unlost generosity and eagerness, translated itself into a beauty I cannot forget.[24]

The O'Briens of No. 65

ALTHOUGH DERMOD O'BRIEN (1865-1935) came from an older generation of artists compared to Jellett, we shall look at his career last, not only be-cause he moved into Fitzwilliam Square relatively late in life, 1920, but also because his artist daughter-in-law, Kitty Wilmer O'Brien (1910-1982), continued to live and work in the house many years after his death. Dermod was a grandson of the Young Irelander William Smith O'Brien, and his father Edward built a grand house at the family es-tate in Cahirmoyle, County Limerick. Lennox Robinson used to spend periods living at Cahirmoyle and he wrote a biography of Dermod

The hallway in No. 65

O'Brien entitled *Palette and Plough*, referring to O'Brien's work as artist and gentleman farmer. O'Brien went to school in Harrow and studied at Cambridge but did not decide to take up art as a profession until he was twenty-two years of age. In 1887, he entered the Antwerp Academy where, according to Robinson, the lessons were neither inspired nor inspiring. Robinson wondered what effect on O'Brien's style might have accrued if he had at first studied in Paris:

This Impressionist movement, this new world of art and literature and music.... He would have found a gaiety there which until the last years of his life was lacking from his painting. For he did towards the end achieve a lovely freedom of touch. Then he painted rapidly and, as it were, carelessly ... I mean that by this time he was so master of his craft that he could afford a little to break the rules and to forget his old teachers' dictum and sometimes paint beyond what he saw.... His painting is too honest to be really great, he painted too much from the eye and mistrusted his heart and his sense of humour.[25]

O'Brien did go on to study in Paris and London before returning to Dublin in 1901, where he set up in No. 42 Mountjoy Square as a portraitist.

In 1905, he was elected an associate member of the Royal Hibernian Academy and only five years later became president, a post he held until his death. The demands of his official position impinged on his time for composition, but he came to rival Sarah Purser as Ireland's official portrait painter. More often than not his subjects were judges and generals, clerics and academics, and at times he grew despondent at the limits of portraiture:

158

Seeing pictures depresses me. Sometimes I feel that I must chuck it all, that it's no damn good pretending to paint when I might be reducing the size of my belly by digging potatoes or cutting down trees or some useful work that requires a bit of brute force.

The drawing room of No. 65

However, it was the selling of the Cahirmoyle estates and a permanent move to Dublin and No. 65 Fitzwilliam Square that led to the most contented and creative years of his life. Robinson wrote:

There was to be a green old age but not spent in County Limerick, a greenness which lasted more than twenty years. The new Dublin home was in Fitzwilliam Square, in a large gracious house where Dermod could spread himself, hang all his pictures ... shelve his books and have a large studio at the end of the back garden. After these years and years of wandering he had at last reached home.

His new artistic freedom came from having no longer to rely on portrait commissions and the inspiration from regular trips to the south of France.

One can see a distinct break in his landscape work about 1924, a break for the better. Some months each winter would now be spent in the South of France....The quick sunshine and bright air, the brilliant blue sea and the grey grass and rocks seemed to come as readily to his brush as the heavy greens and dull skies of Ireland. Perhaps the Irish landscape was like a too placid sitter, a 'good' sitter, a person who would sit immovable day after day, taking the exact position on Wednesday as had been taken on the previous Monday. The foreign landscape was a little less complacent, it had its moods, it demanded more rapid work.

O'Brien happened to be in the south of France in January 1939, only a few miles away from where W.B. Yeats died. He assisted George Hyde Lees with the funeral arrangements and described the events in a letter to Robinson:

> We buried W.B. yesterday in a little cemetery on the highest point of Roquebrune that dominates Cap Martin and Monaco.... We [O'Brien and his wife Mabel] were very fortunate in that we had called on Willy and George after a drive up country the Sunday before. George was out but he received me in his bedroom where he was at work in his dressing-gown. He made me shove his MS. into a drawer and bring Mabel in when he gave us tea and delightful talk as he lay in bed, full of life apparently and in good spirits and at work on poetry of which he was full and to which he could give his time.... It really was a delightful half hour or so of gay chat and amusing gay comment and reminiscences.

> On Saturday George rang me up to say that he had died and would I arrange for clergyman, etc.

> After dinner we motored over, picking up the padre on the way, George took us into his room where he lay looking indescribably noble and beautiful and as if he had fallen asleep with some happy thought on his lips. I had never realised what a beautiful head he had when his features were at rest.

The perspective of a portrait painter evident in the last comment. Dermod O'Brien died in early October 1945, after years of grandchildren crawling in the drawing room of No. 65. Lennox Robinson ended his biography praising O'Brien's ability to capture character in his portraits but with this observation:

> One wishes he had painted portraits of such people as...some old stone-breaker on the road between Ardagh and Rathkeale, or an old woman stirring a pot of meal over a turf fire or giving the boneens their evening feed. This might have made him our Irish Goya, our Rembrandt, our Van Gogh, our Daumier.

Conclusion

ONCE MORE WE'VE REACHED AND BREACHED the year 1922 and so should end our search for Fitzwilliam Square artists. As mentioned elsewhere, the increasing number of flats in the square leads to a greater chance of commenting on some relatively minor painter living in a certain house, while completing overlooking a more renowned sub-tenant starving in her basement. However there are three other painters that should be noted. Pamela Kathleen Wilmer was born in Quetta, now in Pakistan, in 1910 but moved to Dublin at a young age. While studying at the Royal Hibernian Academy Schools she was tutored by Dermod O'Brien and would later marry his son Brendan, becoming known as Kitty Wilmer O'Brien. Brendan and Kitty continued living in No. 65 after the death of Dermod. From 1962 to 1981, Kitty was president of the Watercolour Society of Ireland. In 1951, she exhibited a work entitled 'Spring, Fitzwilliam Square', a view from the first floor window of No. 65 in which Jack B. Yeats's home at No. 18 can be seen across the square. According to a Whytes' catalogue, this painting was used as the basis for an etching that Wilmer O'Brien used annually for the family Christmas card, which her children used to colour in.

In the 1950s, the landscapist, graphic designer and illustrator Norah McGuinness (1901-1980) was living in No. 13 on the east side of the square. McGuinness studied in Dublin and London and, upon advice from Mainie Jellett and Evie Hone, under Andre L'Hote in Paris. After

Kitty Wilmer O'Brien in No. 65

Jellett's death in 1944, McGuinness became president of the Irish Exhibition of Living Art.

And of course, as already mentioned, Jack B. Yeats lived and worked
in No. 18 Fitzwilliam Square from 1929. His is not a career that can be
described in a paragraph or two, but his studio home on that Fitzwilliam Square corner became a meeting place for Dublin's artistic and
literary figures. Deirdre Bair wrote:

> Yeats held 'Thursdays' each week in his studio at 18, Fitz-
> william Square, where guests were invited to drink Malaga
> wine with a twist of lemon and to talk about art and lit-
> erature. Among the regular visitors were Terence de Vere
> White, Austin Clarke, Arland Ussher, Padraic Colum, and
> Joseph Maunsell Hone.[26]

A young Samuel Beckett also attended these gatherings. His stri-
dent presence became abrasive however and he took to meeting Yeats
privately. Beckett was a great admirer of Yeats's paintings and they
became good friends – though Yeats was sure to keep the relationship
professional when it came to valuing his own work:

Samuel Beckett ran up against Jack the businessman in the same way, with a similar result. At one of his intimate talks with Jack at Fitzwilliam Square, Beckett fell in love with a new painting by Jack called Morning. It carried a price tag of £30, which Beckett didn't have. He let Jack know how much he liked the picture and how much he wanted to have it. Jack said nothing, made no move. A week later they met by chance at the National Library, and Beckett mentioned the picture again, 'but still Yeats said nothing'. The price was £30, and, until the money was produced, the picture would not be given up. Finally Beckett brought two friends to Fitzwilliam Square, asked if he could have the picture and pay for it by instalments. Jack instantly yielded, and Beckett borrowed the money from his friends, preferring to owe them rather than Jack.[27]

It's a test of imagination now to picture that studio in No. 18, but we have at least the following recollection by Shotaro Oshima, a Japanese translator of William Yeats's poetry, to go on:

It was on July 7, 1938, that I visited him. I was caught in heavy rain on the way, and at four o'clock in the afternoon I knocked at the door of his house in Fitzwilliam Square, Dublin, with my dripping hat drawn down over my eyes. The artist who received me warmly looked taller and more slender than his brother. He was long-faced and his thin hair hung about his forehead.

' ... Would you care to come to my studio upstairs?' I followed him upstairs, hearing the sound of rain pattering on the roof and window ...

'This picture represents the gloomy houses of poor people in Dublin. That is a public house where the tenants of tenements gather. In that picture I tried to paint a port in Kerry full of cargo boats. This is a scene in the countryside of Galway. My brother William once lived here with his family. This is a shore landscape in the south-east part of Ireland. That picture in the corner represents O'Connell Bridge. You must have crossed it several times' ...

Jack B. Yeats in his studio

The rain was falling incessantly outside. The verdure of the leaves seen through the window looked all the more fresh in the rain. Jack rose to his feet and tried to pull out a larger piece from a bundle of pictures propped up against the wall near the window. It was very large, but with my help he just managed to pull it out. It was five feet wide and four feet tall, and was titled 'Helen of Troy'. [Yeats described the painting in some detail to Oshima]

He smiled. He was so intent on what he was saying that he did not notice that the kettle he had put over the fire to serve tea was boiling over. So I ran to the fireplace and removed the lid of the kettle.

'Ah! the water was boiling over? Thank you,' he said, turning to me from the picture ...

The rain was still falling when I said good-bye to the painter. The little square where we stood presented a lonely and deserted appearance. He shook me warmly by the hand, asking me to revisit Dublin and see him again. After he had entered the house, I stood alone on the pavement of the square and looked up at the lighted window of his studio. It was the only light in Fitzwilliam Square. In the steady fall of rain I left the place, picturing to myself the figure of the artist sitting alone among images of his own creation.[28]

Endnotes

1. Ithell Colquhoun, *The Crying of the Wind: Ireland*, p. 15.

2. Kenneth Ferguson, 'The Irish Bar in December 1798', *Dublin Historical Record*, Vol. 52, No. 1, Spring 1999, pp. 49-50.

3. Rudolph Ackermann, *The Repository of arts, literature, commerce, manufactures, fashions and politics* (1809), pp. 38-39.

4. Willcocks Huband, *Critical and familiar notices on the art of etching upon copper*, 1823.

5. Adam's Irish Art Sale Catalogue, 26 May 2004, Lot No. 15.

6. John Crampton Walker, *Irish Life and Landscapes*, p. 72.

7. Raymond Brooke, *The Brimming River*, pp. 82-84.

8. Anne Crookshank, *Irish Watercolours and Drawings*, p. 224.

9. Rose Barton, *Familiar London* (1904), pp. 4-5.

10. James Scannell, 'The Funeral of William Dargan', *Dublin Historical Record*, Vol. 46, No. 1, Spring 1993, pp. 53-54.

11. William Le Fanu, *Seventy Years of Irish Life*, pp. 222-227.

12. Peter Somerville-Large, *The Story of the National Gallery of Ireland*, pp. 35-43.

13. *The Viceregal Speeches and Addresses of the late Earl of Carlisle, K.G.*, ed. J.J. Gaskin, pp. 123-124.

14. Hester Travers Smith, *Voices From the Void*, pp. 33-34.

15. Ann Saddlemyer, *Becoming George: The Life of Mrs W.B. Yeats*, p. 366.

16. Michael Purser, *Seven Generations, Four Families*, pp. 154-155.

17. Bruce Arnold, *Mainie Jellett and the Modern Movement in Ireland*, p. 7.

18. Arnold, Mainie Jellett 1897-1944, Neptune Gallery Catalogue 1974.

19. Purser, *Seven Generations*, pp. 153-154.

20. Elizabeth Bowen, *People, Places, Things; Essays by Elizabeth Bowen*, ed. Allan Hepburn, p 115

21. Thomas MacGreevy, *The Irish Times*, 17 February 1944.

22. Bowen, *People, Places, Things*, p. 119.

23. Cyril Barrett, *Irish Arts Review Yearbook* Vol. 9, 1993, p. 170.

24. Bowen, *People, Places, Things*, pp. 115-116.

25. Passages quoted in this section are from Lennox Robinson's *Palette and Plough: A pen-and-ink drawing of Dermod O'Brien*, pp. 60, 130, 185, 131, 187-188, 190.

26. Deirdre Bair, 'No-Man's-Land, Hellespont or Vacuum: Samuel Beckett's Irishness', *The Crane Bag*, Vol. 1, No. 2, 1971, p. 17.

27. William M Murphy, *Family Secrets; William Butler Yeats and his Relatives*, p. 322.

28. Shotaro Oshima, 'An Interview with Jack Butler Yeats', in *Jack B. Yeats: A Centenary Gathering*, ed. Roger McHugh, pp. 51-56.

6

Soldiers and Sailors

FOR THE MOST PART, DENIZENS OF FITZWILLIAM Square pottered in the political, legal and cultural circles of Dublin in the main, perhaps London and a few other centres in Europe. The most far-flung lives were those that pursued careers in the army and navy, generals retired from eighteenth century battlefields and their soldier sons enlisting and serving in remote outposts and theatres. The military life of Fitzwilliam Square residents is also the most stark indication of the general loyalty of the square's inhabitants and their broad support of the union with Great Britain. The enlisted and their families would have worn and displayed the insignia and emblems of the British Army naturally and with pride. Even at times when nationalist upheaval was seizing the country, many residents would pay more heed to the newspaper reports of foreign battles, anxiously scanning the lists of dead and wounded for the names of loved ones. As such, the tales of their exploits in this chapter will seem the furthest removed from Irish history, a world away in both senses from the concerns of the majority of Dubliners. These separate worlds were noted by Major General Edward May who grew up in No. 13 Fitzwilliam Square, when he described his childhood excitement at the activities of the Fenians in the 1860s.

> Later on, when the Fenians came to be tried, there was much talk of their doings, and we heard a good deal from our servants about the rebels and their intentions. In our daily walks with a governess we often passed Mountjoy Prison. 'Cease to do evil, learn to do well!' was inscribed

upon it, and we were told stories of James Stephens, the leader, who was there interned with his men.... Some of the servants at home used to tease us by recounting what had occurred in 1798, so that, in strange contrast to what went on in England, we children became quite familiar with the idea of rebellion and lawlessness.[1]

As we shall see, the soldiers that lived in Fitzwilliam Square (those who grew up in the square, were on active service while living here, or had retired here), were present at battlefields from the late eighteenth to the early twentieth centuries. Commanders, commodores and commissioned soldiers served in the American and French revolutionary wars, the Napoleonic wars, the Crimean, Boer and Great wars. We shall also look at the military career of The O'Gorman Mahon, decidedly not a British officer, famed in the nineteenth century as an international mercenary. The sedition that heralded the United Irish Rebellion of 1798 meant that the first houses of Fitzwilliam Square were built at a time when Dublin was singing of arms and insurrection, and so it seems best we begin by looking at residents caught up in those events.

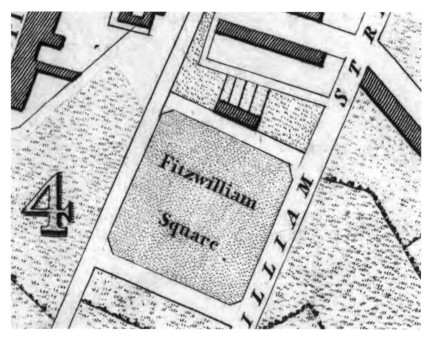

Detail of Faden's Plan of the City of Dublin, 1797

Peter Roe and the Trinity College Corps (1798)

RICHARD, SEVENTH VISCOUNT FITZWILLIAM, began leasing the plots of Fitzwilliam Square in 1791, the same year as the first meeting of the Dublin branch of the Society of United Irishmen in the Eagle Tavern on narrow Eustace Street. As noted in the first chapter, building on the square was slow. While government forces countered the spread of the now clandestine Society with martial law and brutal counter-insurgency tactics, only four houses stood remote on the north side of the square before 1797 (what are now No.'s 56 to 59). Fitzwilliam had leased two plots to Peter Roe in June 1792 and he built and resided in one of the original four houses, No. 58.

Peter's nephew, also Peter Roe (1778-1842), resided in the house as well while he was studying in Trinity College. Young Peter was born in Gorey, County Wexford. His father Henry Roe, a prominent physician, still resided there with his wife Ann and daughter Mary. Peter would go on to be a well-known theologian and was the subject of a biography by Rev. Samuel Madden in 1842. Madden described Roe's involvement in the formation of a college yeomanry corps after the threatened invasion of Wolfe Tone's French fleet at Bantry Bay in 1796:

> It was hardly to be expected that the excitement of the day should be excluded from the university. The love of military affairs is a very general characteristic of young men of birth. Now it penetrated within the walls of college, and soon evinced its existence in no equivocal or undecided manner. In November 1796, Mr Roe writes thus: 'On Thursday there was a private meeting of a few lads in the college, in order to draw up resolutions expressive of our wish to arm at this important crisis in defence of our country; and mentioning that the times usually allotted for recreation we would employ in learning the military discipline ... the resolutions, which were drawn up in an exceedingly mild and proper manner ... were signed by a vast number of lads, among whom were several candidate fellows'.[2]

Their first petition to form a corps was rejected, but with the French fleet visible from the coast in December 1796 their second petition was granted by the lord lieutenant. They met in the room of the Historical Society and a corps of around 220 was formed.

> Of the corps now formed Mr. Roe was an original member and took his place in the third company, which was under the command of Mr. Phipps, a fellow. We may well imagine that, for a time at least, literary pursuits gave way to military ones. How indeed could it be otherwise, when out of a body composed of young and ardent spirits, 220 had enrolled themselves as defenders of their king and country against all enemies. For a time books were well nigh forgotten; all seemed to be of one mind with their drill sergeant, who, in the enthusiasm of his heart, told them one morning 'that it was a pity such fine young men should be wasting their time upon books'.

Madden quoted letters from Roe to his father in Gorey, detailing life in the college corps:

> 'January 3d 1797 – We are ordered by our captain to attend drill for near four hours every day, and to use our utmost endeavours to be so perfect in the exercise as to be ready, if possible, to be reviewed with the other corps on the 29th instant. It is impossible to read: for what with attending drill from eight till near ten in the morning, then breakfasting and preparing for the other drill at twelve, and remaining at it till past two, we cannot possibly attend to our reading, as we are in general so weary as to be more inclined to sleep than to read.' - 'Government is greatly praised for allowing the students to embody; as, if there was an insurrection, or any ferment in town among the lower orders of people, we would contribute more to the restoration of peace than any corps in the kingdom, as the name of college carries terror along with it.' – 'January 10th 1797 – Yesterday the college corps received their arms from government, and we have even now made some progress in our exercise. Our officers are particularly attentive. I was on guard in the college the whole of Saturday night, as the arms were lodged that day in a room. I was very comfortable and happy, as the whole sergeant's guard was very pleasant and entertaining. I stood sentry two hours; the

remainder of the time I was in the Historical Society room, which was converted into a guard-room.

The naïve tone of Peter's letters suggests he was seduced by the fraternal nature of this undergraduate military life. He was probably not aware of, or at least not engaged in, the type of vicious counterinsurgency tactics being employed in the country at large. Peter described an incident of personal peril in an undated letter to his father, presumably from early 1797. When walking home from the college to Fitzwilliam Square one night he was set upon by a gang, probably members of the United Irishmen, drawn by his bayonet and scarlet uniform.

> I shall briefly relate the whole affair. I was going home from the Historical Society about twelve o clock, and when I had gotten about five yards into the street going up to my uncle's [the late Peter Roe of Fitzwilliam-square, Esq. with whom Mr Roe resided during his collegiate course, and for whom he ever entertained the deepest affection (Madden)], I was accosted by five men, who told me they were manufacturers, and wanted charity. I told them I had no money and desired them to begone, as that was no time to be begging. Before I could utter another word, one fellow collared me by the back of the neck, upon which I immediately called 'watch!' They then stopped my mouth, and caught hold of my arm, endeavouring to wrench the bayonet from me, which they were not able to effect. They then began to kick the backs of my legs, upon which I fell upon one knee, in order to protect myself a little, still holding a fast gripe of the bayonet. At length, after a struggle of about three or four minutes, I, by some means, how I know not, slipped from them, drew my bayonet, and, as I was recovering, hit one of them in the face by a back-handed blow, which felled him instantly. Two fellows immediately went to his assistance, and carried him off. In the meantime I got my back against the wall, and kept parrying with the other two. I did not choose to leave the wall, as I feared I might be again surrounded. After hitting them a few smart blows they ran – one into town, the other towards the canal; the former of whom I pursued, and on his turning the corner, I found myself within reach, and made a thrust at him, and drove the bayonet into his back, which rather

increased than retarded his progress. After pursuing him for some little time, I was obliged to give over, as he escaped me through the darkness of the night, and by running through by-lanes. Thus ended the affair, and without any unpleasant circumstances more than that my legs and ribs were very sore for two or three days.

A brave account, perhaps grown a little in the telling. Any action that might have involved Roe during the insurrection in May 1798 has gone unrecorded. This was simply because his main correspondent, his father Henry, had fled Gorey with his wife and daughter to seek sanctuary with his brother in Fitzwilliam Square. As such, the family were, once more, under the one roof. Remarkably, Peter's sister Mary was harbouring a secret. Her betrothed, a Samuel Sparrow, also of Gorey, had taken the oath of the United Irishmen and so ostensibly her fiancé and brother were fighting on opposite sides of the conflict. However, it emerged that Sparrow's commitment to the Society was merely idealistic. He went into hiding during the conflict, appealed to the lord lieutenant for clemency after hostilities, and later emigrated with Mary Roe to the United States.

Veterans of 1798

IN THE FIRST HALF OF THE NINETEENTH CENTURY there were other 1798 Rebellion veterans living in Fitzwilliam Square. For instance, Christopher C. Patrickson was a colonel in the 43rd regiment when he lived in No. 12 from 1831 to 1834. In 1798, he was a 20-year-old lieutenant in the 9th Dragoons and was present at the battle of Ballymore-Eustace on 24 May 1798. James Gordon mentions Patrickson in his *History of the Irish Rebellion*:

> About one o'clock, captain Beevor was awakened by the cry of a person, that the rebels would have his blood. He instantly got out of bed, when he perceived two men rush into the apartment, the one armed with a pistol, the other with a pike. As the former fired at and missed him, the captain seized a pistol which lay by his bedside and shot him through the body. He instantly received a slight wound in the shoulder from the pike of the other; but as he was

reaching for a second pistol, the pikeman closed with him, and seizing him in his arms, carried him towards the top of the stairs, where a number of rebels were ready to receive him on their pikes. By a violent effort of strength, however, the captain succeeded in getting himself extricated, when he dragged his adversary into a room where he was run through the body by lieutenant Patrickson.[3]

Other member of the 9th Dragoons were stationed at Dunlavin, County Wicklow. In retaliation for the attack on Ballymore-Eustace, the Dragoons summarily executed 36 rebel prisoners on Dunlavin Green.

Not all Fitzwilliam Square veterans of 1798 had fought on the loyalist side, however. Take, for example, William Sterne Hart, who lived in No. 17 west (what is now No. 36) from around 1832 until his death in 1842. In *The Correspondence of Daniel O'Connell, 1815-1823* he was described as a major in the insurgent forces.[4] Sterne Hart was a Protestant lawyer and a friend of O'Connell's. *The Proceedings of the Catholic Association* notes that on 18 November 1824:

> Mr. O'Connell proposed as a member, William Sterne Hart, Esq., a Protestant, and sincere lover of his country, and who had endured persecution for being such.[5]

The closeness of their friendship is evident in a footnote of another collection of O'Connell's correspondence. In January 1815, John D'Esterre had challenged O'Connell to a duel when the latter described Dublin Corporation as 'beggarly'. They met at Oughterard, County Kildare where D'Esterre was mortally wounded, an incident that would forever haunt O'Connell. William John Fitzpatrick wrote:

> Sterne Hart was one of the friends who stood beside him during the duel with D'Esterre, and the pistols used on the occasion formed a prominent object among other curiosities displayed at his house in Fitzwilliam Square.[6]

As it happens, the biographer William John Fitzpatrick, born 1830, lived on the same west side at No. 49 Fitzwilliam Square from 1882 until his death in 1895.

Prominent Soldiers and Sailors

OF COURSE OTHER MILITARY RESIDENTS OF Fitzwilliam Square were veterans of battles pre-dating 1798. For example, Lieutenant General Thomas St Quintin L'Estrange of No. 34 fought throughout the American Revolutionary Wars (1775-1783). Lieutenant Colonel John Hart (not related, at least closely, to William Sterne Hart) lived in No. 4 from around 1824 until his death in 1833. He was an inspecting field officer based in Dublin Castle, but during the 1790s he fought with the Enniskillen Dragoons during the French Revolutionary Wars. Sketches could be given of quite a number of military men residing in the square in the first decades of the nineteenth century. However, there were five particularly notable members of the armed forces and their exploits should be recorded. Two of these noteworthy generals resided in No. 5 Fitzwilliam Square on the east side between 1820 and 1831. We may recall that No. 5 was also home in quick succession to two distinguished lawyers, Justices Pennefather and Monahan. Mary Bryan explained the reason behind the cachet of that particular house.

> Lord Fitzwilliam retained the plots of no. 4 and no. 5 until his death, and it would appear that he had intended to build a house for himself on the double site; certainly the 17 foot frontage of no. 4 looks like the gap intended for a special stable lane.[7]

Narrow No. 4 does indeed look as if it was inserted into the east side as something of an afterthought. But Viscount Fitzwilliam's association with No. 5 no doubt meant it was one of the most desirable plots on the square.

Sir Edward Paget of No. 5

A DUBLIN DIRECTORY FOR 1820 RECORDS that No. 5 was home to Lieutenant General Sir Edward Paget, GCB (1775-1849). He was a member of parliament at the age of 21, a veteran of the Peninsular Wars and was later commander-in-chief of the forces in India. The Peninsular War (1807-1814) was a conflict between Napoleon's France and the allied forces of Spain, Portugal and the United Kingdom for control of the Iberian peninsula. In 1809, Paget was promoted to the rank of Lieutenant General and commanded two brigades in the advance on Oporto, a campaign led by Sir Arthur Wellesley, the Duke of Wellington. During the campaign Paget was severely injured and lost his left arm. This necessitated a return to England, the first of two blows to the advancement of his career in quick succession. For when he returned to the Peninsula in 1812, as second-in-command under Lord Wellington, he was captured by the French within a matter of days. Cole related the story in his *Memoirs of British Generals Distinguished during the Peninsular Wars*:

> While the British divisions were scattered and divided in passing through a thick forest not far from Ciudad-Rodrigo, he was intercepted by a patrole of French cavalry, and carried off, as it might be said, from the midst of his own men. At first they thought they had secured the English commander-in-chief; and the evil fortune might have occurred as readily to Lord Wellington, as he also was continually riding between the columns, and without an escort. Paget was hurried off to France, and remained a prisoner until the close of the war. His brilliant prospects were terminated by captivity; and his name was no more to be coupled with the exploits of his gallant countrymen ...

Capture of General Edward Paget, 1812. Note that his left arm is missing.

The capture of General Paget is thus mentioned in Lord Wellington's public despatch to Lord Bathurst: - 'I am sorry to add, that we have had the misfortune to lose Lieutenant-General Sir Edward Paget, who was taken prisoner on the 17th of November. He commanded the centre column; and, the fall of rain having greatly injured the roads and swelled the rivulets, there was an interval between the 5th and 7th divisions of infantry. Sir Edward rode to the rear alone to discover the cause of this interval; and as the road passed through a wood, either a detachment of the enemy's cavalry had got upon it, or he missed the track, and fell into their hands in the wood. I understand that Sir Edward was not wounded, but I cannot sufficiently regret the loss of his services at this moment.' The following kind letter was written to the captive general by his commander:

'Headquarters, 19th Nov., 1812.

My Dear Paget,

I did not hear of your misfortune till more than an hour after it had occurred; nor was I certain of it till the enemy attacked our rear-guard, and the firing had continued for some time, and I found you were not on the field...I cannot account for your misfortune, excepting that you were alone, and could not see the approach of the enemy's cavalry. That which must now be done is to endeavour to obtain your exchange. I have no French general officer in the Peninsula; but I beg you to make it known to the King, and to the Duke of Dalmatia, that I will engage that any general officer they will name shall be sent from England to France in exchange for you. If you should find that there is any prospect of your being exchanged, I recommend to you to endeavour to prevail upon the King not to send you to France...You cannot conceive how I regret your loss. This is the second time that I have been deprived of your assistance at an early period after you had joined us, and I am almost afraid to wish to have you again; but God knows with what pleasure I shall hear of your being liberated, and shall see you with us.

Believe me, &c.,
Wellington.'[8]

Eight years later Paget was residing briefly in Fitzwilliam Square, Dublin. He served in Burma and India during the early 1820s before returning to England. In 1837, he became a full general and was appointed governor of the Royal Hospital Chelsea, the nursing home for British soldiers who are known as the Chelsea Pensioners. He remained in that position until his death in 1849.

In 1828, the Duke of Wellington became Prime Minister and appointed another of his generals from the Napoleonic Wars as commander-in-chief of the forces in Ireland. Lieutenant General John Byng lived in No. 5 Fitzwilliam Square from 1829 until he left Ireland in 1831. Wellington also appointed Henry Paget, Edward's elder brother, as Lord Lieutenant of Ireland. Byng joined the army in 1793 as an ensign in a regiment commanded by Wellington, then Colonel Arthur Wellesley. He was injured during the 1798 Rebellion and fought in Spain and southern France during the Peninsular War. In 1815, Byng commanded a brigade of guards in the Battle of Waterloo, the decisive battle of the Napoleonic Wars. After leaving Ireland and No. 5 Fitzwilliam Square, Byng entered politics. He became the Earl of Strafford in 1843 and rose to the highest military rank of Field Marshal five years before his death in 1860.

The O'Gorman Mahon of No. 64

WE CAN IMAGINE THESE HIGH RANKING British officers attending salons and dinner parties during their brief residence in Fitzwilliam Square, other guests enthralled by tales of battles, gallantry and capture during campaigns that would have already entered British military legend. However, the most remarkable military man to live in the square never entered the British army. His life was so extraordinary that he shall feature in two chapters of this book, for his political career spanned the rise of O'Connell and the fall of Parnell. In this chapter we shall look at his exploits as international mercenary and adventurer. He was James Patrick Mahon (1800-1891), known as The O'Gorman Mahon, a Roman Catholic born to a prominent family in Ennis, County Clare. His adopted name was a combination of his parents' surnames, preceded by the determinate article to suggest he was chief of a clan. Late in his parliamentary career he rose in the

Commons in response to a disparaging remark made of such ancient Irish titles:

> Only three men living are entitled to be called by the designation 'The' – The Pope, The Devil and The O'Gorman Mahon!

Rumours were he would challenge to a duel any man who condescended to call him mister, perceiving an intolerable lack of honour in that honourific. In 1826, he joined the Catholic Association and was instrumental in Daniel O'Connell's parliamentary election victory in 1828, as we shall see in Chapter 8. His biographer, Denis Gwynn, described how he came to live in Fitzwilliam Square:

Vanity Fair *caricature of* The O'Gorman Mahon, 1885

> In the early summer of 1830, when his reputation as the hero of the Clare election was at its height, O'Gorman Mahon decided to marry a Dublin heiress. Miss Christine O'Brien, of Fitzwilliam Square, had property in her own right amounting to £60,000. By his marriage he thus obtained ample means of entering Parliament.

O'Gorman Mahon lived in No. 64 Fitzwilliam Square on the north side, with his wife and three sisters-in-law. A Scottish politician, Robert Graham, described visiting his Fitzwilliam Square house in his memoirs, *A Scottish Whig in Ireland, 1835-1838*:

> 21 May 1835: I went on to Fitzwilliam Square and made a visit to Madame O'Gorman Mahon's. You know he is the

man who would shoot anybody who would call him Mr
O'Gorman Mahon and, with that knowledge, I should have
run some risk of being puzzled in what way to denominate
his wife, but as on his first visit he called her Madame, I
was in some degree relieved from my dilemma, tho' I was
not quite certain till I saw her that she was not a foreigner
instead of an Irishwoman. She is a very pleasant and lively
person and, after I had sat with her sometime, in the course
of which she said O'Gorman Mahon had not yet appeared,
having been out very late at a ball, she rang the bell and told
the servant to bring word whether he was likely to be down
soon. The order was given in so unusual a way that I did
not know whether it was her husband she alluded to and
not wishing to hurry him down.... I began to say 'Is it Mr -,
I was very nearly getting into a scrape'. She laughed good-
humouredly and said 'Oh he would allow you to call him so.'
I stuck to my ground, that I was only nearly getting into a
great scrape, and she told me to take care again, as he had just
been laying in a fresh stock of bullets and these were then
at my elbow. I pressed with my finger a paper parcel on the
table and found it hard enough to contain leaden bullets.[10]

In the same year, the restless O'Gorman Mahon left Ireland to begin
years of travels and adventures abroad. His wide ranging was sum-
marised by Gwynn:

In Paris he became a personal friend of Louis Philippe
[the 'Citizen King' of France], and he fought a number
of duels while he frequented the court of the Second Empire....Wherever wars broke out, he volunteered for service
at once. Louis Philippe made him an honorary Colonel,
and after Louis Philippe's downfall he served, with ranks
varying from Captain to General, under most of the flags
of Europe. He had fought also against Arab tribes in Africa
when he returned to Ireland during the great famine.... For
five years he remained in Parliament again until 1852. Once
more, with the world before him, he set out in search of
adventure. France had grown quiet since the Revolution of
1848, and he passed on to Russia, where the Czar made him
a Lieutenant in his international bodyguard. He went on
bear-shooting expeditions with the Czarevich, and under

the Russian flag he took part in war against the Tartars, travelling east afterwards to China and returning by India and Arabia.

Approaching his sixtieth birthday he returned to France where his wife and son now resided. However his restiveness soon saw him depart again, this time for the Americas. His exploits there became legendary among his younger parliamentary colleagues during his third stint in the House of Commons late in life. Gwynn continued:

> The legend which was generally repeated, and which he certainly would have been the last to discourage, was that he had become Commander-in-Chief of the army in Uruguay and had immediately afterward gone on to Chile, where he became Admiral of the Fleet in a war with Bolivia; and that having exhausted all possibilities of active service in both these commands, he passed on to Brazil, where he found further service as a Colonel. Later again, according to general report, he was a volunteer on the Northern side in the American Civil war.

A feature on O'Gorman Mahon in the *Daily News* in 1879 commented on this remarkable career:

> His brilliant success per mare et terram is, as far as we are aware, without parallel in the records of adventure or even of romance. The hardiest romancer would not dare to raise his hero to the chief command of the army in one State and of the navy in another. But once more, truth is stranger than fiction."

Perhaps this is so, but the extent of O'Gorman Mahon's exploits in South America are not so easy to verify. We shall look more fully at his parliamentary career later. The O'Brien sisters remained living in No. 64 Fitzwilliam Square until 1858.

Admiral Robert Dudley Oliver of No. 55

So, WHILE IN NO. 64 THERE POSSIBLY RESIDED a future commander of the Chilean navy, in No. 55 Fitzwilliam Square there lived a bona fide retired admiral of the British Navy. Robert Dudley Oliver was born in

1766 and lived long-term in the square from June 1816 until his death in 1850. He joined the navy as a fifteen-year-old boy aboard the *HMS Prince George* and was a shipmate of the young prince William, later King William IV. Oliver was battle-hardened as a young sailor during the American Revolutionary War. His ship was heavily engaged in the battles of St Kitts and the Saintes in 1782, and he advanced through the ranks of the navy in the final years of the eighteenth century. Oliver was a senior lieutenant aboard the *Artois* under Captain Edmund Nagle when on 21 October 1794 they captured the French Seine class frigate *Revolutionnaire*. For his conduct Oliver was made a commander on the very same day. He captained a number of vessels in waters off Britain, Ireland, Canada and in the Mediterranean before March 1803, when he received command of the *Melpomene*. This was the first year of the Napoleonic Wars. In 1804, Captain Oliver led a squadron to attack a number of French vessels stationed in Le Havre. He described the attack in a letter to William Marsden, first secretary of the Admiralty, written aboard the *Melpomene* on 2 August 1804:

> My Lord,
>
> The wind having changed yesterday to the N. E. I determined to make another attack on the numerous vessels in Havre Pier, as well as those which were moored outside, amounting to 18 brigs, and as many luggers, and stood in with the squadron, as per margin. At half-past seven p.m. the bombs [bomb vessels] were well placed off the pier heads, when they began a well-directed fire, which was kept up with great spirit for about an hour and a half. The town was very soon observed to be on fire in two places; and seven brigs, which were on the outside of the Pier, found it necessary to move; one lost her main mast. As the wind came more off the land, and a strong ebb tide setting out, I ordered the bombs to discontinue firing. At half past nine we anchored with the squadron about five miles from the Light-houses ... I am, &c.
>
> R.D. Oliver[12]

The *Melpomene* was not engaged during the Battle of Trafalgar (21 October 1805) but was employed in towing damaged vessels from the

Detail of painting by William Clarkson Stanfield of HMS Mars *at the Battle of Trafalgar, 1805.*

site of battle. The *HMS Mars* had been engaged during Trafalgar and her captain, George Duff, had been lost during the fighting. Oliver was appointed his successor as commander of the *Mars*. During that command was the engagement for which he is mentioned in British naval history books. 'Lamellerie's expedition' was a French naval operation launched in February 1806. Captain Louis de Lamellerie of the *Hortense* escaped with three other French frigates, remnants of the Battle of Trafalgar, from the British blockade of Cadiz. During the next six months the four vessels cruised the Atlantic, looking to disrupt British trade at every opportunity. On 27 July the rogue squadron was spotted by lookouts aboard the *Mars* near the coast of Rochefort. The *Mars* had been stationed near the port specifically to intercept French vessels and Captain Oliver immediately ordered pursuit. William James takes up the story in his *The Naval History of Great Britain*:

> On the 27th of July, at 6 P.M., when in about latitude 47° north, longitude 7° west, steering south-east by east, which was a direct course for Rochefort, the Hortense and her three companions were discovered by the 74-gun ship Mars, Captain Robert Dudley Oliver, the look-out ship of a British squadron of five sail of the line, under the command of Commodore Richard Goodwin Keats, in the Superb.

The Mars, making the necessary signals, which the Africa 64 repeated to the commodore ... crowded sail in chase. The French frigates immediately set all the additional sail they could, and continued their course to the south-east. Soon after dark the Mars lost sight, as well of them as of all the ships of her own squadron, except the Africa, who was seen on her lee quarter till 11 P.M., when she also disappeared. The Mars now shaped her course so as to prevent the enemy from getting to leeward; and, as a proof with what judgment she was steered, daylight on the 28th discovered the four frigates on the same bearing as on the preceding evening, but, except one, at a greater distance. Upon that one, which was the Rhin, the Mars evidently gained.

Observing this, and that the British 74 was entirely alone, the French commodore, with what appeared a proper spirit, put about, and, on joining the Rhin, formed his four frigates in line of battle on the larboard tack. Finding, however, that the Mars was not in the least intimidated by the approach of four heavy French frigates, but was hastening on to engage them, M. La Marre-la-Meillerie (sic) failed in his resolution, and at 3 P.M. made off with three of his frigates, leaving the fourth to her fate. Having already run a distance of 150 miles, and the day being far spent, the Mars continued in pursuit of the nearest frigate; when at 6 P.M., in the midst of a heavy squall of wind and rain, and just as the Mars, having gained a position on the frigate's lee quarter, had fired a shot and was preparing to open her broadside, the Rhin hauled down her colours.

Soon after the Mars had taken possession of the Rhin, the squall cleared up, and the Hortense, Hermione, and Thémis were seen standing to the south-east; but the approach of night, the proximity of the French coast, and the stormy state of the weather, owing to which not more than a third of the prisoners could be removed, rendered any further pursuit impracticable. Captain Oliver, thereupon, accompanied by his prize, steered in the direction of his squadron; and which, so far had he outrun it in 24 hours' chase, the Mars did not rejoin it until the forenoon of the 31st. Great credit was due to Captain Oliver for having persevered in the chase so long after he had got out of reach of support from any ship of his squadron; and, had the four frigates been commanded by a Bergeret, a Bourayne, or one of many other French captains whom we could name, an opportunity would doubtless have been afforded to the officers and crew of the Mars, to show what could be effected, under such circumstances, by a well-appointed, well-manned British 74.[13]

Captain Oliver described the engagement to his squadron leader, Captain Keats of the *Superb*, in a letter from the *Mars*, dated 29 July 1806. In it, he specifically mentions the excitement aboard at the possibility of engaging all four of the French frigates. He describes gaining on the rear-most ship, the Rhin:

> ... this induced the French Commodore to tack with his three headmost ships, and join her, and formed in line of battle on the larboard tack, I thought, and hoped, with a determination to try the fortune of war, which is what everyone on board the Mars most anxiously wished; but, after making some signals, about three in the afternoon he made off with three frigates; the other continued her course under an extraordinary press of sail, and finding that she was the only one we had gained on during a chase of 150 miles, and the day far spent, I still kept after her till six o'clock, when in the midst of a violent squall of wind and hail we were ranging upon her lee quarter: after the first shot she struck her colours, just at the moment our broadside was about to open on her. She proved to be La Rhin, a very fine French frigate, of 44 guns, 18 pounders on the main deck, and 318 men; only four years old.[14]

From 1810, Oliver was commanding the *HMS Valiant* and was involved in the British blockade of New York during the War of 1812. Oliver resigned his commission in 1814 and eventually retired to Dublin. He lived for more than thirty years in No. 55 Fitzwilliam Square, during which time he was an active member of religious societies in the city. Oliver continued to rise in rank during his retirement. He became a Rear-Admiral on 12 August 1819; a Vice-Admiral on 22 July 1830; and a full Admiral on 23 November 1841. In 1805, he had married Mary, the daughter of Sir Charles Saxton, commissioner of the royal dockyard at Portsmouth. Mary died in No. 55 on 17 June 1848. Admiral Oliver died at Dalkey, County Dublin on 1 September 1850. The tales he could tell of his life on the high seas seem so incongruous to the small Georgian square to which he retired. No doubt, throughout his time there, No. 55 was filled with any number of exotic artefacts, the jetsam of a remarkable maritime career.

George Bingham of No. 66

WE SHALL BRIEFLY LOOK AT THE FINAL notorious military man residing in Fitzwilliam Square in the first half of the nineteenth century. A Dublin directory for 1830 notes a Lord Bingham MP residing in No. 66 Fitzwilliam Square. This was George Charles Bingham (1800-1888), the third Earl of Lucan. Between 1826 and 1830 he was the MP for County Mayo so No. 66 was probably his residence when business brought him to Dublin. Bingham is remembered in Ireland for his contemptible reaction to the Famine in Mayo, using the catastrophe as an excuse to clear his estates of what he considered unprofitable tenants. He was Lord Lieutenant of Mayo from 1845 until his death.

Bingham is more generally remembered for his actions during the Battle of Balaclava (25 October 1854) during the Crimean War, where he was commander of the cavalry division. His brother-in-law, Lord Cardigan, was in command of the Light Brigade. When Lord Bingham received a muddled order from the British commander, Lord Raglan (to 'advance rapidly to the front, follow the enemy, and try to prevent the enemy carrying away the guns'), he in turn ordered Cardigan to lead the fateful 'Charge of the Light Brigade'. This was because the only guns visible to Bingham from his position were a large mass of Russian guns at the end of a valley about a mile away. Both Cardigan and Bingham knew the action would be suicide, but Cardigan led 673 cavalry men straight into the valley between the Fedyukhin heights and the Causeway heights, famously dubbed the 'Valley of Death' by the poet Tennyson. Bingham was to lead the Heavy Brigade and follow in support, but when he observed the Light Brigade being decimated in front of him he decided to halt and spare the Heavy Brigade a similar fate.

The charge became synonymous with the folly of British commanders and the bravery of her soldiers. Raglan lay the blame squarely on Bingham:

> ... from some misconception of the instruction to advance, the Lieutenant-General (Bingham) considered that he was bound to attack at all hazards, and he accordingly ordered Major-General the Earl of Cardigan to move forward with the Light Brigade.

Cardigan survived the charge and returned home a hero. Bingham never again saw active service but he did advance through the ranks, becoming Field Marshal a year before his death in 1888. His great-great-grandson, Richard Bingham, seventh Lord Lucan, famously went missing in 1974 after murdering his children's nanny, Sandra Rivett, and attacking his estranged wife at her London home.

A young veteran of the Crimean War was Lieutenant Lawrence Edward Knox (1836-1873) who was promoted to captain in the 11th

Lawrence E. Knox, founder of The Irish Times, *of No. 53*

Regiment in the year following that conflict. When he was only 22 years of age he founded *The Irish Times* newspaper in Dublin, a journal then with moderate conservative principals and distinct unionist leanings. The first editorial on 29 March 1859 described the paper's intended readership as those:

... indifferent to the manoeuvres of faction, disgusted at the arts of demagogue, and sincerely desirous of laying aside their mutual prejudices and labouring together for the good of their common country.... They desire to see measures discussed with reference to their essential merits rather than to their party bearings.[15]

While he was proprietor of *The Irish Times* Knox resided in No. 53 Fitzwilliam Square, the first house on the north side. He died there on 24 January 1873 from scarlet fever. At twenty past four in the afternoon, 'clasping the hand of a near relative, he gave one short sigh and died'. The first report of his death in his own newspaper ended:

> We can only record his loss; we are unable to express our sense of it.[16]

Soldier Sons of Fitzwilliam Square

AFTER 1850 IT IS THE MILITARY SONS OF Fitzwilliam Square with whom we are concerned, rather than the generals, admirals and mercenaries who would reside here from time to time. Young men who joined the armed forces and found themselves fighting in the Crimea, in South Africa and in the Great War. Edward Sinclair May was the son of George Augustus Chichester May, the judge who stepped down at the opening of Parnell's trial in 1880 (described in Chapter 2). They lived in No. 13 from 1863. Edward May would attain the rank of Major General and wrote an auto-biography entitled *Changes and Chances of a Soldier's Life*. The description of his early military training could easily apply to any of the young men from Fitzwilliam Square who went to join the armed forces. He began by describing his home and a youthful interest in military affairs:

> We Mays lived on the east side of Fitzwilliam Square, Dublin, during the winter and spring. There were ten of us – six sons and four daughters.... Within a quite small radius there lived thirty-nine first cousins. And those of us who were old enough all marched to church at St Stephen's, Mount Street, with our fathers and mothers walking arm-in-arm behind us after the fashion of the day.... Then came the war between Prussia and Austria, and I was old enough to read the papers and can remember the description of the white-coated Austrians and my surprise at their choosing such curious garments.[17]

May detailed his struggle with mathematics in order to qualify as a cadet at the Royal Military Academy at Woolwich. He discovered that his application was successful at home in No. 13:

> With the hated sums out of the way I was happy enough, and, when the trial was over.... I went home to Ireland in trepidation all the same. I might qualify, but there were lots of others who had done so too, and there were only forty places to be filled. Some time afterwards we were at dinner at home when the London post came in, and there in The Times was a list of successful candidates for Woolwich, and my name in it was tenth. My father was so pleased that he drew his signet ring off his finger and gave it to me there and then. I therefore became a cadet when I was just seventeen, and joined at the 'Shop' [a nickname for the academy] in March, 1873.

He went on to describe life within the academy; well-trodden tales of institutional hardship and homesickness:

> The place was run on rougher lines than prevail nowadays. Iron cylinders filled by taps of icy water, in a shed in a backyard, provided the only bath accommodation for the Junior Terms. We ... rushed from our rooms without slippers or dressing-gowns to the icy cauldrons, plunged in and rushed back without a stitch of clothes on to dry ourselves before the fire the servant had lit in our rooms.... Then there were concerts in the passages of the various houses, when a new-comer stood on a table and sang, asserting – however depressed and gloomy his countenance – that he was 'off to Philadelphia in the morning,'... If he sang well, he was encouraged by an encore; if not, he was 'toshed' with a bucket of water. If a boy were above himself and offended against any of the rules ... he was 'turned up.' Our beds were hinged near the head and were turned over against the wall during the daytime, but when the victim was in bed that process was effected by the cadets during the night.

May completed his training in 1876 and was ordered to join a field battery in India as a lieutenant. The break this entailed between the cadet and his family was highlighted by May's description of his send-off from Dublin:

> I left for India, accompanied as far as London by my mother, who was to spend a month with some old friends there. On April 12th, a bitter day, when, I recollect, snow was falling in London, she saw me off at Waterloo. Like the foolish boy I was, I pictured India a region of unvaried heat, where the sun blazed every day, and all one had to consider was how to keep cool.... My mother realised that I should be cold on the way to Southampton, obtained a rug from her carriage, and flung it in through the window to me just before the train moved off. I never saw her or heard from her again, and in that rug I preserve my last link with her. She got a chill at the station, she returned to the house at which she was staying, became seriously ill, went to bed, and never again got up. The first letter I received when I reached India was from my father, telling me that she was too ill to write, and almost the next one announced her death.

That must have been a bitter blow for a graduate cadet newly arrived in a strange land. It highlights that the soldier sons of Fitzwilliam Square must each have gone through periods of the utmost misery; they must have been heart-sore and home-sick even prior to the possible horrors that awaited them on the battlefield.

The contrast of the cosiness of a childhood in Fitzwilliam Square and the loneliness of the battleground is illustrated by a child's drawing that survived in a family archive. Marshal Neville Clarke of Graiguenoe Park, County Tipperary was a barrister who moved into No. 11 Fitzwilliam Square in 1864 – we already encountered his family in the first chapter. His wife Mary Pearson gave birth to their six children in the house; the eldest was Charles Neville Clarke, born 1866. A childhood picture-book belonging to Charles survives dating from around 1875, when Charles was nine years old. One drawing depicts the nursery of No. 11, which was on the third floor.

It shows a nanny named Saunders and two of Charles's younger brothers. Saunders is washing baby Marshal Falconer in a small bath in front of an open fire. Two-year-old George Vernon, dressed as a lit-

Childhood drawing by Charles Clarke
of the nursery of No. 11, 1875

tle girl (typical of the time), plays with a toy cart. Other toys are strewn in the foreground: building blocks, a ball and a miniature farmyard with animals. Simple furnishings and ornaments are also visible: the small bath, the cot with netting and a modest table in the background. Charles entitled this drawing, 'Saunders washing the baby and George with his cart and bricks'.

It is poignant to consider that the toddler George grew up to be educated at Wellington and, like Edward May, commissioned into the Royal Field Artillery at Woolwich before serving in the Boer War. On 8 April 1902, Captain George Vernon Clarke was killed in action while trying to rescue a wounded man at Uitvlugt. The baby would become Lieutenant Colonel Marshal Falconer Clarke. He survived the Boer War and the Great War, received the Distinguished Service Order and retired to Glasbury, Wales. The young illustrator, Charles Neville Clarke, inherited Graiguenoe upon the death of his father in 1884. Graiguenoe Park became a target for local republicans and was eventually burned down in 1923. Charles moved to England and was killed with his wife Bertha at the Regina Hotel during the German's third blitz of Bath on 26 April 1942.

The Boer War experiences of George Clarke (the toddler in the picture) were set out in a series of letters he sent home to his family.[18] He intended the letters to form a diary of sorts and they are a very detailed account of his time in South Africa. On 14 November 1899, he wrote of his first glimpse of Cape Town aboard the *SS Armenian*:

At 7 o'clock yesterday morning we sighted land and saw Africa for the first time. In another couple of hours Table Mountain rose out of the mist, and by one o'clock we were anchored outside Cape Town Harbour to wait for orders.... I was very much disappointed with the appearance of Cape Town. It was so overpowered by the height of Table Mountain that it looked like a little seaside watering place squashed in between the hills and the sea. The country all around

George Vernon Clarke, 1889

looked lovely and uninhabited, so different from an English coast.

Clarke's letters go on to describe his various engagements and manoeuvres as an artillery gunner spanning almost the entire length of the war. An example is this fairly graphic missive to his mother, Mary Elizabeth Clarke, dated 1 August 1900 from Standerton:

My dear Mother, I had an interesting day on Friday last ... Major Adams came to tell me that there were a lot of Boers on our right.... Four scouts were sent out to watch that flank, and they presently opened a very rapid fire and ran back as hard as they could and my man galloped back in a great hurry to tell me that there were 50 Boers behind a certain hill. I searched the hill with my glasses and presently saw two heads appearing. I laid a gun at 5,000 yards on the two heads which kindly waited for me. I fired, and after waiting a few seconds saw them suddenly disappear and the shell burst behind them. Undoubtedly the heads were cut off by the passing shell. I sent a second shell presently to burst in the air behind the hill, and three or four Boers broke cover.

He ended the letter:

We are trying to get a bit civilized again. Have started white tablecloths and glass tumblers.

George Clarke was killed in the penultimate month of the war. His final letter was to his brother Charles (who had drawn him as an infant in the nursery of No. 11 Fitzwilliam Square):

Botha's Pass, April 6th 1902.

My dear Charlie, Your parcel of clothes arrived at a very opportune moment. We finished the last drive yesterday and are now off again on another. They don't give us a moment's peace now-a-days. Thanks very much indeed for sending the clothes.

In haste, Yr. Affte. Brother, G.V. CLARKE.

Two days later he was shot while trying to rescue Corporal A.H. King of the 79th Battery. King described the incident in a letter dated 8 October 1902. Both King and another officer were injured and stranded close to enemy lines when the horse they were riding together collapsed on top of them. The Boers captured both men but King's guard was killed by gunfire from the British side. So he took the opportunity to crawl back towards his own troops despite broken ribs. The Boers trained their guns on him but none of them hit. King was exhausted though, and after a few hundred yards could only lie exposed in no man's land.

All at once I was much surprised to see a man which about 2 months after I found to be Captain Clarke 87th Battery, walking along on my right leading his horse coming from the direction of our men. He would be about 100 yards from me and about 400 yards from the enemy who were returning the fire of our men. How he got so far out with his horse is a mystery to me. The Boers caught sight of him as soon as I did and turned their rifles on him. I made across to him as well as I could but he seeing me move came to me. He asked me if I was wounded. I told him I had not been hit but thought my shoulder or ribs were broken.

He got me across his horse and advanced a few paces, but I could not keep on the horse. He then advised me to hold on by the stirrup iron and we got along a dozen paces or so when a bullet struck the pony in the hoof, laming it. He said 'That's done for the pony.' The same instant another struck it in the body. It kicked out and caught me on the hip, knocking me down. I had just time to say 'I'm hit' when the pony fell on its side.

Almost as soon as I spoke I heard a bullet crack and the Captain fell. He groaned rather heavy, and I crawled round the pony which was still struggling and kicking, and got to him. He lay on his back inclining a little towards his right side. I took his hand and spoke to him, but I could not distinguish any answer. I had an idea he could tell I spoke to him but he could not answer. I took his hat off to see where he was hit, made a hurried examination of his head but could not see any mark of a bullet or any blood. I then unbuttoned his serge to look at his breast when a couple of bullets passed the side of my head like a hot iron [King was then shot in the thigh] ...

The whole affair from me seeing the Officer first and myself getting shot I don't think exceeded two minutes. I do not think the Captain suffered any pain at all as he never moved. He groaned a few times and was quiet. The Doctor tells me he was hit by 2 or 3 bullets. If so the Boers must have hit him again after me.... When the Captain came to me all the arms he had was a revolver in his hand. When I pointed out where the Boers were, he did not get excited but remained quite cool and calm throughout.

King's description is of a gallant but foolhardy end to a life begun in Fitzwilliam Square. That Clarke would decide to lead his horse on foot into the teeth of enemy fire strikes one as strangely, tragically, heedless. The psychological effects of three years of warfare may have bred in Captain George Clarke a fatalistic recklessness.

The Great War

AND OF COURSE A PALL HUNG OVER the names of many young boys recorded in the 1901 census for Fitzwilliam Square, and young men in the 1911 census. For many would volunteer to fight in the European war of 1914 and some would die in the trenches. Just some of their stories are set out below.

Captain Maurice Cecil Walker of No. 38

In the previous chapter on artists we met John Crampton Walker who grew up in No. 38 Fitzwilliam Square. Two of his brothers were soldiers and both survived the war. Captain Garret Walker was a signal officer in the 7th Royal Inniskilling Fusiliers. He was decorated with the military cross and later compiled a history of his battalion entitled *The Book of the 7th Service Battalion Royal Inniskilling Fusiliers from Tipperary to Ypres*. His brother Captain Maurice Cecil Walker also received a military cross and wrote a history of his unit, *A History of 154 Siege Battery, Royal Garrison Artillery*. Both Walkers were careful not to recount graphically the battles in which they fought, mindful that the families of the lost would read their accounts.

Maurice, however, was able to relate the following anecdote of a miscommunication during an eerie lull in the German spring offensive of 1918:

> The scene at the battery was the officers' mess, the tiny pillbox in Manor Farm, in which Captain Walker [he refers to himself] and 2nd Lieut. Greene were playing chess. Suddenly the telephone buzzed and the C.O. Brigade spoke the following message:

> 'I have some very serious news for you, so serious indeed that I cannot dare to tell you over the phone. The fact is that the enemy are very near us! You have now no chance of escape or saving your [artillery] guns. You must fight to the last, and then blow up the guns. You perfectly understand that you will fight to the last man? I expect that I shall be scuppered before you, but that cannot be helped. Good-bye and Good Luck!'

The sudden arrival of this rather dramatic and mysterious message rather upset the game of chess, but it came rather as a relief to know that something definite had at last happened. A few extra preparations were made for receiving the Huns....The scene at the Brigade end of the telephone was something like this. All the Brigade transport on the road and the C.O.'s car ready to leave at a moment's notice. The C.O. himself feverishly ringing up all his batteries and ordering them to fight to the last and his Adjutant burning all the secret papers....To give the Colonel and his staff their due, the sequel to this event must be related. It transpired later that Corps had sent a false message to Brigade, to the effect that the enemy were in Vierstraat, a small village about a mile distant from Brigade H.Q....The origin of this false rumour ... arose from a party of English troops relieving a Scottish battalion and mistaking them for Huns on account of their unkempt appearance and strange dialect.[19]

The unionist politician Andrew Beattie lived in No. 46 Fitzwilliam Square for many years after 1898. His son was Sydney Herbert Beattie. The Northampton Museum holds a photo of Beattie with the following description of his career:

Born 1888 in Dublin and educated at Dublin University. He was commissioned in February 1911. Sydney Herbert Beattie was made a Lieutenant in May 1912 and a Captain in March 1915. At this time he was attached to the 10th Battalion Royal West Kent Regiment. In August 1917 he was awarded the Military Cross for conspicuous gallantry and devotion to duty. Made a Captain in 1917 and attached to the 10th Battalion Royal West Kent Regiment. Served in Russia from May 1919 to Oct 1919. Wounded three times in World War I. Returned to the 2nd Battalion and died of accidental injuries received at Templemore, 10 August 1920.

The London Gazette of 25 August 1917 recorded his receipt of the military cross:

For conspicuous gallantry and devotion to duty. He took over command during consolidation and by his personal coolness, initiative and resource, supervised the work under fire, remaining at his post although wounded and setting a splendid example of what an officer's conduct should be at all times and especially in an emergency.

Sydney Herbert Beattie's death was noted in *The Times* on 20 August 1920:

> Trapped in a burning house.
>
> Colonel's life sacrificed in attempt at rescue.
>
> Our Dublin Correspondent telegraphed last night:-
>
> News reached Dublin today of the death in the military hospital at Tipperary of Lieutenant Colonel Beattie, a son of Sir Andrew Beattie of Dublin. It appears that Colonel Beattie was in Templemore on the night when District Inspector Wilson was killed, and hearing that a man was imprisoned in a burning house, he entered it and searched for the man, whom he failed to find. When he tried to escape he found that he was trapped by the flames in the upper storey, and he jumped from a window to the street. He was removed to the military hospital suffering from severe burns and concussion, and he died this morning.

The Gamble family were long-term residents of No. 51 Fitzwilliam Square. A Richard William Gamble took up residence there in 1868. Richard Keene Gamble, born 1861, was the main occupant from 1893. His eldest son Richard Maurice Brooks Gamble served with the 7th Battalion of the King's Liverpool Regiment. Gamble's name appears on the memorial plaque in the 1937 Reading Room of Trinity College Dublin. Details of his death were given in *De Ruvigny's Roll of Honour*:

> Eldest son of Richard Keene Gamble of 51 Fitzwilliam Square, Dublin ... born at Leeson Park, Dublin, 16 July, 1893. Educated at M. Le Penton's School, Dublin, afterwards at Tonbridge School, Kent, and Trinity College, Dublin, where he had matriculated in Arts and Medicine, and was about to take his degree when war broke out. He was a member of the Officer's Training Corps, and immediately volunteered and was gazetted to the Liverpool Regiment, 5 Sept, 1914. He went with his regiment to the Front in March, 1915, and was killed in action, when leading his men

in an attack on the German trenches at Richebourg, on the night of 15-16 May, 1915 and was buried at the Rue de Bois, half a mile south of Richebourg St Vaast, with eight brother officers killed in the same attack. His Commanding Officer described the circumstances; 'We were ordered to take the German trenches. Under heavy fire he led his men with the greatest bravery, and had reached the parapet of the German trenches when he fell with two Germans under him, death being instantaneous.'[20]

Noting that Gamble cut short his studies in Trinity College to go and fight, we can recall Peter Roe of No. 58, enthusiastically forming a Trinity College corps in the lead up to Rebellion in 1798. In his battalion history, Maurice Walker of No. 38 recalled the ending of hostilities in Europe:

Late in the evening of November 10th came news of the signing of the Armistice. We celebrated it as well as circumstances permitted. Verey Light pistols were fired in the air and bonfires lit. Our surroundings were too dismal and uncomfortable for carrying out celebrations suitable for such a happy day. On the 20th we moved to Tourcoing, with guns and column complete. There we settled down to live a more civilised life. Thus the war ended as far as we were concerned.[21]

World War II

To CONCLUDE THIS CHAPTER WE WILL LOOK at some associations that Fitzwilliam Square had with World War II. By deed dated 27 June 1884, the widow Mary Clarke sold No. 11 Fitzwilliam Square to the barrister Robert Seeds, and the house would be home to three generations of the Seeds family. William Seeds was born in 1882, grew up in Fitzwilliam Square, and from an early age aimed for a foreign-service career that would include Russia. He spent the period from September 1899 to June 1900 in St. Petersburg, where he lived with several Russian families, studying the culture and language. In 1904, he entered the diplomatic service and was posted to Washington DC, and later to capitals in Europe, the Far East and South America. On 2 April 1938, Seeds was offered the position of British ambassador to the Soviet Union, fulfilling his life-long ambition. He arrived in Moscow on 21 January 1939 to present his credentials to Mikhail Kalinin, chairman of the Presidium of the Supreme Soviet, and impressed his audience by speaking Russian. However, Stalinist Russia was very different from the one of Seeds' youth and he quickly became disillusioned. He wrote to Lord Halifax, British secretary of state for foreign affairs, on 29 August 1939:

> I am precluded by my guardian-devils of the police who dog my every movement abroad from any possibility of acquiring first-hand knowledge, or even impressions.[22]

Seeds' main concern on the eve of World War II was the intended policy of the Soviet Union with regards international relations – whether Moscow would come to an accord with Britain and France, Germany or retreat into isolation. Seeds worked tirelessly in tripartite discussions with members of the Russian, French and British governments, suspicious, but genuinely unaware that a Nazi-Soviet non-aggression pact would be signed on 23 August 1939. Seeds wrote in his diary on the evening of August 22:

> At 8pm I had interview with Molotov [Russian Commissar for foreign affairs] when he pretended that it was our insincerity which had forced Russians to treat with Germany and I had at any rate satisfaction of talking to him of Russian 'bad faith' which annoyed him extremely.

On 2 January 1940, Sir William Seeds and his wife returned to England on leave and they would not return to Moscow. Seeds eventually retired to Greece and died on the 2 November 1973. His sister, Roberta Seeds Roe, continued living in No. 11 Fitzwilliam Square until 1954. Her grandchildren remember 'Cuddy', as she was known, as an extravagant and larger than life character, extremely wealthy and distinguished. She enjoyed riding and hunting and was a grand lover of rugby.

In 1942, the consulate of the Polish government-in-exile moved to new offices at No. 1 Fitzwilliam Square. The Consulate General was Waclaw Tadeusz Dobrzynski. No. 1 also became the repository for the Polish Foreign Ministry archives. It was felt these documents would be safer in Dublin rather than London, and each year a large quantity of boxes arrived, causing severe shortages of space. The consulate office continued in Fitzwilliam Square until it closed in 1958. As it happens, a distinguished Polish émigré was living in Fitzwilliam Square at the same time as the consulate. Jan Lukasiewicz was one of the twentieth century's foremost mathematicians and logicians. He took up residence in No. 57 Fitzwilliam Square in 1949 and remained until his death in 1956. Lukasiewicz was a Pole born in the Ukrainian city of Lwow in 1878. He studied mathematics and philosophy

Jan Lukasiewicz of No. 57

at his local university until 1915, when he accepted a lectureship at the University of Warsaw, then under German control. In 1919, he became Polish Minister for Education and was also Dean of Warsaw University's School of Philosophy. He and his wife Regina suffered terribly during World War II. His house was burned with the loss of his library and manuscripts. He started giving lectures at the underground university and was part of a clandestine Warsaw government during German occupation. He escaped Poland with his wife shortly before the abortive Polish uprising of 1944 and was hiding in Münster, Germany when it was liberated by the Americans in April 1945.

However, it was the Stalinist regime in Poland that Lukasiewicz fled when he accepted the offer of the Chair of Logic at the Royal Irish Academy. Professor J. Slupecki wrote:

> The problem to which Lukasiewicz was most interested and which he strove to solve with extraordinary effort and passion was that of 'determinism'. It inspired him with his most brilliant idea, that of many valued logics.[23]

His ideas were so influential that logic theories from Aristotle to 1930 are now known as 'classical' logic, while theories after 1930 are know as 'many-valued' or, more informally, 'fuzzy' logic. Slupecki continued:

> ... the logical systems constructed by Lukasiewicz are masterpieces of simplicity and formal elegance.

Lukasiewicz's time in Fitzwilliam Square was productive. He continued working and publishing papers right up to his death. Following his passing, his wife Regina left Ireland. In the preface to the second edition of his most famous work, *Aristotle's Syllogistic*, Lukasiewicz wrote:

> The whole work I dedicate to my beloved wife, Regina Lukasiewicz née Barwinska, who has sacrificed herself that I might live and work. Without her incessant care during the war, and without her continual encouragement and help in the loneliness of our exile after it, I could never have brought the book to an end. (Dublin 7th May 1950)[24]

Elsewhere, Lukasiewicz eloquently described his own work:

> Whenever I work even on the tiniest logistic problem, I always have the impression that I am confronted with a mighty construction, of indescribable complexity and immeasurable rigidity. I sense that structure as if it were a concrete, tangible object, made of the hardest of materials, a hundred times stronger than steel and concrete. I cannot change anything in it; by intense labour, though, I discover in it ever new details, and attain unshakable and eternal truths. Where and what is this ideal structure? A believing philosopher would say: it is in God and His thought.[25]

So No. 57 Fitzwilliam Square was a retreat for an exquisitely logical mind, one that had endured the most barbaric moments of European history. The house had been one of those original four, standing alone on the newly laid out Fitzwilliam Square in 1798. In the intervening years we have seen numerous distinguished generals and admirals residing in the square, and young soldiers who left Dublin to embark on their perilous careers. All of their tales, no matter how seemingly gallant or adventurous, tragic or foolhardy, all that effort and sacrifice seems so wasteful when considering Lukasiewicz's simple description of his noble work. It is heartening that a man confronted with the mindlessness of twisted ideology, and brutal soldiery, could find a haven to continue learning.

Apparently, the ending of hostilities in Europe was announced to Fitzwilliam Square by the author Eamonn Mac Thomais, when he was just a delivery lad. He recalled:

> Now, as true as God is in his Heaven, and cross my heart and hope to die, I declared Peace in Fitzwilliam Square and I didn't get or make a brass farthing. I remember it as if it was yesterday! It was around D-Day 1945, and as I pedalled the bike around Fitzwilliam I kept repeating the words that had come over the wireless. I wanted to knock on every door to tell them the good news and sure I shouted it so loud at the house that I delivered to, the maids and receptionists could hear me down in the basement. Fitzwilliam, which was always so quiet, so beautiful and so lonely, some days I wouldn't see a cat, was now humming with excitement, smiles and loud laughs, as they listened to my Declaration of Peace.[26]

Endnotes

1. Sir Edward May, *Changes and Chances of a Soldier's Life*, p. 8.

2. Passages quoted in this section are from Samuel Madden's, *Memoir of the Life of Peter Roe* (1842), pp. 17, 19-23.

3. James Gordon, *History of the Irish Rebellion in the year 1798* (1813), pp. 178-179.

4. Irish Manuscripts Commission, *The Correspondence of Daniel O'Connell; 1815-1823* (1972), Vol. 2, p. 28.

5. *Proceedings of the Catholic Association in Dublin from May 13, 1824 to February 11, 1825*, p. 706.

6. William John Fitzpatrick, *Correspondence of Daniel O'Connell, the liberator* (1888), Vol. 2, p. 381.

7. Mary Bryan, *The Georgian Squares of Dublin*, p. 113.

8. John William Cole, *Memoirs of British Generals distinguished during the Peninsular Wars* (1856), Vol. 1, pp. 158-160.

9. Denis Gwynn, *The O'Gorman Mahon; Duellist, Adventurer and Politician* (1934), pp. 13, 110.

10. Robert Graham, *A Scottish Whig in Ireland, 1835-1838*, ed. Henry Heaney (1999), p. 23.

11. Gwynn, *The O'Gorman Mahon*, pp. 9-11.

12. James Ralfe, *The Naval Chronology of Great Britain* (1820), Vol. 1, pp. 53-54.

13. William James, *The Naval History of Great Britain* (1859), Vol. 4, pp. 165-166.

14. *The Gentleman's Magazine* (1806), Vol. 76, Part 2, p. 854.

15. *The Irish Times*, 29 March 1859.

16. Ibid., 25 January 1873.

17. Passages quoted in this section are from Edward May's *Changes and Chances of a Soldier's Life*, pp. 5-7, 19, 21-22, 25-26.

18. Passages quoted in this section are taken from a typescript bound volume of letters from George Vernon Clarke to members of his family written during the Boer War, preserved by the Clarke family. The letters were transcribed by Penny Lindley and are available online at www.marshalclarke.com/GeorgeClarkesDiary.

19. Maurice Cecil Walker, *A History of 154 Siege Battery, Royal Garrison Artillery*, p. 59.

20. Marquis de Ruvigny, *The Roll Of Honour* (1916), Vol. 1, p. 147.

21. Maurice Cecil Walker, *A History of 154 Siege Battery*, p. 83.

22. Sidney Aster, 'Sir William Seeds: The Diplomat as Scapegoat', *in Leadership and Responsibility in the Second World War*, ed. Brian Farrell, pp. 124, 142.

23. Jerzy Slupecki, *Jan Lukasiewicz; Selected Works* (1970), ed. Ludwik Borkowski, p. vii.

24. Jan Lukasiewicz, *Aristotle's Syllogistic, from the standpoint of modern formal logic* (1951), p. ix.

25. Jan Lukasiewicz, *W Obronie Logistyki* (In Defence of Logic) 1937, quoted by Eckhart Menzler Trott, *Logic's Lost Genius: The Life of Gerhard Gentzen*, p. 180.

26. Eamonn Mac Thomais, *Fitzwilliam Days*, clipping found amongst Rose Dunne papers, Irish Architectural Archives.

7

Doctors – Medical, Academic and Divine

S CHOLARLY MEDITATION, PHYSICAL MEDICATION and divine mediation concerns us in this chapter; those residents of Fitzwilliam Square who devoted their lives to study, academic discovery, religious devotion and medical practice. Some have already been noted in other chapters and in different capacities, such as the cuckold Lord Branden, doctor of divinity in No. 3, and the poet James Henry, doctor of medicine in No. 6, however there were many others. It is often noted that in the twentieth century, Fitzwilliam Square was to Dublin what Harley Street is to London: a place for doctors' clinics and consulting rooms. However, this prevalence of medical practitioners was not at all apparent for much of the nineteenth century. Back then, names preceded by doctor were more likely to belong to professors of the University of Dublin and the religious. In particular, the square was home to a number of prominent mathematicians, including Thomas Meredith, the father and son Bartholomew and Humphrey Lloyd (both provosts of Trinity College), Charles James Hargreave, several members of the Graves family and, by association, William Rowan Hamilton. William M. Dixon referred to this profusion of mathematics in nineteenth century Dublin:

> The mathematicians of the Continent, following in the wake of Descartes, were pursuing studies destined to revolutionise the methods of modern science. While Cambridge slept, unconscious of the dawn of a new day, Dublin was awake.[1]

Other residents were naturalists, economists, historians and astronomers, members of institutions such as the Royal Irish Academy and contributors to scientific journals and periodicals. Some of those working in the offices of today's Fitzwilliam Square are in the same rooms where once there were book-lined, well-appointed studies overlooking the central garden; gentlemen of varying disciplines and talents surrounded by tomes sacred, medical and scientific, cluttered desks beside glowing hearths and locked doors past which children had learned to tread softly. A.P. Graves, noted in Chapter 4, described sneaking into the study of his father, Rev. Charles Graves, in No. 41 Fitzwilliam Square:

> When I was about five years old, I used to steal into my father's study, darkened in his absence by the closing of the shutters to protect his books from the sun. Opening enough of one shutter to allow a single crack of light to fall upon the writing-table, I would climb the step-ladder, take down Spencer's Faerie Queene and open it upon the table, to the level of which my shoulders just reached. There I would stand to read, with my arms clasping the heavy volume. I believe I got through the whole of the poem without being discovered.[2]

While looking at religious inhabitants of the square in this chapter we shall also consider the early meetings of the religious group the Plymouth Brethren, which took place in the drawing-room of No. 45 during the late 1820s. Later, we shall sketch the square's most prominent physicians, surgeons and general practitioners.

Rev. Thomas Meredith DD of No. 53

As far back as May 1809, Thomas Meredith (1777-1819) took possession of No. 1 Fitzwilliam Square north, what is now No. 53. Meredith had entered Trinity College in 1791, graduating with a BA in 1795. Ten years later he was awarded with an MA and was also elected a fellow of the college. In July 1807, Meredith married Elizabeth Mary Graves, a cousin of the Graves family that would live in No. 41. Among their children born in Fitzwilliam Square was a daughter, Anne Meredith, 'both beautiful and accomplished. A born actress, she could move her hearers to tears or laughter, and a musician too' (she died relatively young). Also born there was William Collis Meredith (1812-1894), who was later Chief Justice of the Superior Court for the province of Quebec. Thomas Meredith was highly regarded in the college as a mathematician and lecturer. One of his pupils was the poet Charles Wolfe (1791-1823), with whom he maintained a close friendship in subsequent years. A biographer of Wolfe described Meredith:

Rev. Thomas Meredith of No. 53

> He was esteemed one of the most distinguished scholars in the university to which he belonged. His genius for mathematical acquirements especially, was universally allowed to be of the first order; and his qualifications as a public examiner and lecturer were so eminent, as to render his early retirement from the duties of a fellowship as a serious loss to college.[3]

While living in Fitzwilliam Square (where he kept a large library of rare books and antique maps) Meredith became a doctor of divinity in 1812. The same year he was appointed rector of Ardtrea in County Tyrone and he resigned his Trinity College fellowship.

He died relatively young in Ardtrea in 1819 from apoplexy, which evidently in those days referred to any sudden attack such as a stroke or haemorrhage. However, curious tales have arisen surrounding the circumstances of his death. These seem to have sprung from the last lines of an epitaph written by Charles Wolfe and inscribed on a memorial in Ardtrea:

He was summoned from a family of which he was the
  support and delight
And from the flock to which he was eminently endeared
On 2nd May 1819 in the 42nd year of his age
By a sudden and awful visitation but he knew
That his Redeemer lived.[4]

A century later, Rev. Ernst Scott was the rector of Ardtrea. He wrote a letter in 1924 to a Colborne Powell Meredith, one of Thomas's grandsons, setting out the local legend surrounding this awful visitation:

> In the parish of Ardtrea, in the County of Tyrone, Ireland, stands the big rectory in which I took up my abode, with my family, on my appointment to the living in 1914. It is a curious house, with a curious history – a huge, grim, rambling building standing in the midst of forty-five acres of grounds. Erected over a century ago for a wealthy incumbent, the atmosphere of the place seems to be impregnated with that peculiar blend of mystery and superstition which surrounds so many old houses of the kind ...
>
> If its situation and appearance bears the impress of the unusual, so likewise do its traditions. One of its first inhabitants, Dr. Thomas Meredith, a former Fellow of Trinity College Dublin, Rector of Ardtrea for six years, and great-grandfather of my wife, died within its doors in 1819 from a 'sudden and awful visitation', as his tombstone states.
>
> Exactly what this was no one seems to know, but the story runs that a governess employed by Dr Meredith was troubled by a ghost, which took the form of a lady arrayed in white – possibly, averred local tradition, the Virgin Saint Trea, who lived hereabout in the fifth century. This apparition greatly troubled the good doctor, and on the advice of a friend he charged a gun with a solid silver bullet and lay in wait for the midnight visitor. In due course a report was heard, and next day the Rector lay dying upon the flagged floor of a basement room. From that hour the country-people looked askant upon the 'haunted' house, and avoided it whenever possible.

A variation of this story appeared in J.D. Seymour's *True Irish Ghost Stories*:

> A local legend explains this 'visitation,' by stating that a ghost haunted the rectory, the visits of which had caused his family and servants to leave the house. The rector had tried to shoot it but failed; then he was told to use a silver bullet; he did so, and next morning was found dead at his hall-door while a hideous object like a devil made horrid noises out of any window the servant man approached. This man was advised by some Roman Catholic neighbours to get the priest, who would 'lay' the thing. The priest arrived, and with the help of a jar of whisky the ghost became quite civil, till the last glass in the jar, which the priest was about to empty out for himself, whereupon the ghost or devil made himself as thin and long as a Lough Neagh eel, and slipped himself into the jar to get the last drops. But the priest put the cork into its place and hammered it in, and, making the sign of the Cross on it, he had the evil thing secured. It was buried in the cellar of the rectory, where on some nights it can still be heard calling to be let out.[5]

Wretched scepticism leads one to think Wolfe merely described Meredith's sudden and fatal affliction when he referred to the 'awful visitation', but the words were obviously seized upon by local romancers to concoct the legend. Wolfe's esteem for Meredith was evident in a letter he wrote dated 4 May 1819, describing the days following his erstwhile tutor's death:

> I am just come from the house of mourning! Last night I helped to lay poor Meredith in his coffin, and followed him this morning to his grave. The visitation was truly awful. Last Tuesday (this day week) he was struck to the ground by a fit of apoplexy, and from that moment until the hour of his death, on Sunday evening, he never articulated. I did not hear of his danger until Sunday evening, and yesterday morning I ran ten miles, like a madman, and was only in time to see his dead body. It will be a cruel and bitter thought to me for many a day, that I had not one farewell from him, while he was on the brink of the world. Oh, one of my heart-strings is broken! The only way I have of describ-

ing my attachment to that man, is by telling you, that next to you and Dickinson, he was the person in whose society I took the greatest delight. A visit to Ardtrea was often in prospect to sustain me in many of my cheerless labours.[6]

Rev. Bartholomew Lloyd DD of No. 13

WHILE MEREDITH WAS RESIDING IN No. 53 Fitzwilliam Square, a colleague fellow had acquired two plots on the east side of the square. Rev. Bartholomew Lloyd (1772-1837) lived in No. 13, one of two houses he had constructed. Lloyd was born in New Ross, County Wexford, entered Trinity College in 1787 and was elected fellow in 1796. An obituary later noted:

> ... he soon outstripped all competition at the college examinations; and when a candidate for his Fellowship, delighted the profound Professor Young, afterwards Bishop of Clonfert, by giving the solution to a problem which had been passed unanswered at several previous examinations.

Rev. Bartholomew Lloyd of No. 13

During his time in Fitzwilliam Square, Lloyd was Professor of Mathematics from 1813 to 1822 and Professor of Natural and Experimental Philosophy from 1822 to 1831.

Weakness of voice prevented Dr Lloyd from becoming very popular as a lecturer; but few were more deservedly admired as an examiner. The paternal kindness of his manners relieved those who suffered from awkwardness and timidity, and his eagerness to encourage modest merit was proverbial.... In his house were generally to be found all the gentlemen of Dublin who took an interest in the advancement of science – the geologist, the chemist, the natural philosopher, and the mathematician. He used frequently to say, that exclusiveness was the bane of science.[7]

In 1831, Dr. Lloyd left No. 13 Fitzwilliam Square for the Provost's House of Trinity College. Luce wrote:

> Change was in the air when Provost Kyle resigned in the Spring of 1831. Catholic Emancipation had been achieved in 1829, a new Whig government was in power, and the great Reform Bill was about to come before parliament. The installation of Bartholomew Lloyd as the new Provost on 9 April 1831 was in keeping with the spirit of the times, for it was the prelude to two decades of major reform and development in the College.[8]

Elsewhere it has been noted:

> So far as Trinity was concerned, the nineteenth century began only when Bartholomew Lloyd became Provost in 1831. A determined if conciliatory reformer, his provostship was marked by a number of important changes, of which the most significant was the introduction of the modern system of honour studies in 1833.[9]

He also altered the term structure of the college, which had remained unchanged since 1637. Lloyd introduced the trimesters of Hillary, Trinity and Michaelmas terms to the college in 1834. Lloyd also placed a renewed emphasis on advanced teaching and research for the college chairs. He proposed that his replacement in the chair of Natural and Experimental Philosophy should solely be engaged in advanced research, be exempt from normal tutorial work and receive a salary of £700, more than triple the normal rate. Luce again:

> The proposal might have gone through without much opposition but for the fact that his preferred candidate for the new post was his own son, Humphrey, who had been elected to fellowship in 1824. Not surprisingly, a storm of controversy was stirred up, but the Provost eventually got his way, and Humphrey, who was an excellent physicist

(and a future Provost), soon justified his appointment by some original and successful experimental work.[10]

Humphrey Lloyd was also a resident of Fitzwilliam Square and we shall look at his career later. His father, Bartholomew, died on 24 November 1837, once more from a fit of apoplexy. He had been president of the Royal Irish Academy for two years prior to his death.

The Plymouth Brethren

OTHER REVEREND RESIDENTS OF FITZWILLIAM SQUARE in the first decades of the nineteenth century included Rev. Truell of No. 15, Rev. Thomas Kelly of No. 16 and Archdeacon Saurin of No. 64. However,

John Nelson Darby, founder of the Plymouth Brethren

the square was not just a place of abode for the religious, but also a place of worship. The Plymouth Brethren was an evangelical Christian movement began in Dublin around 1827. The first of its English assemblies was later held at Plymouth from where the movement took its name. Members wished to move away from the liturgical framework of the established church, or any other, and simply meet in private houses to discuss the bible and celebrate holy communion without the need for clergy. One of the most prominent founding members was Rev. John Nelson Darby (1800-1882), who was the brother-in-law of Edward Pennefather (of No. 5 – described in Chapter 2) and tutor to his children. Another tutor in the Pennefather household was Francis William Newman (1805-1897), younger brother of 'Blessed' John Henry Newman. Seán O'Faoláin described Francis Newman's encounters with John Nelson Darby in his book *Newman's Way*:

Frank [Newman] lived with Pennefather in Fitzwilliam Square after a brief preliminary sojourn in the Wicklow hills.... He found in his employer a kind and generous friend. He also found in the Fitzwilliam Square house an odd-looking man named John Nelson Darby, whose sister Pennefather had married. The man exercised a strange magnetic influence over the whole household.... Darby was by this date a physical wreck. He went hobbling on crutches around Pennefather's house, blood-shot, unshaven, in shabby clothes, a virtual cripple. To this he had been reduced by his selfless zeal in God's service.[11]

Another Plymouth Brethren founder was John Giffard Bellet (1795-1864) who later recalled being introduced to a Francis Synge Hutchinson, also of Fitzwilliam Square:

I continued, however, in Dublin, and he [Darby] more generally in the county Wicklow, but he had introduced me to dear F. Hutchinson, whose memory is very dear to me and much honoured by me. He and I found we had much in common.... Dissatisfied as I was, we went occasionally to the dissenting chapels together, but we had not much sympathy with the tone prevalent. The sermons we heard had generally, perhaps, less of the simplicity of Christ in them than what we had in the pulpits of the Established Church, and the things of God were dealt with more for the intellect and by the intellect, than, as we judged, suited the proper cravings of the renewed and spiritual mind.[12]

Many Brethren histories say Mr Hutchinson (1800-1832) was living in No. 9 Fitzwilliam Square, but his house was No. 8 on the west side, which is No. 45. Bellet went on to describe his association with other founders such as Anthony Groves and Edward Cronin, and Hutchinson's offer to host meetings in his drawing room.

But on returning to Dublin in the November of that year, F. Hutchinson was quite prepared for communion in the name of the Lord with all, whosoever they might be, who loved Him in sincerity, and proposed to have a room in his house in Fitzwilliam Square for that purpose. He did so, designing, however, so to have it that if any were disposed to attend the services in the Parish Church or Dissenting chapels they might not be hindered; and he also prescribed a certain line of things as to the services of prayer, singing and teaching that should be found among us each day.

John Nelson Darby, in a rather disjointed recollection, described the very first meetings in Fitzwilliam Square, referring to an early dispute:

> Five of us met at Fitzwilliam Square – Bellett, Cronin, Hutchinson, the present Master Brooke (who was frightened away by Hutchinson), and myself. As Hutchinson was willing, I proposed meeting next Sunday. We did at H.'s house. Brooke did not come.[13]

It's not recorded what Hutchinson said or did to frighten Master Brooke away. Edward Cronin suggests that there had already been similar meetings in his home in Pembroke Street and that there were more than five at the initial gatherings. He wrote:

> Here [at Pembroke street] Francis Hutchinson joined us, and as we were becoming numerous, offered us the use of his large room in Fitzwilliam Square.[14]

The Fitzwilliam Square meetings quickly grew in number. Grayson Carter wrote:

> According to the Brethren historian Henry Pickering, considerable interest was awakened as a consequence of this meeting, and those who ventured to it were struck by the sight of hundreds of people coming together to worship without a clergyman, yet there was no confusion, but 'all things were done decently and in order'.[15]

To say there were hundreds of members in that Fitzwilliam Square *piano nobile* may have been an exaggeration, but the increase in numbers did lead to the removal of the meeting rooms to Aungier Street. It was also intimated that poorer members felt out of place in the genteel surroundings of the square. Cronin wrote:

> We soon began to feel, as humbler brethren were added to us, that the house in Fitzwilliam Square was unsuited,

which led us to take a large auction room in Aungier Street for our use on Sundays.[16]

The Fitzwilliam Square meetings only lasted from November 1829 to May 1830. Francis Synge Hutchinson died a young man only two years later. The first English meetings of the Brethren were held in December 1831 in Plymouth. The movement spread worldwide and, though split in various ways because of theological differences, is still widespread in North America and elsewhere.

Stephen Creagh Sandes, Bishop of Cashel of No. 17

WHILE MEMBERS OF THE BRETHREN CAME AND went at No. 45, there lived Rev. Stephen Creagh Sandes across the square in No. 17 (the last house on the east side). He purchased No. 17 in October 1826 (though directories say he had lived there since 1821) and died in Fitzwilliam Square on 15 November 1843, aged sixty-three. He had been a fellow of Trinity College for many years and was a doctor in both law and divinity. In 1836, he was consecrated Anglican Bishop of Cashel and Emly, and in 1839, was invested with episcopal jurisdiction over the sees of Waterford and Lismore. An obituary noted:

> Dr Sandes' appointment was one of very few which gave general satisfaction to all parties; for, although an avowed Whig, and to the last degree a Liberal in politics, but he was yet, from his manifold good qualities and the unassumed simplicity of his character, a great favourite in every quarter where he was known.[17]

Richard Whately (1787-1863), Archbishop of Dublin was less generous in his opinion of Sandes. Nigel Yates described the archbishop's blunt views:

> Whately was also very contemptuous of some of his colleagues among the Irish bishops. He describes Sandes of Cashel as 'remarkably illiterate ... does not even pretend not to have the sight of a book'.[18]

Sandes' career in Trinity College is recalled in his connection to the election of William Conyngham Plunket (later lord chancellor of Ireland) to parliament as the member for the university in 1812. Plunket's candidacy was dogged by a controversy surrounding his prosecution of Robert Emmett in September 1803; that he had argued the case with undue severity against his former friend in order to curry favour and advance his career. In 1804, Plunket successfully sued the *Weekly Register's* William Cobbett, who printed that Emmett had described Plunket as 'that viper my father warmed in his bosom'. The travelogue writer John Gamble repeated Emmett's alleged statement in a book published in 1811. Another legal action by Plunket saw that book withdrawn from the shelves and meant the controversy was fresh in the minds of Trinity College electors in 1812. Charles Phillips, in his sympathetic sketch of Plunket in *Curran and his Contemporaries*, described the role Sandes played in the election, reflecting the esteem in which he was held within the university:

> I willingly conclude ... with an anecdote, which can only be known to very few, and which was related to me by a loved and ever-to-be-lamented friend, the late Bishop of Cashel – a man who combined with talents the most transcendent every virtue which could adorn humanity. A very close contest was proceeding in the year 18[12] between Mr. Plunket and. Mr. Croker for the representation of the University of Dublin: either candidate would have done honour to its choice. It was quite understood that Dr Sandes, from his well-won popularity, had the election in his hands. Mr. Plunket called to canvass him, and the bishop related to me what followed: 'I locked the door,' said he, 'to avoid all interruption, and at once said, 'Mr. Plunket, I know, of course, the nature of your visit. I need not say I admire your talents, and coincide in your political opinions; but I will deal quite candidly with you. My vote and interest you shall never have, until you fully satisfy me respecting the part you took on the trial of the unfortunate Robert Emmett.' He sat down, entered upon an elaborate explanation, and at the end of an hour I promised the support which made him member for the University.' The election which founded the fortunes of Mr. Plunket was carried by a very narrow majority (as I believe, only five), and there could be no doubt that Dr. Sandes decided it.[19]

As mentioned elsewhere, David Plunket, one of William C. Plunket's sons, was living in No. 29 from 1839. As such, he was a Fitzwilliam Square contemporary of Bishop Sandes who died in No. 17 in 1843.

> Having been long in an extremely delicate state of health, he had only returned from England four days before his death, and from that period continued speechless. His inability to articulate was caused by paralysis. He was, however, perfectly conscious of his approaching dissolution, and to the last recognised his friends. His death was in every sense that of a sincere believer in the merits of his Saviour's atonement. His remains have been deposited in the vaults of the University.[20]

Graves, Lloyd and Hamilton

IF WE RETURN TO MATTERS MATHEMATICAL, we find distinguished members of the generation that followed Thomas Meredith and Bartholomew Lloyd residing in Fitzwilliam Square. Lloyd's son Humphrey (1800-1881), lived as a young man with his father in No. 13 and later lived in No. 34 from 1843 to around 1855. Meanwhile, the Graves family were long-term residents of No. 41 on the west side. As already mentioned, John Crosbie Graves took possession of the house around April 1814. Humphrey Lloyd and three of John C. Graves' s sons were close associates of William Rowan Hamilton (1805-1865), one of Ireland's greatest mathematicians and scientists. Lloyd, John Graves (1806-1870) and Charles Graves (1812-1899) were themselves mathematicians and colleagues of Hamilton. Robert Perceval Graves (1810-1893) was the author of *Life of Sir William Rowan Hamilton, Andrews Professor of Astronomy in the University of Dublin, and Royal Astronomer of Ireland*, a three volume biography and compilation of Hamilton's correspondence. Their sister Clarissa Graves (1808-1871) married the eminent German historian Leopold von Ranke in 1843. She had also been a friend and correspondent of the English poet Felicia Hemans, who was living in Dublin prior to her death in 1835.

We can recall that Humphrey Lloyd succeeded his father as Professor of Natural and Experimental Philosophy in Trinity College in 1831 amidst talk of nepotism. However, Lloyd the younger soon excelled as a scholar and mathematical scientist. He took up residence in No. 34 in 1843 and while there, was president of the Royal Irish Academy. In 1867 he became Provost of Trinity College. Luce wrote:

> Humphrey Lloyd was a Dubliner, a son of the reforming Provost of the 1830s, and probably the most distinguished scholar to hold the office since Narcissus Marsh. An eminent mathematical physicist with a long list of publications, he was a Fellow of the Royal Society, held an honorary doctorate from Oxford, and had been President of the British Association as well as the Royal Irish Academy. Lloyd was in advance of his time in the importance he attached to research as a function of the University.[21]

Rev. Humphrey Lloyd of No. 34

He was a close friend and colleague of William Rowan Hamilton. In particular, they are associated through Hamilton's prediction, and Lloyd's experimental discovery, of the conical refraction of light in 1832. The importance of the discovery lay in the fact that Hamilton had predicted a hitherto unimagined physical phenomenon purely through mathematical equations and theory. An English philosopher remarked that it was 'in the teeth of all analogy'.[22] Lunney and Wearie wrote:

> For Hamilton it was a crowning achievement, a realisation of his precocious promise. For mathematical physics in general it was a significant milestone: arguably the first mathematical prediction of a novel physical property that was subsequently confirmed by experiment. It has been said that Hamilton claimed that his theory was so secure that it had no need of experimental validation. If he did say this, it must have been a rare jest from this serious man, for he did

not regard the theory as a closed book. He did everything he could to encourage and assist Lloyd in his difficult task.[23]

As an aside, it's worth mentioning that Hamilton's 'precocious promise' was spotted at an early age by the subject of our first sketch in this chapter: Rev. Thomas Meredith. Robert P. Graves wrote:

> We well remember to have heard, long before we ever saw our friend [Hamilton], of Dr Meredith, formerly Fellow of Trinity College, and a man of great learning and ability, reporting with expressions of astonishment, that he had examined in the country a child of six or seven, who read, translated and understood Hebrew better than many candidates for fellowship; this child was young Hamilton.[24]

Robert Graves' collection of Hamilton's letters records the correspondence surrounding the 1832 discovery. The difficulty for Lloyd's experimentation was finding a biaxial crystal of sufficient quality in which to observe the theorised cone of refracted light. However, on 14 December 1832 he was able to write to Hamilton with a breathless report:

> Dear Hamilton,   Trinity College, December 14.
> I write this line to say that I have found the cone. At least I have almost no doubt on the subject; but must still verify it by different methods of observation. I have no time to say more at present than that I observed it in a fine specimen of arragonite which I received from Dollond in London since I saw you last.[25]

Four days later, Hamilton described the discovery in a letter to the English astronomer John Herschel:

> I applied to Professor Lloyd, son of our Provost here, to submit the matter to experiment. For some time he could do nothing decisive, not having any biaxal crystal of sufficient size and purity; but having lately obtained from Dollond a fine piece of arragonite, and having treated it according to my theoretical indications, he has perceived a curious and beautiful set of new phenomena, which, so far as they have yet been examined, appear to agree with the theory, and

at any rate are worthy of study. I thought this intelligence would interest you.[26]

Upon the death of Rev. Bartholomew Lloyd in 1837, Hamilton became president of the Royal Irish Academy. He distinguished himself in that post for nine years. It turned out his incumbency was a bridge between the Lloyds, for upon Hamilton's retirement from the post Humphrey Lloyd was elected president of the RIA.

Hamilton recorded the election, and a note of congratulations he delivered to Lloyd, in a manuscript book:

> My recollection of the note to Lloyd, is that it ran as follows:
>
> 'Library of the R. I. A., Monday night (about 11 o'clock), March 16th, 1846.
>
> My dear Lloyd, allow me to be the first to communicate to you, at least to be the first to do so in writing – for I presume that you will hear from others in some way the same result – that I have just now had the honour and the high gratification of declaring, from the Chair of the Academy, that you have been elected President. Accept the assurance of my cordial (though humble) co-operation in your exertions for the future welfare of the Academy: though I can never hope to give you any assistance so valuable as that which I have on several occasions received from you. I have some Minute Books to hand over whenever it may be your convenience to receive them; and, as it is now late, shall only add that I remain, with the most sincere congratulations to you and the Academy on the result of this night's election, my dear Lloyd, your faithful friend.'
>
> I dropped this note in Lloyd's letter-box, 17, Fitzwilliam-square, south, at about 11.30 P.M., before I ordered my car home-ward.[27]

It speaks much to their friendship, and in general to Hamilton's reputation as a courteous and humble man, that he would hand-deliver this congratulatory missive at so late an hour. We can picture his carriage approaching No. 34 on the dark and deserted south-west corner of Fitzwilliam Square; the renowned scientist gathering his coat and taking his message quickly to the door. He looks up to see if any lights flicker in the rooms above, then slips the note in the letter box and returns to his carriage. His journey home is quite a long one, through the city streets at the midnight hour before 17 March 1846, to the Dunsink Observatory in the countryside north-west of the city (though Hamilton, born in Dominick Street and, as such, a true north-sider, does not consider it so remote).

When Lloyd's five year term as president elapsed, Hamilton was involved in a slight controversy as to who should be his successor. Dr. J.T.R. Robinson of the Armagh Observatory was a favourite among academy members and seemed likely to be elected unopposed. However, Hamilton felt the president should be Dublin-based and wished to propose Professor Charles Graves of No. 41. Graves was described by his son Alfred in the latter's autobiography:

> I remember my father as a spare, well-proportioned man, a little below the average height but with a dignity of carriage that made him appear taller. He had that shade of blue eyes which usually goes with auburn hair. His forehead was high and dome-shaped, the nose aquiline, the mouth straight and stern, though it relaxed at times into an engaging smile. His hands were small yet capable, with long, slender fingers. He was most peculiar about his dress, and orderly in all his habits.... He was so fine and well-grounded a scholar, that he was able to converse freely in Latin with one of the brothers Grimm whom he met while travelling on the Continent.... He was better known as a mathematician, attaining European reputation as an original discoverer.... It may be that his classical tastes were responsible for the elegant form in which he presented his new algebraic and geometrical formulae and theorems, which have been described as instances of the 'Poetry of Mathematics'... He was the secretary to the Brehon Law Commission, [and] took a leading part in the translation into English of the Old Brehon Laws.[28]

Charles Graves was Professor of Mathematics in Trinity College from 1843 to 1862. He left Fitzwilliam Square around that time and from 1866 until his death he was Bishop of Limerick, Ardfert and Aghadoe.

Hamilton felt Graves was more suited to the post of RIA president than Robinson of Armagh. However, it was intimated to him that a contest would lead to ill-feeling within the academy and ultimately Dr. Graves urged Hamilton to withdraw his advocacy. Hamilton did so with little rancour and on the day of the election was the proposer of Dr. Robinson. He explained his initial support for Graves in a letter to the Earl of Dunraven, a backer of Robinson's candidacy, dated 11 February 1851. The letter was written from No. 12 Fitzwilliam Square west:

> It was not in any spirit of hostility to Robinson ... that I took some steps towards supporting Graves. My grand point was that I thought the President ought to be on the spot, and to be, if possible, a working member of the Council.... And looking within the Council, I had long since come to the conclusion that Graves combined the necessary qualifications to a greater degree than anyone else I knew.... Still I should not have chosen to withdraw my own move, such as it was, if Graves himself (perhaps partly influenced by you) had not earnestly requested me to do so, in a full and free conference which we had here together yesterday. To his request (backed as it were by yours) I yielded.

In a separate note Hamilton added:

> It is true that Graves and I are old friends, and indeed that I am bound to the whole Graves family by ties of old affection.... It has always been my opinion that the election of a President partakes in a high degree of the nature of a judicial act. It should be, as I think, performed without fear, favour or affection.[29]

Of course, we know that No. 12 west was the home of Dr. Charles Graves, and that Hamilton must have visited and perhaps lodged there while discussing the issue. What it demonstrates is that Fitzwilliam Square was host to a veritable knot of mathematicians in the first half of the nineteenth century, and that the lives of Meredith, the Lloyds, the Graves' and Sir William Rowan Hamilton were quite entangled.

Before moving on, we should briefly note some other academics living in the square. In the late 1820s, John Caillard Erck was living in No.

19 and Edward Smith was living in No. 53. Erck was an early archivist and calendar publisher and the father of Wentworth Erck (1827-1890). Wentworth was an amateur astronomer who made some notable discoveries at his own observatory in Sherrington, County Wicklow. Edward Smith was the father of Joseph Huband Smith, who lived in No. 53 in the early 1830s. Huband Smith was an antiquarian, a member of the Royal Irish Academy and author of many articles on archaeology. Samuel Mountiford Longfield moved into No. 47 Fitzwilliam Square in 1838 when he was Regius Professor of Feudal and English Law in Trinity College. He was the first holder of the Whately Chair of Political Economy in the university, named for Archbishop Whately, who, we can recall, was so contemptuous of Bishop Sandes of Cashel. Charles James Hargreave was an Englishman, mathematician and judge of the Landed Estate Court. He lived in No. 12 Fitzwilliam Square from 1859 until his death in 1866. His biographical entry notes that he died from an exhaustion of the brain, a fate most take great pains to avoid.

Medical Doctors

WE'VE COME A LONG WAY IN THIS CHAPTER without the mention of a medical doctor. The first such practitioner was the physician Charles William Quin (1755-1818), who lived in the square from 1804 to 1817. Quin was a fellow and president of the Royal College of Physicians in Dublin, and was Physician General of the army in Ireland in the late eighteenth century. In 1790, he published his thesis *A Treatise on Dropsy of the Brain*. When Rev. Thomas Meredith left No. 53 for Ardtrea in 1813 he was replaced in that house by the physician Robert Lloyd, possibly a relation of the Lloyds of No. 13. Dr. Lloyd moved to London in 1818. After that, medical doctors in Fitzwilliam Square were scarce. *Thom's Directory* notes a William Warren, MD who took up residence in No. 42 prior to 1834. However, it appears that his doctorate was in music, and that he was actually William Warren Mus.D. (1770-1841). He was the organist at various times in Christchurch Cathedral, St Patrick's Cathedral and the chapel of Trinity College. In 1809, he was described as 'the best organist in the empire'.[30] If so, then the next medical doctor on the square was the classical scholar James Henry of No. 6, described in Chapter 4.

On 28 May 1841, a Dr. Thomas Massey sub-leased No. 4 Fitzwilliam Square from Miss Osborne, daughter of Melinda Osborne, recently deceased, who had lived there since 1839. Massey was described in directories as an apothecary and an accoucheur (an obstetrician). The house was owned by Peter La Touche, and the landlord was the honourable Sydney Herbert. Dr. Massey had told Miss Osborne that his wife had taken 'a particular fancy'[31] to the situation and houses of the square and, after proving his good character and solvency, the lease was struck. However, in a matter of months Dr. Massey converted the front parlour of No. 4 into an apothecary shop, complete with moulded windows, business counter, shelving and glass door. Such a venture was in violation of the terms of the lease, which specifically forbade setting up an apothecary (among many prohibited trades) and the other residents of the square were quickly alarmed. Dr. Massey was at pains to explain his position. On 12 August 1841, he wrote a letter from No. 4 simply addressed to 'Sir', seeking to counter 'misrepresentations made to you':

> In the first place I beg to remark that the surgery which I have opened at my house for the purposes of compounding my patients' prescriptions can in no wise be construed into a public shop, not having the smallest appearance of such externally, it being quite of a private nature, consequently not coming under the denomination of an Apothecary's or Druggist shop.

His neighbours were not convinced. Nicholas French lived next door in No. 3, and he wrote to Cornelius O'Sullivan, Mr. Herbert's agent, on 23 February 1842:

> As I am in the most immediate neighbourhood of the Apothecary shop lately established here you will excuse me troubling you on the subject.... We find the value of our residences materially deteriorated by receiving so unwelcome a neighbour as an Apothecary and I, in common with all the residents in Fitzwilliam Square, do strongly protest.... If any one establishment of this kind is admitted, it will become the nucleus around which others will spring up and

so change the whole appearance and undervalue this square as a fashionable and desirable residence.

Legal proceedings were instigated, primarily by the landlord Herbert against the owner Peter La Touche. In consequence of that action, the following order of court was hand-delivered to Dr. Thomas Massey in No. 4 Fitzwilliam Square on 16 January 1844:

> ... that the said Thomas Massey do forthwith alter the exterior of said premises fronting Fitzwilliam Square by removing the moulding placed by him round the front parlour window of said house, and that he do alter the interior by removing the glass door in the hall and do replace same by the door for which it was originally substituted, and that he do remove the counter in the front parlour, and that he do not permit the hall door of said premises to remain open at any time for any longer time than shall be necessary for all reasonable ingress and egress.

An early challenge to the square's residential character was thus quashed.

Organist William Warren's widow was replaced in No. 42 in 1846 by James Goodshaw, MD. Two years later, Goodshaw moved to No. 33 on the south side of the square and set up a practice there with fellow doctor John Blyth (they were neighbours of Humphrey Lloyd). Treatment of patients in Fitzwilliam Square had begun in earnest (though both Goodshaw and Blyth had forsaken medical orthodoxy in order to practise homeopathy, so some might say patients would have been as well going to one of Mr. Warren's recitals). *The British Journal of Homeopathy* recorded his death in 1851:

> Homoeopathy has to lament the loss of one of its most earnest and successful practitioners in the death of Dr. Goodshaw, at the comparatively early age of 54 ...

> We cannot dismiss this brief notice of our departed fellow labourer without adverting to the fact, that Dr. Goodshaw must have been considerably beyond 40 years of age before he commenced the study of homoeopathy, and thus, when the opinions of most other men are stereotyped, he appears

not merely to have mastered the new system of therapeutics, but to have had the moral courage to avow his convictions, and carry his principles into practice. His success in his district soon brought him crowds of patients – and in order to extend the benefits of his newly acquired powers of healing as widely as possible, he established the Homoeopathic Dispensary in Abbey Street, Dublin, in the year 1844, at his own expense. This was the first institution of the kind in Ireland; it has continued open ever since, and is still in vigorous operation ...

Of course, this success made him an object of dislike and almost persecution, amongst his allopathic brethren, who could not believe in the purity of his motives, or the sincerity of his convictions. Their aspersions often wounded Dr. G[oodshaw]'s feelings, which were of the most sensitive character; and the death of a well-known individual under homoeopathic treatment gave the public and the profession an opportunity of denouncing both him and the system with the most unmeasured violence. We have no doubt the effect of this was most baneful to our departed friend.[32]

Another journal noted:

The success attending Dr Goodshaw's efforts on behalf of the sick, excited the envy and animosity of many of his Allopathic brethren in Dublin, who seldom shrunk from denouncing him as guilty of all manner of baseness and quackish practices. Such asperities told powerfully on the sensitive mind of Dr Goodshaw.[33]

The mention of 'the death of a well-known individual under homoeopathic treatment' no doubt refers to another former Fitzwilliam Square resident, Richard Benson Warren, who lived in No. 7 from c.1822 to 1835. His obituary in 1848 noted:

His death is attributed to the homeopathic treatment. About January last he exhibited a tendency to paralysis arising from the softening of the brain. Two homeopathic doctors were called in [we can guess at their identity] and continued their infinitesimal prescriptions. The day before his death two eminent physicians (Crampton and Admas) declared his recovery impossible, and ascribed his sudden decline to the treatment he had received.[34]

After Goodshaw's death in 1851, John Blyth continued to live and work in No. 33 for several decades until his own passing in 1892.

The Bensons of No.'s 42 and 57

THE 1860S SAW THE SETTLEMENT OF TWO medical families who would reside long term in the square. Charles Benson took up residence in No. 42 in 1856. He was a Sligo man who studied medicine in Trinity College, becoming an MD in 1840. He was a member of the Royal College of Surgeons in Ireland from 1825, and in 1832 was one of the founders of the City of Dublin Hospital on Baggot Street. During the 1830s he was Demonstrator of Anatomy in the school of the RCSI and was elected the chair of medicine in 1836. He retired from that post in 1872 because of failing eyesight. He died in No. 42 on 21 January 1880. His two sons were also prominent doctors. The younger was Arthur H. Benson, also a surgeon, who continued living in

Dr. Charles Benson of No. 42

No. 42 until his death in 1912. He worked as an ear, nose and throat surgeon primarily in the Royal City of Dublin Hospital. In 1894, one of the ophthalmic wards in that hospital was named the Arthur H. Benson ward.

The elder brother was John Hawtrey Benson who removed to No. 57 Fitzwilliam Square in 1877. He would live in that house for 54 years until his death in 1931. After graduating from Trinity College, Hawtrey Benson was appointed assistant physician in 1866 at the hospital his father helped found. He worked primarily in the Drummond wing of the Baggot Street hospital which dealt with the treatment of infectious diseases, a wing inundated during the smallpox epidemic in Dublin of 1872. As an expert on infectious disease, Hawtrey Benson had cause to write in the *British Medical Journal* in April 1889, contradicting an earlier article which had asserted that 'there is no evidence that leprosy is spread by contagion in England' (BMJ 30 March 1889). Benson detailed a case he dealt with of a man (identified as T.H.) who returned from India in 1872, presented himself with the symptoms of leprosy and soon after died. A year later the man's brother, M.H., was also referred to Dr. Benson with the same affliction. Benson wrote:

> M.H. had never been beyond the shores of the UK, had never been out of Ireland, and no case of leprosy, except his brother's, had occurred in his neighbourhood, if tradition can be taken, for some centuries. To my mind the proof of contagion afforded by this case possesses a force little short of that of a mathematical demonstration (BMJ 13 April 1889).

Dr. John Hawtrey Benson of No. 57

From 1891, Hawtrey Benson was consulting physician for her majesty's colonial office. He was president of the Royal College of Physicians of Ireland for 1910 and 1911 and was knighted in 1912.

The family that had been living in No. 57 immediately prior to John H. Benson were the Smiths, landowners in Clonmult, County Cork. John Shaw Smith bought the house from the barrister Arthur Bushe in 1865. His son, John Augustus Smith, was a medical student earning an MB from Trinity College and a licentiate degree from the RCSI. John Shaw Smith was an accomplished early photographer, renowned for his studies of archaeological sites in North Africa and the Middle East. Unfortunately, he suffered from mental problems, including a neurosis that he was living far beyond his means, when in fact he was quite comfortably off. The pressures of these imagined financial woes ultimately told, and he shot himself in No. 57 Fitzwilliam Square in 1873. *The Irish Times* gave details when reporting on the inquest. Smith's law adviser, Robert Meade (of No. 32 Fitzwilliam Square), deposed that he had seen the deceased the night before.

> He was in great distress about his means and his affairs, for which there was not the slightest occasion.

The report continued:

> Mr John Augustus Smith, of 57 Fitzwilliam Square, son of the deceased, stated that his father was a private gentleman, about 61 years of age, and living in the house with witness and his mother.... About half-past eight o'clock on the previous morning witness went into his father's room. He was speaking to him, and seemed in his usual health. He was talking about getting up to breakfast. Witness hearing the postman knock at the door, went down stairs to get the letters, and returned with them, going past the deceased's room to his mother's room, on the floor above. He was giving her the letters when he heard a crash, and thought that his father had fallen over the bath. He ran into the room, and found the deceased in bed, bleeding from a wound in the right temple, and having in his hand the revolver now produced. He was quite dead, but, thinking that he might not, he ran for Dr McDonnell, who came at once, and pronounced life extinct. The time which elapsed between the witness speaking with the deceased and hearing the noise was no more than about two minutes. The witness had no idea that the deceased had a revolver in his possession.[35]

The poor man may have recently bought the weapon for his rash purpose and must have been very ill to take advantage of so brief a window while his son retrieved the mail on a normal Fitzwilliam

Square morning. As far as one can tell, John Augustus Smith never went on to complete his doctorate in medicine.

The Moore Family of No. 40

WILLIAM DANIEL MOORE, MD (1813-1870) moved into No. 40 Fitzwilliam Square on the west side in 1868, two doors up from the Bensons. His son, John William Moore, continued to live in the house until his own death in 1937. William D. Moore qualified from the Apothecaries' Hall in 1833. He had to leave his course of medical studies in Trinity College in 1828, probably for financial reasons. He re-entered Trinity College in 1840, attained his BA and MB, but only became an MD in 1860. Somerville-Large notes that 'his only professional appointment was the very humble one of physician to the Molyneaux Home for the Female Blind'. However, W.D. Moore made his name through his genius for languages. His wide fluency, particularly in the Scandinavian tongues, meant he made great contributions in the translation of medical articles and texts. His translations had a reputation not only for accuracy, but also for grace and fluency. As can be imagined, his work earned him special gratitude from a number of eminent physicians whose papers he brought to a much wider audience. Professor Anders Retzius wrote to him from Stockholm on 30 December 1859:

> It is a great advantage for an author in a language so little known as ours, to see his papers translated in the first and most spread languages in the world in so correct a manner. I truly wonder your power in that way, so much more as the special anatomy demands so exact knowledge in the matter itself.[36]

In recognition of his effort, Moore was elected an honourable fellow of the Swedish Society of Physicians in 1855 and the Norwegian Medical Society in 1857. At the age of 54 he was struck by progressive muscular atrophy and declined to the point that by 1870 he was confined to his Fitzwilliam Square home. He died there on 28 October of that year.

John William Moore graduated from Trinity College with his MD in the year following his father's death. In 1875, he was appointed consulting physician for the Meath Hospital, succeeding the famous physician William Stokes (1804-1878) in that post. Moore remained in that position for the remainder of his long life and was president of the RCPI from 1898 to 1900. Aside from medicine, he took a keen interest in meteorology and was a member of the Royal Meteorological Society. An obituary noted, 'Morning and evening for seventy years he read his barometer and thermometer and recorded the rainfall', using the resulting data to produce a book entitled *Meteorology Practical and Applied*. In 1887, he described witnessing a meteor arcing over Dublin in a letter to the British periodical *Nature*:

Dr. John William Moore of No. 40

> At 8.52 p.m. (Dublin time) of yesterday, Tuesday, September 13, my wife and I while walking home were startled by a sudden bright flash like lightning, but slower and more regular in its movement. Simultaneously an intensely brilliant meteor shot majestically across the sky from north-north-west towards south-south-east, passing near, but to the eastward of, the zenith in its route. It seemed to take its origin from between the Pointers and the constellation Perseus, and died out at a height of 25° or 30° above the horizon.[37]

He mentions that he was out walking and apparently Dr. Moore cut quite a distinctive figure in his daily perambulations. Professor T.G. Moorehead wrote the following in an appreciation following Moore's death in 1937:

> Dublin has lost one of its best-known and best-loved figures. There can be few inhabitants of the city who have not been familiar for many years with Sir John as he walked with

rapid stride from his house in Fitzwilliam Square to his beloved Meath Hospital or to the meeting place of one of the many committees of which he was a member. For he was a great walker, and attributed much of his good health and his longevity to his regular exercise and to his simple habits. To all whom he met on his walks he gave a cheery greeting and salutation, and often paused to exchange a word. Familiar also to those who lived near him and were early risers was his appearance as he stood on the steps of his house in the early morning, pleasantly smiling, surveying the day and assessing its possibilities.[38]

Carrying on a Hospital

WE CAN RECALL THAT IN THE 1840S AN ATTEMPT was made to establish an apothecary shop on the east side of the square and the proprietors were quickly ordered to desist. Well, in the 1890s residents of Fitzwilliam Square were once more troubled by efforts to establish an enterprise, this time a private hospital in No. 28 on the south side. Mrs. Elizabeth Perry subleased the house from her sister Mrs. Mary Shekleton, most probably late in 1894. The house had been in some disrepair and Perry carried out renovations in order to transfer her business, that of a private hospital, from her previous address at No. 74 Harcourt Street. At that time the house next door, No. 29, was occupied by James Monahan QC (son of Chief Justice Monahan who had lived in No. 5). Monahan was very concerned that the hospital would prove to be most prejudicial to the comfort of the square's residents, particularly his own. He informed the Earl of Pembroke's agent, Mr. Vernon, of the developments and court proceedings were instigated (Pembroke was still owner in fee of all the houses on the square).

> Mr Monahan QC in his affidavit stated that on account of the thinness of the partition between his house and No 28 any unpleasant noises that occurred in the latter would be heard in the former, and an affidavit of a servant, who slept in a top room in Mr Monahan's house, stated that one night since the transfer of the hospital business she heard screaming in No. 28 for an hour, and coughing during the rest of the night.[39]

Many of the square's residents were loud in their opposition to the hospital, including John William Moore, subject of our previous sketch:

> Dr JW Moore and others deposed to the likelihood of the value of the houses being depreciated by what was being done, and to the danger of patients suffering from infections being brought to No. 28... Mrs Perry as sub-lessee of the house, would be entitled to keep a key for the square, and there could be no doubt that the result of that would be that the square would be used by the convalescent patients to which the residents most strongly objected.

An injunction against the hospital was granted on 18 April 1895, and that ruling was upheld in the Court of Appeal on 20 December that year. The final judgement was delivered by Lord Chief Justice Fitzgibbon in which the terms of the original Fitzwilliam Square leases were minutely interpreted; in particular the clause that forbade the use of:

> ... any part of the front of said houses as a shop, or [to] carry on ... the business of a tavern, alehouse, soap boiler, chandler, baker, butcher, distiller, sugar baker, brewer, druggist, apothecary, tanner, skinner, lime burner, hatter, silversmith, coppersmith, pewterer, blacksmith, or any other offensive or noisy trade, business, or profession whatsoever.

The defendants' counsel had argued that a private hospital was not mentioned in the trades listed as prohibited, and could not even be considered *ejusdem generis* (of the same kind or class) with those enumerated; and that a private hospital was not an 'offensive business'. Lord Fitzgibbon held that the rule of *ejusdem generis* would not apply in this case as the plain object of the deed was 'to make the test of what was prohibited the attribute of noise and offensiveness'.

Fitzgibbon decided that the word 'offensive' was introduced into the covenants to preclude those trades that would be annoying and hurtful, not alone to the physical eye but to the mind's eye; annoying not merely to the eye and nose, but to the feelings and the minds of the occupiers of the houses in Fitzwilliam Square. He then described the patients that Mrs. Perry had treated:

Every description of patient was received into the hospital except those suffering from contagious diseases, or actual insanity. Ladies came to be confined there. Patients suffering from hysteria were admitted there, and surgical operations of all kinds were performed there.

Surprisingly, Fitzgibbon examined the noise issue from the point of view (or hearing) of the patients within the hospital. He argued that occupants residing next door would be compelled by common humanity to curtail their usual entertainments, knowing that the noise of their revelry would add to the despair of those unfortunates a wall's breadth away.

Most forms of entertainment are attended with noise. Suppose there are ladies next door who have been confined. That there are patients suffering from hysteria, and others upon whom surgical operations have been performed.... What I ask would be the position of the next-door proprietor. If he were a person of ordinary humanity he would not use his house for the purpose of giving practically any entertainment. He would not give a ball or musical party, which, I assume, it is the privilege of those resident in Fitzwilliam Square to give – both would be attended with considerable noise – noise not alone from the music and dancing, but noise from the crowding of carriages and conveyances and people outside the house.

Perhaps this overestimated the selflessness of the neighbours but it has a peculiar logic, and displays a consideration for the plight of the patients that was admirable. But the fact that Fitzgibbon prioritised this as the first annoyance accruing from living next door to a hospital strikes one as very odd. Later, he describes what would seem to have been more common concerns:

I think it is eminently calculated to affect the nerves and give unpleasant sensations to be next door to an establishment in which the epileptic [apologies to sufferers] or hysterical patient whose hysteria may develop into insanity are treated, and in which ... deaths may result with far more than ordinary frequency. But the matter does not at all rest here. I own, I think, the apprehensions of those who fear infection from the existence of such an establishment are not far-fetched or unreasonable.

The long and the short of it was that the original injunction was upheld, and Mrs. Perry was compelled to cease her trade as a private hospital within Fitzwilliam Square. No. 28 was soon after the home of the lawyer and politician Sir Denis Henry.

Twentieth Century Doctors

OF COURSE, THERE WERE MANY OTHER MEDICAL men residing in all corners of the square in the years before and after the turn of the century, too many to name. A quick scan through the directories would reveal, for example, William Josiah Smyly, master of the Rotunda Hospital living in No. 56 in the 1880s. His sister, Louisa Stewart, and infant niece and nephew were brutally murdered in the Kucheng massacre of Christian missionaries in south east China in 1895. Appallingly, another baby nephew had his eye gouged out.

Prominent surgeons living in the square around the turn of the century included Richard Bolton McCausland, Thomas Eagleson Gordon, Leveson Gower Gunn and William Taylor. Yet more prominent doctors took up residence during the years of the Great War, such as Louis Cassidy, who lived in No. 24 from 1915 until his death in a hunting accident in 1928. Cassidy had served in Gallipoli as an army doctor, returning to Ireland after suffering shrapnel injuries. Cassidy courted peril of a different kind a few months before his death. *The Irish Times* reported:

> 'We are probably the worst cooks in the world. You will not, in the length and breadth of the world, get worse cooking than in Ireland or a worse lot of housekeepers,' said Dr Louis Cassidy yesterday at the annual general meeting of the Women's National Health Association at Ely place... The more you ponder, said Dr Cassidy, the more you come to the conclusion that many of the troubles of this country can be directly traced to these two facts: There is too much tea and baker's bread consumed and vegetables are hardly ever thought of.[40]

*Dr. William Ireland De Courcy
Wheeler of No. 23*

Also in 1915, Ireland's first neurosurgeon, Adams Andrew McConnell, took up residence in No. 69, the last house on the square.

The same year, Surgeon Rear-Admiral William Ireland De Courcy Wheeler (1879-1943) began living in No. 23. In 1944, a bequest of his library together with a large bookcase that had belonged to Richard G.H. Butcher (1819-1891), was made to the RCSI, of which he had been president. The Wheeler-Butcher collection contained many books belonging to Wheeler's father and namesake, a famous nineteenth century doctor of Merrion Square. His grandfather, George Wheeler, had met an unfortunate end:

> George Nelson Wheeler of Annsborough, Robertstown 'met a tragic end while shooting on the bog at Robertstown. He was shooting game with a muzzle-loading hammer. He fired once and the gunpowder failed to ignite. Then he did just what one is taught not to do. He looked down the barrel to see what was going on, and – boom – off went his head!'[41]

Back to Fitzwilliam Square, Wheeler's wife, Lady Elspeth Wheeler née Shaw, had founded an arts club in Dublin called 'The Ladies of the Round Table'. She was referred to rather witheringly in correspondence between the poet Thomas McGreevy and George Yeats, W.B.'s wife. McGreevy wrote on 30 December 1925:

> The ladies of the Round Table sound pretty ghastly, but what could they be when Elspeth de Courcy Wheeler was one of them? I hear she went to Egypt to die. I shall be surprised if she does however.

Yeats wrote on 15 March 1926:

> Lady Wheeler is back, she didnt die in Japan or India as one rather expected. She is looking well and less hysterical and is so amiable and full of love that I suspect she is conscience stricken.[42]

Two other doctors to note. William Doolin, surgeon and medical historian, lived in No. 50 Fitzwilliam Square from 1915, and in No. 2 from 1922. Doolin's library and archive also makes up one of the special collections of the RCSI library. The prominent Jewish gynaecologist Bethel Solomons moved into No. 42 in 1917. In 1928, he sublet the upper floors to W.B and George Yeats. Solomons was master of the Rotunda Hospital from 1926 to 1933. He was also a rugby player, earning ten caps for Ireland. His father Maurice Solomon's optician practice was mentioned in *Ulysses* while Bethel himself was given a mention in *Finnegans Wake*: 'in my bethel of Solyman's I accouched their rotundaties'. We can recall

Dr. Bethel Solomons of No. 42 by his sister, Estella Solomons

the accoucheur Thomas Massey, who lived in No. 4 in the 1840s. Bethel Solomons was president of the RCPI in the 1940s. His sister, Estella Solomons (1882-1968), was a renowned artist.

Conclusion

WE BEGAN THIS CHAPTER LOOKING AT DOCTORS academic and divine, provosts of the University of Dublin and Church of Ireland bishops. In 1911, another university leader began living in No. 41. Denis Coffey was the first president of University College Dublin, formed following the University Act of 1908. He was also a medical doctor and prior to his appointment as president he had been Dean of the Catholic University Medical School. We shall look at his career again in the following chapter, in particular an incident involving the British Army and the UCD college roll during the War of Independence. There was another Church of Ireland bishop living in No. 34, Dr. Humphrey Lloyd's old house. James Bennett Keene (1849-1919) had been Bishop of Meath since 1897. Fitzwilliam Square was his Dublin home when war was breaking out in Europe, at which time Keene made some unfortunately naïve remarks regarding the possible consequences of conflict. Keith Jeffrey wrote:

> At the end of 1914 James Bennett Keene, Church of Ireland Bishop of Meath, while noting the grievous costs of the war, echoed the theme of purification. 'We believe', he said, 'that this fiery trial will prove to be a purifying discipline. If it lead to a moral and spiritual renewal of our nation the loss will end in gain.'[43]

By this time the trend of doctors locating their consulting rooms within their Fitzwilliam Square homes had begun. Mary Bryan wrote:

> It was a convenient and economical arrangement and the houses adapted well. The two main rooms on the ground floor became surgery and waiting room while the return could house a receptionist and toilet facilities. In some cases the ground floor back room served as a waiting room during the day and reverted to being the dining room in the evenings...By 1968 the cream of the medical profession was located in Fitzwilliam Square with no less than ninety five doctors practicing there, leaving only four houses in private residential occupation.[44]

The medical doctors had truly taken over the square. However, we know that for much of the nineteenth century, MDs were few and far between. We've seen that in their absence (or abeyance) Fitzwilliam Square had a strong tradition of scholarship associated largely with the University of Dublin, particularly in the discipline of mathematics. Those careers aptly represent the aspects of the square conducive to scholarship: tranquillity, stillness and hush. By contrast, the Fitzwilliam Square lives of our next and final chapter will be those caught up in the turmoil of political ferment and nationalist agitation.

Endnotes

1. William M. Dixon, *Trinity College, Dublin* (1902), p. 184.

2. A.P. Graves, *To Return to all That*, p. 12.

3. John Russell, *Remains of the late Rev. Charles Wolfe* (1826), p. 155.

4. Richard Hastings Graves, *The Whole Works of Richard Graves* (1840), p. cxxxii.

5. J.D. Seymour, *True Irish Ghost Stories*, p. 79.

6. Russell, *Remains of the late Rev. Charles Wolfe* (1826), pp. 155-156.

7. *The Gentleman's Magazine* Vol. 9 (1838), p. 209.

8. J.V. Luce, *Trinity College Dublin: The First 400 Years*, p. 81.

9. History of Trinity College: Academic Development (1831-1918), www.tcd. ie.

10. J.V. Luce, *Trinity College Dublin: The First 400 Years*, p. 84.

11. Seán O'Faoláin, *Newman's Way: The Odyssey of John Henry Newman*, p. 128.

12. Letter from J.G. Bellett to James McAllister, 7 June 1858, *Interesting Reminiscences of the Early History of 'Brethren'*, p. 4.

13. *Interesting Reminiscences of the Early History of 'Brethren'*, p. 9.

14. Ibid., p. 10.

15. Grayson Carter, *Anglican Evangelicals: Protestant Secessions from the Via Media c. 1800-1850*, p. 199.

16. *Interesting Reminiscences*, p. 10.

17. *The Gentleman's Magazine* Vol. 19 (1843), p. 529.

18. Nigel Yates, *The Religious Condition of Ireland, 1770-1850*, p. 70.

19. Charles Phillips, *Curran and His Contemporaries* (1850), p. 313.

20. *The Gentleman's Magazine* Vol. 19 (1843), p. 529.

21. J.V. Luce, *Trinity College Dublin: The First 400 Years*, p. 100.

22. *The Dublin University Magazine* 1842, Vol. 19, p. 105.

23. James Lunney, Denis Weaire, 'The Ins and Outs of Conical Refraction', *Europhysics News*, Vol. 37 (2005), pp. 26-29.

24. *The Dublin University Magazine* 1842, Vol. 19, p. 95.

25. Robert Perceval Graves, *Life of Sir William Rowan Hamilton* (1882) Vol. 1, p. 626.

26. Ibid., p. 627.

27. Graves, *Life of Sir William Rowan Hamilton* (1882) Vol. 2, p. 516.

28. A.P. Graves, *To Return to all That*, p. 17.

29. Graves, *Life of Sir William Rowan Hamilton* (1882) Vol. 2, pp. 659-660.

30. Ita Margaret Hogan, *Anglo-Irish Music, 1780-1830*, p. 207.

31. Passages quoted in this section are from documents in the Pembroke Estate Papers, National Archives, Dublin.

32. *The British Journal of Homeopathy* (1852), Vol. 10, pp. 174-175.

33. *The British and Foreign Homeopathic medical directory and record* (1853), p. 208.

34. *The Gentleman's Magazine* Vol. 30 (1848), p. 322.

35. *The Irish Times*, 31 January 1873.

36. *Arch Ophthal* Vol. 75 (1966) p. 436. L.B. Somerville Large, *William Daniel Moore 1813-1871*.

37. *Nature*, Volume 36, Issue 935 (1887), p. 508.

38. *British Medical Journal*, 23 October 1937, pp. 831-832.

39. Passages quoted in this section are taken from reports in *The Irish Times*, 26 March 1895, 21 December 1895.

40. *The Irish Times*, 3 July 1928.

41. *Leinster Leader*, 29 August 2002

42. Letter from Thomas MacGreevy to George Yeats, 30 December 1925 and from George Yeats to Thomas MacGreevy, 15 March 1926. The Thomas MacGreevy Archive, www.macgreevy.org.

43. Keith Jeffrey, *Ireland and the Great War*, p. 24.

44. Mary Bryan, *The Georgian Squares of Dublin*, p. 108.

8

Politics and Patriots

Tʜɪs ʜɪsᴛᴏʀʏ ᴏꜰ Fɪᴛᴢᴡɪʟʟɪᴀᴍ Sqᴜᴀʀᴇ has come full circle. We began by looking at the square's lawyers, invariably engaged in action against Ireland's agitators, conspirators and militants. In this chapter we shall look at Fitzwilliam Square inhabitants more directly associated with Ireland's political and popular movements. Retelling Irish history through the prism of a single Georgian address obviously requires telling it slant. But following Fitzwilliam Square inhabitants we find important associates of O'Connell's agitation; a prominent Young Irelander in his declining years; a slew of inhabitants who were victims, investigators and spoilers of Fenian plots; two colourfully-reported tales regarding Parnell's family and political life; field-hospitals during the 1916 Rising; and safe-houses during the War of Independence. Observing Irish history from these Fitzwilliam Square homes will give a curious sense of both the domestic and public lives of national figures. It will allow us to flesh out the stories of those killed by Fenian design or agrarian unrest, which are otherwise historical footnotes. It will give us a sense of the intimate hush and secrecy when conspiracy is brought into the drawing room.

The O'Gorman Mahon of No. 64

Iɴ ᴛʜᴇ sɪxᴛʜ ᴄʜᴀᴘᴛᴇʀ ᴡᴇ ᴍᴇᴛ ᴛʜᴇ sᴡᴀsʜʙᴜᴄᴋʟɪɴɢ James O'Gorman Mahon who married the wealthy heiress Christine O'Brien of No. 64 Fitzwilliam Square in 1830. We may recall that he was something of a firebrand, insisted on being called by the designation 'The' O'Gorman

Daniel O'Connell and The O'Gorman Mahon, 1828

Mahon, and was quick to demand satisfaction in matters of honour. By 1830, he was famed for the part he played in the victory of Daniel O'Connell in the Clare by-election of 1828. The election had been triggered by the appointment of the incumbent William Vesey Fitzgerald as president of the Board of Trade by Prime Minister Wellington. Fitzgerald was required to re-contest his seat and had expected to be returned unopposed. O'Connell's triumph signalled the collapse of landlord control over Catholic voters and hastened the Catholic Relief Act of April 1829, known as Catholic Emancipation. O'Gorman Mahon's biographer, Denis Gwynn, gave a colourful account of the young man's nomination of O'Connell in June 1828. Crowds were packed into the market town of Ennis where the Sheriff was to read the writ announcing the election. The assembled landlords looked on bitterly as O'Connell arrived to popular acclaim. The courthouse was thronged with his supporters:

> Among them, seated in the most conspicuous position he could find – for he had thrown his legs over the balustrade of the gallery, and sat thus suspended over the crowd below – was one young Catholic landlord.... Even the Sheriff, agitated by the suspense of so unusual a scene, and painfully anxious to proceed to business, could not fail to notice this remarkable young man who was so truculently defying all the conventions of the court.... 'He had a coat of Irish tabinet, with glossy trousers of the same national material,' an eye-witness wrote afterwards; 'he wore no waistcoat; a blue shirt, lined with streaks of white, was open at his neck; a broad sash, with the medal of 'The Order of the Liberators' at the end of it, hung conspicuously over his breast; and a profusion of black curls curiously festooned about his temples, shadowed a very handsome and expressive countenance a great part of which was occupied by whiskers of a bushy amplitude.'

> 'Who, sir, are you?' demanded the Sheriff, assuming the authoritative manner of the East India service.... The young firebrand, with his sash and medals and the bushy side-whiskers that clustered around his Byronic collar, was not overawed. 'My name is O'Gorman Mahon,' he answered.

> 'I tell that gentleman,' retorted the Sheriff, in frigid mono-syllabic tones, 'to take off that badge.' The crowded court buzzed with excitement. It was the insolent young man who had prepared the ground for all the raging demonstrations of the previous week. His quickness in repartee was well known, and he had every opportunity of playing to the gallery. There was a brief silence. Then, in insolent mimicry of the Sheriff's own intonation, he spoke with deliberate emphasis. 'This gentleman,' he replied solemnly, laying his hand on his blue shirt-front, 'tells that gentleman,' – and he pointed with a familiar provocative gesture to the Sheriff – 'that if that gentleman presumes to touch this gentleman

or any other gentleman, then this gentleman will defend himself or any other gentleman, while he has got the arm of a gentleman to protect him.'

That remarkable sentence provoked a loud burst of applause. A riot seemed to be imminent ...

Only O'Connell himself could have quelled the excitement that these exchanges provoked.... He saw that the only chance of averting a riot was to win cheers for himself. 'Yes, green is no party colour,' he shouted. 'It may be hateful to the eyes of our opponents, but that darling colour shall flourish when the bloodstained Orange shall fade and be trodden under foot.' Such a frenzy of applause greeted his intervention that the Sheriff saw that further insistence was hopeless ...

Only when Sheriff Molony had put the question whether any other candidate was to be proposed, did the young man rise magnificently to announce that he desired to nominate Daniel O'Connell. The applause, according to the newspaper reports, was deafening.... The great fight had begun.[1]

O'Gorman Mahon fell out with O'Connell during the election of 1830 that followed the demise of George IV (and by that reckoning, the Georgian era). O'Connell relinquished his seat in Clare in order to stand in Waterford. It was assumed O'Gorman Mahon would be his successor in Clare, but O'Connell wished for his son Maurice to contest the seat. O'Connell had also considered Christine O'Brien of Fitzwilliam Square to be an ideal wife for Maurice, who must have considered O'Gorman Mahon a bitter rival when the latter claimed both prizes: the seat and the heiress. However, Maurice soon had revenge, unseating O'Gorman Mahon in the election of 1831. The latter had not made a good impression during his short time in Westminster. He rarely attended votes and was suspended temporarily over accusations of bribery and corruption. The O'Gorman Mahon spent the next four years in Fitzwilliam Square, qualifying as a barrister in 1834. The following year he began his years of wandering, becoming a soldier of fortune, as described in Chapter 6. We shall catch up with his political career later in this chapter, when once more he would stand for election in county Clare, this time with the unknown Captain William O'Shea as his running mate.

John O'Neill of No. 43

WITH CATHOLIC EMANCIPATION ACHIEVED, O'Connell turned his political focus to repeal of the Act of Union, but little progress was made during the 1830s. Wishing to emulate the tactics and success of the Catholic Association, O'Connell founded the Loyal National Repeal Association in 1840. Its first meeting was held in the great room of the Corn Exchange on Burgh Quay on 15 April 1840, but turnout was disappointingly low. The chairman of that first meeting was a Fitzwilliam Square contemporary of O'Gorman Mahon. John O'Neill was a wealthy old Protestant who was a Volunteer in 1782 when legislative independence was achieved. Now residing in No. 43 Fitzwilliam Square, and in his declining years, he lent his support to this attempt to retrieve that lost autonomy. W.J. O'Neill Daunt, in his *Eighty Five Years of Irish History*, described that first repeal meeting:

> The room was not one-fifth part filled; there was a discouraging display of empty benches – a commencement that might well have disheartened a leader less sanguine than O'Connell ...

> 'As soon,' said O'Connell, 'as they begin to find out that I am perfectly in earnest, they will come flocking into the Association.'

> The chair was taken by Mr. John O'Neill, of Fitzwilliam Square, a Protestant merchant of great wealth and sterling patriotism. He had been in early youth a member of the Volunteer army of 1782. 'I was then,' he said to me, 'too young to be of much use to Ireland, and now I am too old.' But, young or old, his country had always commanded his best services. That good old Protestant patriot is long since dead. He descended to the tomb full of years, and deeply honoured by his fellow-countrymen.

> For more than half-an-hour the few who had congregated at the Corn Exchange anxiously awaited the opening address of the Liberator; but he still lingered, apparently unwilling

to commence, in the hope of a more numerous attendance. But no reinforcement came. There were manifestations of impatience among those who had assembled. O'Connell at length rose, and with the air of one deeply impressed with the high and solemn responsibility which he incurred, spoke as follows:

'My fellow-countrymen, I rise with a deep sense of the awful importance of the step I am about to propose to the Irish people, and a full knowledge of the difficulties by which we are surrounded, and the obstacles we have to contend with ...'[2]

O'Connell's instincts proved correct once more, and the Repeal Association grew from these humble origins into a mass movement. However, the momentum was broken when O'Connell succumbed to government demands to cancel the mass meeting planned for Clontarf, County Dublin, in October 1843. The circumstances of O'Connell's subsequent arrest and trial were described in Chapter 2. We may recall the state trial was presided over by Edward Pennefather, then of No. 5 Fitzwilliam Square, while James Henry Monahan, later also of No. 5, was one of the counsels for the defence. The end of the agitation and O'Connell's pragmatic overtures to Irish federalists and British Liberals saw the split between what was known as Old Ireland and Young Ireland. Also in Chapter 2 we noted Attorney General Monahan's prosecutions of Young Irelanders arising from the abortive rebellion of 1848. However, one member who escaped prosecution was John Blake Dillon (1814-1866), who successfully went into hiding immediately after the revolt, and then fled to the United States. He returned to Ireland in 1856 under amnesty and took up residence in No. 51 Fitzwilliam Square. He joined the ranks of the square's other veteran rebels such as the 1798 insurgent William Sterne Hart of No. 36. But John Blake Dillon was the only leader of a revolutionary movement ever to reside long term in Fitzwilliam Square.

John Blake Dillon of No. 51

THE SLUGGISH START TO THE REPEAL AGITATION was given a boost by the formation of the weekly newspaper the *Nation* in 1842. The founders

Birth of 'The Nation'

were Charles Gavan Duffy, Thomas Osborne Davis and John Blake Dillon. The poet James Clarence Mangan, who had worked for several years in No. 47 Fitzwilliam Square, was also an original contributor. Gavan Duffy described Dillon in his *Young Ireland: A Fragment of Irish History, 1840-1850*:

> In person he was tall and strikingly handsome, with eyes like a thoughtful woman's, and the clear olive complexion and stately bearing of a Spanish noble. His generous nature made him more of a philanthropist than a politician. He was born and reared in Connaught among the most abject and oppressed population in Europe.... Dillon desired a national existence primarily to get rid of social degradation and suffering which it wrung his heart to witness without being able to relieve.

Gavan Duffy also described the meeting that led to the formation of the *Nation*:

> I met Dillon in the Hall of the Four Courts; he made me acquainted with Davis, and as we were pleased with each

245

other he proposed that we should walk away together to some place fitter for frank conversation. They put off their gowns and we strolled into the neighbouring Phoenix Park.... After a long conversation on the prospects of the country we sat down under a noble elm within view of the park gate leading to the city, and there I proposed a project which had been often in my mind from the first time I met them, the establishment of a weekly newspaper which we three should own and write.[3]

John Blake Dillon, 1866

The Young Irelanders split from the Repeal Association in 1846. Militant rhetoric, the wretched state of Famine-stricken Ireland and the inspiration provided by popular uprisings in Europe meant rebellion, headed by William Smith O'Brien in July 1848. He travelled around the south of the country with Dillon and Thomas Meagher, urging the population to muster. Dillon's biographer Brendan O'Cathaoir described the naivety of the rebel leaders:

The people were told to prepare for the expected rising in Kilkenny and were urged by Dillon to prevent O'Brien's arrest. It rained heavily on the way to Kilkenny. The trio stopped occasionally for shelter, and the famished peasantry left them in no doubt about the lack of revolutionary fervour. They halted to inspect the antiquities in Gowran. This charming interlude shows that seldom can an insurrection have been conducted with more idealism and less realism.[4]

O'Cathaoir noted that Smith O'Brien was completely incapable of initiating hostilities, and on 28 July Dillon suggested he should travel to his native County Mayo and raise the people there. In so doing, he left Smith O'Brien's side the day before the ignominious engagement at the Widow McCormack's house in Ballingarry, County Tipperary.

Dillon recounted his subsequent adventures as a fugitive in a lengthy letter to his wife, Adelaide Dillon née Hart, dated 30 August 1848. He finished by saying plans for his escape from Ireland were well advanced. His bitterness at the failure of the rebellion and his complete misjudgement of the spirit of the ravaged Irish population were apparent:

> As for the people I have lost all faith in them. They are treacherous and cowardly, and if Ireland is ever destined to be free, her freedom must be the gift of strangers. It is in this connection I said my career as a patriot was almost closed. After what we have witnessed I think it would be madness to hope for any manly effort on the part of the Irish people; and the attempt to emancipate by foreign agency, a people who have not the spirit to raise an arm in their own defence, appears to me rather quixotic. All these are secret thoughts but no thought of mine is a secret from you.[5]

Dillon first escaped to France before settling in New York where he practiced as a barrister. Upon his return from exile to Ireland in 1856 he kept a townhouse at No. 51 Fitzwilliam Square (his principal residence was Druid Lodge, Killiney). Dillon formed the National Association, a constitutional alternative to Fenianism in the 1860s, and was elected MP for Tipperary in July 1865. He was the first of a political dynasty; his son John Dillon (1851-1927) was a prominent nationalist parliamentarian, and his grandson James Dillon (1902-1986) was the leader of Fine Gael. John Blake Dillon died suddenly from cholera on 15 September 1866.

The Murder of Thaddeus O'Callaghan of No. 55

WE MAY RECALL THE MARITIME CAREER OF Admiral Robert Dudley Oliver, long-term resident of No. 55 Fitzwilliam Square (described in Chapter 6) who died in September 1850. He was replaced in that house by a young

Catholic solicitor called Thaddeus O'Callaghan. In common with many Fitzwilliam Square residents, O'Callaghan was a landlord of estates outside of Dublin, in his case County Galway. In 1852, he purchased an estate at Ballinamona, close to Lough Derg, through the Court of Bankruptcy. The lands had numerous tenants who O'Callaghan wished to remove in order to carry out supposed improvements, particularly the construction of a police barracks. He employed a Scottish steward to effect the necessary evictions but he also visited and resided in the area from time to time. Unsurprisingly, he was the subject of great resentment among his tenantry, who in this instance could not be quelled by local spiritual leaders. The *Nenagh Guardian* noted:

> ... though [O'Callaghan] was himself a rigid Roman Catholic, he had the temerity to dispossess a priest and the mother of two other Roman Catholic clergymen.[6]

His associates urged him to remain away from the locality when such open hostility existed. But O'Callaghan would not heed their warning, merely smiling and pointing to the revolver he kept at his side, which he called his 'protector'. His recklessness proved costly when he left his Fitzwilliam Square home to travel to his Galway estates in the spring of 1856. The *Nation* reported on 8 March:

> A dreadful murder was perpetrated a few days ago near Portumna, Mr Thaddeus Callaghan, solicitor, of 3 Fitzwilliam Square [north], Dublin and Ballinruane, in county Galway, having fallen a victim.

A correspondent to the paper was quoted in the same edition:

> It is my painful duty to announce to you the perpetration – in this hitherto peaceful district – of the horrid crime of murder, under circumstances that leave little doubt but that the victim fell before the wild justice of revenge.[7]

The *Nenagh Guardian* seemed to revel in its graphic description of the killing:

> [O'Callaghan] continued to frequently visit his Galway estate, and was only after arriving there the day preceding

his tragic and melancholy end. Not being in the habit of making any lengthened stay, he kept no servants there, and on Friday evening, the cream for his tea not coming at the required time, he went on to his steward's house, not far distant, to ascertain the cause of the delay. On his return, in a short time afterwards, he had not proceeded far before some person or persons – the number is not known as no one witnessed the deed of blood, but those immediately concerned in the dreadful act – sprung on him from behind a ditch, and struck at him with a hatchet or some other sharp instrument [other reports say he was attacked with stones]. From the suddenness of the attack, and the deadly character of the weapon with which he was assailed, the ill-fated gentleman must have been easily overcome, and the demons, adding barbarity to their fiendish ferocity, were not satisfied with depriving their victim of life, but afterwards beat him about the head. When discovered he presented an awful spectacle, his skull being smashed to pieces, and his brains bespattered about the place.[8]

The *Nation* reported that for some time O'Callaghan was in receipt of threatening letters and was also quick to link the killing with the tradition of agrarian unrest in the country. 'The shadow of another awful murder rests upon the system of Landlordism in Ireland.' O'Callaghan's murder had unusual elements, however. It occurred during a relative lull in agrarian violence between the Great Famine and the Land War of the late 1870s. Also, the fact that he was a Catholic middle-class professional apparently aping the worst excesses of the Protestant landlord class may have increased resentment. The *Nenagh Guardian* reported the reaction of the local Catholic clergy to O'Callaghan's demise:

A correspondent of the Galway Express supplies the following information respecting the after-death denunciations to which the assassinated deceased has been made liable. 'On last Friday,' he says, 'the priest alluded 'to the murder' (of Mr Callaghan) – and prayed for the victim and his murderers, and expressed a hope that his fate would be a warning to other landlords, and that no more blood might be shed!!! Mr Callaghan was a Roman Catholic and was very generous in his contributions towards the chapel, having presented a splendid pair of candlesticks, vestments, mass-books, &c, &c. But all these were ordered by the Priest to be taken away, that nothing belonging to such a fellow should any longer pollute the Holy Alter. He even said that he would send back the usual dues paid by Mr Callaghan at Christmas.' How far such anathemas, and prayers, and hints, encourage to crime or suggest it, let the reader contemplate.[9]

The reader can also contemplate the reliability of this report, but it demonstrates that O'Callaghan's faith was to the front of commentary on his murder. His assailants were never discovered.

The Parnell Sisters

FITZWILLIAM SQUARE WAS THE SETTING FOR two colourfully reported tales relating to Charles Stewart Parnell's family and political life. The first was a very public dispute between two of Parnell's brothers-in-law in the mid 1870s. Alfred McDermott was the solicitor of Parnell's father, John Henry Parnell (1811-1859) of Avondale, County Wicklow. Upon Parnell senior's death, McDermott went to Avondale to manage the family's affairs, under the direction of the Court of Chancery. He eventually married Sophia Katherine Parnell (1845-1877), who was a year older than her brother Charles, and described by her brother John as 'a beautiful bright haired girl'. Alfred and Sophia took up residence in No. 43 on the west side of Fitzwilliam Square in 1872. Sophia's immediate elder sister was Emily Parnell (1841-1918). Marie Hughes described the estrangement between Emily and her father that resulted from her choice of husband:

> [Emily] was a lively girl, with considerable talent as a musician. She was her father's favourite until she displeased him by forming an early attachment for the son of a neighbour. This was Arthur [Monroe] Dickenson, whose family lived at a house called Kingston near Avondale. Emily's father did not approve of the family as he considered the boys wild and unstable. He eventually forbade them to visit Avondale, but despite this ban and perhaps partly because of it, the romance progressed and the couple entered into a secret engagement.... [Her] uncle Sir Ralph Howard dis-

covered the secret engagement and reported it to Emily's father. The latter reacted as might have been expected and promptly made a will by which he disinherited Emily from any shares in his estate. As his sudden death occurred short-ly afterwards – it was the year 1859 – this rash action was never undone.... It must be said to her credit that despite ev-ery obstacle she remained loyal to her choice and eventually her widowed mother consented to the marriage. It would be pleasant to be able to report that her father's prejudices proved unfounded, but unfortunately they were destined to be fully justified by subsequent events.[10]

Emily lived with her hus-band, Arthur Monroe Dick-enson, at No. 22 on Lower Pembroke Street, which is the continuation of Fitzwil-liam Square west leading to Baggot Street, so in essence the Parnell sisters were near neighbours.

In 1905, Emily Monroe Dickenson wrote a memoir entitled *A Patriot's Mistake – Being Personal Recollections of the Parnell Family, by a Daugh-ter of the House.* In general, it is an interesting but unreliable history of the family, but in it she describes her antipathy

Emily Dickenson, née Parnell

towards her brother-in-law, Alfred McDermott. This seemed to stem from the fact that Alfred had at first courted and been rebuffed by Em-ily before turning his attentions to Sophia. According to Emily, Alfred would have known that she was already secretly engaged to Arthur Dickenson:

> [My] mother made an acquaintance of one [McDermott] who ingratiated himself into her favour by helping her, as

a friend, in her law business and other matters. My sister and I were thus thrown a good deal in his way. She was now about fifteen and very lovely.... She was exceedingly fair, with an abundance of golden hair, which hung like an aureole around her. Her figure was tall and willowy. She had large and dark blue eyes, the typical Irish eyes, straight features, and a complexion with the delicate pink often seen on the inside of sea shells, forming altogether a bewildering picture that was hardly of the earth. Mother's friend, who excelled in sharpness and cleverness, was an adept in flirting.... He first directed his attention towards me, which culminated in an offer of marriage, although he knew I considered myself engaged. When rejected by me, he transferred his homage and affections to my sister, with whom he made such good use of his opportunities and influence, that on her attaining the age of sixteen he persuaded her to elope with him, without the knowledge of her mother, who was ill at the time, or that of her family, even running the risk of the Lord Chancellor's anger [as a ward of the court Sophia could not marry without the Lord Chancellor's permission]. They were married in Scotland, according to the Scotch fashion, after which my sister returned to her family, she and her husband having decided on keeping their marriage secret until the former should come of age."

The couple successfully kept their Scotch marriage a secret and were publicly married in St. George's Church, that distinctive steeple in the north inner-city, when Sophia turned 21.

Emily's resentment towards Alfred McDermott was mainly the result of an imagined negligence on his part, which she felt resulted in her sister's death. Sophia had given birth to four children, three of whom were still living in 1877. In that year the children contracted scarlet fever and their mother insisted on treating them herself in No. 43 Fitzwilliam Square. Emily wrote:

Whilst I was existing as best I could, my sister was having ample time to repent of her rash marriage – not that she ever confessed to doing so. She, too, was fond of, and loyal to, her husband, to whom she was a very good wife. She was extremely fond of her children, of whom she had three living, and to them she devoted her life ...

She was now about twenty-seven, and was expecting another baby daily, when the three children took the scarlatina. My sister sat up night and day with them, and gave herself no rest. Feeling the fatigue would prove too much for her, and fearing that the expected little stranger would suffer in consequence, she asked for extra assistance, to which reasonable request objections were raised.

The doctor, who had attended her on each previous occasion of childbirth, remonstrated with her husband for allowing his wife to remain in the house under such circumstances. He declared that if she took the scarlatina, and in his opinion this was inevitable, she would certainly die, and he entreated him to exert his marital authority to induce her to leave the house. Her husband, getting very much annoyed by the doctor's interference, informed him curtly that his wife should not quit the house with his consent; moreover, he would know where to find another doctor, and summarily dismissed the kind and anxious old man.

Thus my poor sister met her hour of trouble attended by a stranger. As foretold by the old doctor, she caught the infectious disease. In her exhausted condition she rapidly sank after the birth of a girl, who survived.

We will draw a veil over the husband's terrible remorse and anguish, for which even his worst enemies pitied him, as he hung over the dead body of his late loving wife, his young and lovely helpmeet, who had sacrificed so much for his sake. We will also draw a veil over my deep sorrow for the loss of a loved and favourite sister. I registered a vow to myself that never, never would I forgive the man to whose instrumentality I considered that sister's death was due.

Elsewhere, Emily condescendingly referred to Sophia's 'rash marriage'; in this instance, describing a conversation with Sophia in the latter's Fitzwilliam Square dressing-room, some years before her death:

A very pretty blue-and-white boudoir in a fashionable Dublin square. It is my sister's house, and she is herself seated at a little octagon table, dispensing tea in little blue cups. She is evidently rather angry, and is, speaking earnestly. On a low chair near the fire, I am listening with a curious air of detachment in my attitude, as we listen to the criticisms of those who do not understand us. Both have changed but little since our first season. She looks the more matronly, and is perhaps conscious of it, as she advises her elder sister. [Sophia berates Emily for encouraging the amorous attentions of an older barrister referred to as 'Mr L'.]

I said, laughing, 'My wise sister is developing into a veritable dragon of the British matron type. Do not get cross, dear, and oh, do not lecture me. It does not suit you at all.'

The conversation ended, as it generally did, in her giving in to my views. She, though lovely and interesting, was of a very pliant nature, and her early marriage to a rather ordinary type of man had made her very conventional.

Despite her superior air, Emily must have envied Sophia's conventional, loving family life to some degree. Her own husband, Arthur Monroe Dickenson, proved to be particularly unstable, alcoholic and abusive (as old Parnell feared he would). Emily described episodes in which he would destroy crockery, burn clothes and one incident in which he threatened to strangle her, actually tightening his fingers around her neck. Alfred McDermott also became the victim of his demented actions, his attempt to win Emily for himself in 1860 apparently unforgotten:

At times he displayed a violence which was especially directed against my brother-in-law, for whom he had ever cherished bitter feelings because he had dared to try and rob him of me, and I lived in fear that his repeated threats to shoot him would some day be carried out. Once, returning from a walk, and missing Arthur's gun from its customary place, with instinctive prevision I hastened to my brother-in-law's house, [No. 43 Fitzwilliam Square] where I found Arthur standing on the doorstep with the gun in his hand. Inventing, in the emergency of the moment, an excuse, I coaxed him away, and on getting the dangerous weapon safely inside the house, forthwith placed it under lock and key, on pretence of restoring it to its place. It transpired afterwards the gun was not loaded, but at the time I was ignorant of this. In any case, I knew my brother-in-law would have made a 'case' out of the harmless incident if he had got the chance.

Dickenson's erratic behaviour was occasionally reported in *The Irish Times*. The reports make it clear that Emily would often take refuge in her sister's Fitzwilliam Square house. They also paint a picture of the McDermott family besieged in No. 43 with Dickenson ominously pacing in front of the house, hammering on the door and being pleaded with through the letter-box. On 2 November 1875, McDermott appeared in the Court of Queen's Bench to have a conditional order made against Dickenson. Justice Charles Barry of No. 3 Fitzwilliam Square happened to be on the bench. The court report stated:

> At eight o'clock on Sunday evening, the 15th of November [1874], Mrs Emily Dickenson with her child, aged four years, and Mrs Dickenson, the mother of the defendant, came to Mr McDermott's house during his absence. On his return he was informed by Mrs Dickenson that her husband had been drinking, and she feared he would assault her.

Emily did not wish to remain in No. 43 so Alfred escorted her to a hotel in Kildare Street.

> On returning to Fitzwilliam Square, Mr McDermott found Captain Dickenson at his hall-door, acting violently, trying to break in the door, and terrifying Mrs McDermott and her children, one of whom was dangerously ill. Mr McDermott gave Captain Dickenson into custody.

Dickenson was put in gaol for two days when, according to the report, Charles Stewart Parnell and Alfred bailed him out, having both received a written promise from Dickenson that he would abstain from alcohol in future. There was relative peace for the best part of a year.

> On the 4th of September, after returning from Kilkey, Mr. McDermott was informed that Mrs. Dickenson on the 2nd

of September came to Mrs. McDermott at eight in the evening and stated that her husband had been drinking, and she
feared he would lock her up. She returned to him for a few
minutes, but immediately afterwards rushed back, pursued
by her husband, and took refuge in Mr McDermott's house.
Before the door was locked, her husband came up and said
he 'must see Emily at once.' She said she was afraid to go
out to him. He said then, 'open the door at once; or I will
knock it down,' giving the door a violent drive. He then
required to see Mr McDermott. Mrs McDermott (speaking
through the letter-box opening) told him Mr McDermott
was away. Captain Dickenson replied, 'That is a lie – he
is hiding from me.' He added, 'If the door is not opened I
will force it through and break all McDermott's bones, and
smash everything in the house.' Terrified at this, and there
being no man in the house, Mrs Dickenson, Mrs McDermott, the three children in the house, and the maid servant,
escaped through the stable and coach-house into the lane at
the back, and the children who were partially undressed,
were put into a cabman's house in Quinn's lane, while Mrs
McDermott and Mrs Dickenson looked for a policeman.

What a frantic scene that must have been, those three women and
three children escaping through the long Fitzwilliam Square back garden to the stable lane in the autumnal darkness, while a brute raged
against the front door. In the following weeks Dickenson continued to
come to No. 43, leaving offensive letters. The report continued:

Captain Dickenson returned and Mr McDermott watched
his movements from the front window. For more than an
hour the captain walked up and down before the door using
offensive and threatening expressions, stating that the letters were intended to induce Mr McDermott to fight him,
and for this purpose he offered every insult in his power.

Once more Dickenson was arrested and required to appear before the police court but he absconded from the country. The Court of
Queen's Bench issued a conditional order against him. Matters came to
a head two years later in November 1877. Sophia had died of scarlet fever in April that year. On 24 November, Dickenson successfully forced

his way into No. 43 and confronted McDermott. The latter made the following deposition in court on 4 December 1877:

> I reside at No. 43 Fitzwilliam Square. I know Captain Dickenson. He is married to the sister of my late wife. On the 24th of last month, a little before eight o'clock at night, I was sitting in my dining room after dinner when a very loud knock came to the door; then a ring; immediately afterwards another loud knock. The door then opened, and on turning round I saw Captain Dickenson behind me. There were three children and two old ladies in the room. Captain Dickenson appeared to be much under the influence of drink. In fact he is always so. It is exceptional when he is sober. He staggers by my house frequently. He calls my children – [counsel for the defence objected]. He said, 'Don't disturb yourselves.' I got up and got a pistol, and said, 'If you attack my family or myself I will shoot you.' [Defence counsel: It is very well you did not use it or it is not there you would be.] I told one of my sons to send for a policeman. We all rushed out of the room. He said, 'You are the bloodiest, damnedest coward.' He repeated the expression. I said nothing but told him to leave my house. I kept on my guard with the pistol. I walked to the door to see if the police were coming, and then he walked out making an offensive observation about my wife's grave. His demeanour and manner were contemptuous and the most insulting possible.

Dickenson referred to Sophia's grave because McDermott had not yet erected a tombstone above it. The court ordered Dickenson to find two sureties in £100 each that he would keep the peace, or in default go to gaol for two months. That seemed to settle the matter and there were no further reports of disturbances at that Fitzwilliam Square home.

Parnellism and Fitzwilliam Square

CHARLES STEWART PARNELL ENTERED PARLIAMENT and was enhancing his reputation throughout the years of this unseemly quarrel between his brothers-in-law. In 1879, he became president of the Land League and was elected chairman of the Irish Parliamentary Party in 1880. The 1880 general election also saw the return to parliament of an old Fitzwilliam Square resident, The O'Gorman Mahon, O'Connell's

Photo of The O'Gorman Mahon, c. 1882

early associate, who once again represented Clare. His running mate in the election was the retired captain William O'Shea, recently returned from Spain, where he had squandered a fortune attempting to exploit minerals. Of course, the affair between O'Shea's future political leader and his wife Katharine would split the Home Rule Party. As it happens, William O'Shea's parents, Henry and the Countess Catherine O'Shea, lived in No. 38 Fitzwilliam Square between 1863 and 1870. The O'Gorman Mahon recognised in O'Shea a kindred adventurous spirit and the two were duly elected, being enthusiastic supporters of the New Departure. Kitty O'Shea recalled her first meeting with O'Gorman Mahon soon after the election:

> The O'Gorman Mahon was then a tall, handsome old man with a perfect snowstorm of white hair, and eyes merry and blue as those of a boy. He could look as fierce as an old eagle on occasion, however, and had fought in his day more duels than he could remember.

Both running mates had a confession to make, and O'Gorman Mahon felt Katharine should hear it from her husband.

> The O'Gorman Mahon electrified me by saying, 'Now Willie, 'twill slip easier into her ear from you!'

It was just that neither man was able to meet the expenses from the campaign and so they had to appeal to Kitty's wealthy aunt to help them out. During that same meeting O'Gorman Mahon referred to Parnell.

> 'If you meet Parnell, Mrs O'Shea, be good to him. His beg-
> ging expedition to America has about finished him, and I
> don't believe he'll last the session out.'[13]

Mrs. O'Shea introduced herself to Parnell within a few months of the new parliamentary session and they quickly embarked on a love affair. Captain O'Shea's discovery of the affair occurred within six months and he soon after challenged Parnell to a duel, sending O'Gorman Mahon as his second. Gwynn wrote:

> Few incidents in all O'Gorman Mahon's career are so much
> to his credit as that he should have accepted this thankless
> task of telling his political chief that he had outraged the
> laws of gentlemanly behaviour. If Parnell escaped the ne-
> cessity of meeting O'Shea in a duel, it would appear that his
> escape was entirely due to his own unblushing audacity in
> pretending that no illicit relationship existed between him-
> self and Mrs O'Shea.

A reconciliation between all parties was achieved in the summer of 1881, allowing Parnell and Mrs. O'Shea to secretly continue their relation-ship. O'Gorman Mahon and Captain O'Shea were assuaged by Parnell's assurances, to the point that they both worked hard to secure his release when he was imprisoned in Kilmainham Jail that October – O'Shea was the intermediary when the Kilmainham Treaty was drafted in April and May 1882. Even earlier, The O'Gorman Mahon had approached Joseph Chamberlain seeking the release of his party leader:

> Without hesitation, he promised in his own characteristic
> way ... that he would make himself personally responsible
> for Parnell's good behaviour if he were set free. Chamberlain,
> not unnaturally, asked how O'Gorman Mahon would ensure
> obedience.... O'Gorman Mahon retorted vehemently, 'By
> God! If he doesn't behave, sir, I will shoot him!' Chamberlain
> was perhaps unconvinced by that form of guarantee.[14]

Sir Charles Villiers Stanford

Within a week of Parnell's release the Phoenix Park murders took place. Frederick Cavendish and Thomas Henry Burke were assassinated with surgical knives at the hands of the radical Fenian group the Invincibles on 6 May 1882, outraging public opinion. In November that year the Invincibles attempted to strike again. This time their target was Judge James Anthony Lawson, who we can recall from Chapter 2 was Attorney General during the suppression of the *Irish People* newspaper and subsequent conviction of leading Fenians in 1865. The attempt on Lawson's life by the Invincible Patrick Delaney was foiled by a Fitzwilliam Square cabman, as outlined by Sir Charles Villiers Stanford (1852-1924). Stanford was an Irish-born composer of choral music and long-term professor of music at Cambridge. His mother lived at No. 26 Fitzwilliam Square on the south side throughout the 1880s. Stanford wrote in his *Pages from an Unwritten Diary*:

> During the troublous years in the early eighties, which came to a climax in the Phoenix Park murders, I had paid a few visits to Ireland. The developments which followed this crime came very near home to me, from an incident which closely affected my mother. She lived in Fitzwilliam Square, and had let her stables to a most respectable cab-proprietor who was wont to keep his cab at a stand at the corner of the square, from which the whole length of Fitzwilliam Street was visible. Mr. Justice Lawson, who with [William Edward] Forster and others was the most threatened man in Dublin, lived on the East side of the street, and used to start on foot every morning at 10.30 or so to walk to the Four Courts. One morning the cab-driver saw a doubtful-looking

person pacing up and down opposite Lawson's house, and guessed that he was up to mischief. He proved to have good reason for his suspicions. Shortly afterwards Lawson came out, and as he started towards Merrion Square the man shadowed him. But the cabman left his cab to chance, and followed them picking up a policeman as he went. Just as Lawson was passing Kildare Street Club, the assassin rushed at him with a knife, and was just seized in time by his two pursuers. The knife turned out to be one of the same make and pattern as those used in the Phoenix Park, and helped to convict the murderers. Shortly after, the cabman came to my mother and told her that he had been bombarded with so many threatening letters that he would have to leave the country, and she got up a private subscription to start him and his family in Canada.[15]

The effects of the Invincibles' violence reached throughout the decade, especially when *The Times* newspaper published a series of articles entitled 'Parnellism and Crime' in 1887. The paper printed facsimiles of letters forged by Richard Piggott, purporting to show that Parnell and other Home Rule leaders supported the extreme Fenian violence of the early part of the decade. In one of the forgeries, Parnell apparently wrote to Patrick Egan, then treasurer of the Land League:

> Though I regret the accident of Lord F Cavendish's death I cannot refuse to admit that Burke got no more than his deserts.

Parnell immediately denounced the letters as barefaced forgeries, but the matter was not fully investigated until a special parliamentary commission began sitting in September 1888, known now as the Parnell Commission. *The Times* was well aware that the letters would not stand up to scrutiny, so endeavoured to prove the substantive accusations in their reports: that Parnell and his associates in the Land League were inextricably linked to the militancy of the Fenians, and in particular the Invincibles. *The Times* solicitor Joseph Soames employed a series of solicitors' clerks in Dublin to procure evidence of conspiracy between the physical force and constitutional aspects of Irish nationalism.

One of those agents was John Walker, managing clerk of Robert Beauchamp, solicitor of Foster Place, who resided in No. 25 Fitzwilliam Square. In the course of his investigation, Walker made contact with a Fenian named Patrick Molloy in November 1888 and he would arrange to see this informant in his employer's Fitzwilliam Square home.

> We met and I asked him to come over to 25 Fitzwilliam Square. He came over with me and we went into Mr Beauchamp's study.[16]

Molloy thought Walker was interested in a book that he was canvassing, but Walker quickly told him he believed he had information relevant to the Commission. Molloy initially denied this but agreed to meet again in the same house at eight o'clock the next evening. Walker described that meeting:

> The study in which we were is connected with the dining room by folding doors and he asked, 'Is there anybody in the next room?' I said, 'I think not, but we can go in and see.' We both went in, and he took a look round and said, 'It is all right.' The folding doors were again closed and I asked him to tell me of his connection with the Fenians.

The Parnell Commission

Molloy told Walker that he had been a Fenian since he was sixteen years old and had joined the Invincibles in 1882.

> He told me of meetings of the Invincibles that he had been at. He told me of one in the Winter Palace Garden [pub on St. Stephen's Green], when Judge Lawson's [attempted] murder was discussed. I asked him was it the way it was to be done that was discussed. He said, 'No, the place and time. Those who were to do it knew how.'

What a curious coincidence. In the parlour of No. 25 they discussed an attempt at murder foiled by the cabman of No. 26. Molloy claimed that Patrick Egan of the Land League attended these meetings and Walker, eager to establish this link between the League and the murders, asked if he was sure. Molloy replied, 'Perfectly, I know the man well'. However Molloy would not commit his statement to writing until he received guarantees that both he and his parents would be moved from Dublin and their expenses covered. Walker contacted Soames in London to make these arrangements and met Molloy again some days later. Once more they were in Fitzwilliam Square, but Molloy would not speak until he could confirm Walker's identity. Walker told him he was currently in the house of Robert Beauchamp and if he went to his office in Foster Place that gentleman would identify him. Molloy did so and it was arranged they would meet again at No. 25 that evening.

Walker received Molloy in Beauchamp's study once more. He rang a bell and asked a servant to bring Mr. Beauchamp down. Beauchamp entered his study and addressed the informant:

> 'This is Mr Walker, who is acting for the Times, and whatever he says to you will be all right.'

Molloy said that he was fully satisfied and Mr Beauchamp withdrew. Still ill at ease, Molloy went through the folding-doors into the dining room, looked around, snapped his fingers and listened. Who knows what he hoped to achieve by this. Perhaps he wished to trigger an unwitting response from an eavesdropper; perhaps he felt he could tell if they were alone by the echo; or perhaps he was engaging in some conspiratorial theatre. Walker asked if everything was all right and

Molloy said, 'Yes'. All the doors to the room were locked. Walker took some paper from the desk and asked Molloy to dictate his statement. Walker began writing the informer's name, writing a capital 'P' and lower case 'a' for Patrick, but Molloy refused to allow this. In the statement his name was replaced by the random letter 'A', but Walker kept the original page with the crossed out 'Pa…', and this was subsequently used in evidence. Molloy dictated the statement he had given to Walker some nights before: that he had attended meetings with Patrick Egan during which the assassination of Judge Lawson was planned, and details of other interactions with the Invincibles. When his statement was complete, both men read it over. Molloy was uneasy. Walker asked how he had managed to drift into this way of life and said, 'It is a wretched business altogether'. Molloy looked at his questioner. 'No one can tell how I got into it. Some have made their thousands by it.' He picked up his statement again and slowly leafed through the pages. 'And some have got the rope.'

Molloy was subpoenaed to appear before the Parnell Commission in December 1888 when his evidence would be considered. His appearance elicited some considerable excitement. John McDonald in his *Diary of the Parnell Commission* wrote:

> Patrick Molloy had for some time been exciting curiosity. He has been described as a Times 'dark horse' – as one who could throw strong light on past relations between the leaguers and the invincibles. On the other hand, it had been reported in Dublin that Molloy amused one of The Times agents with imaginary tales, which he would disavow in the witness-box.[17]

Molloy's first appearance was on 6 December to answer why he had at first ignored his summons. Molloy said he had not been given sufficient money to cover his expenses, in which opinion the commission president Sir James Hannen did not concur. Molloy was committed to prison until further notice. His testimony began in earnest the following day.

> When the usher called out for Patrick Molloy, every eye was turned to the entrance through which Mr Patrick Mol-

loy was composedly elbowing his way in the custody of a police officer. Handing his coat to somebody – with the air of a grand duke attended by his valet – Mr Molloy as composedly walked into the witness-box.

He was asked to state his address.

'Well,' replied Mr Molloy, 'my present address is Holloway Gaol, London.' The ghost of a flicker of a smile passes over the usually rigid features of Mr Justice Day.

John Walker sat with the solicitor for *The Times* facing his informant in the witness box. He must have awaited Molloy's evidence eagerly but he was to be bitterly disappointed, indeed humiliated. For Molloy completely disavowed everything he had told Walker in Mr. Beauchamp's Fitzwilliam Square house. The Attorney General kept up a long line of questioning:

But here, in the witness-box, was Patrick Molloy absolutely, contemptuously denying – in his long string of negative answers – that he had said this, that, and the other thing to The Times agent a week or two ago in Dublin. He was charged with having said in Dublin that he was a Fenian. Here he averred that the charge was a fabrication. Nor did he know Carey the [1882] informer – 'never knew the man in my life' – nor was it true that that paper (nodding at it carelessly) from which the Attorney General was reading had been written in his presence; nor was it true that The Times agent read it to him for his approval; nor did he read it himself.

Eventually, in exasperation, Molloy referred directly to Walker, with whom he had been in such close cahoots in No. 25:

'Ach!' said he, pointing carelessly with his thumb to Mr Walker, who sat on the solicitors' bench, 'that man thought I knew a lot about the Fenians, and that I could tell lots of things about Davitt and all that; they supposed I knew a great deal' – and here Mr Molloy laughed, privately, as it were, holding his head down, balancing himself on his elbows, and slowly rubbing his palms together.

Molloy was asked directly if he had been humbugging *The Times* agent. 'Yes, I was humbugging him'. We can imagine what John Walker must have made of this testimony, being taken for a fool in front of the assembled galleries and media. He had no opportunity to slink away however, as he was called immediately after Molloy.

> The last act in this funny piece – about the funniest piece since the trial began – was short. Mr Walker, entering the witness-box, seemed somewhat embarrassed – which was natural, under the circumstances. He informed Sir Richard Webster that the person from whom he got Molloy's name was a Mr. Houston, of the Irish Loyal and Patriotic Union. [Edward Caulfield Houston was the man who originally sold Piggott's forgeries to The Times for £2,530.] 'Our time wasted,' the President remarked. And so the whole case, in so far as the ingenious Molloy was for the time being concerned, fell to the ground. Molloy, from his place in the crowd, watched the collapse.

The statement coaxed from or concocted by Molloy in the locked study of No. 25 Fitzwilliam Square exposed the weak position of *The Times*, relying on crude forgeries and paid turncoats. Walker at least had the satisfaction of seeing Molloy subsequently sentenced to six months' hard labour for perjury. The case against Parnell ultimately collapsed when the forger Piggott was exposed, fled to Spain and committed suicide. Lyons wrote:

> The Liberals exulted and when Parnell first appeared in the House after the Pigott fiasco Gladstone led them in a standing ovation; Parnell, who knew his Englishmen almost as much as he hated them, totally ignored their plaudits and thus mounted higher in their esteem.[18]

Parnell's triumph was short-lived. In December 1889, William O'Shea filed for divorce from his wife Katharine, citing Parnell as co-respondent. The case wasn't heard until November the following year. Gladstone warned that if Parnell remained as leader they could not hope to oust the Conservatives at the next election. During the meetings of the Irish Parliamentary Party to discuss Parnell's leadership,

Parnell dismissed Gladstone's interference by saying, 'Who is the master of the party?' The MP Timothy Healy quipped in response, 'Who is the mistress of the party?' earning a strong rebuke from a disgusted Parnell. Healy continued to strongly condemn Parnell and his new wife in a number of public speeches. After one such address in Longford in November 1891, some months after Parnell's death, Healy was assaulted in the corridors of the Four Courts by a Fitzwilliam Square resident. His attacker was Tudor McDermott of No. 43, son of the late Sophia McDermott and Parnell's nephew. Incensed at Healy's continued vitriol, he awaited him in the passage leading to the coffee room. He grabbed Healy by the collar and proceeded to horsewhip him around the shoulders, body and legs – avoiding the face because Healy was wearing glasses. As can be imagined, this remarkable scene caused quite a stir in the Four Courts. According to *The Irish Times*, McDermott only stopped when a policeman arrived on the scene.

> McDermott presented his card to the constable observing – 'I am after giving Healy a damn fine thrashing. He'll tell you the reason why.'[19]

Healy did not hand McDermott into custody and so the latter was allowed to return home. McDermott's actions garnered much sympathy from Parnellites. At a meeting of the Irish National League reports of Healy's chastisement were met with loud cheers. The American-born artist James McNeill Whistler sent the following telegram to McDermott at No. 43 Fitzwilliam Square:

> A Gentleman's impulse is always the right one. Your delightful act is a perfect example of this beautiful and offensive truth. Permit me also to add my warmest sympathies and hearty congratulations to the many you must have received.[20]

It seems odd to recall that Tudor McDermott was, as a child, spirited through the garden of that Fitzwilliam Square house with his young siblings by his frantic mother and aunt, escaping from the demented Captain Dickenson who was attempting to break in through the front door.

A Witness to the Rising

Parnell's party came within a whisker of achieving Home Rule in 1914 but their efforts were overtaken by international and then national events. Fitzwilliam Square was little affected by the Rising in 1916, despite its proximity to the fighting. In the vicinity, the most famous flashpoints were St Stephen's Green, where the Citizens Army under Mallin and Markievicz dug in; Boland's Bakery on Grand Canal Street, where the 3rd Battalion of Volunteers were under the command of de Valera; and the battle of Mount Street Bridge, where by far the largest number of casualties were inflicted on British forces during the whole of the Rising. One of the houses on the south side of the square, No. 32, was temporarily used as a field hospital during the fighting. The solicitor Robert Warren Meade had purchased the house in 1871. His daughters were living there in 1916, when 25 beds were employed to treat combatants. Neighbours of the Meade sisters in part donated the necessary food and bedding.

During the centenary commemorations of the Rising in 2016, a re-markable document came to light: an eye witness account of the rebellion written by a Fitzwilliam Square inhabitant, Arthur Matheson of No. 20.

The barrister Charles Louis Matheson, his wife Elinor, and their young children moved in to No. 20 in 1889. The 1901 census notes that the eldest son Arthur was a law student at the turn of the century. Twin sisters Eileen and Mary were 20 years old, and the youngest son was Charles Frederick, aged 8.

There was also a daughter not present on the day of the census: Vera Matheson, born 1884, who later won a scholarship to Trinity College where she studied French and modern literature. Elinor, the mother, died in July 1911. Of the twins, Eileen married Charles Thompson, but she died in 1913. Mary married a man named Wilson and left Dublin altogether. Arthur graduated from Trinity College in 1903, attended King's Inns and was called to the Inner Bar. At the outbreak of war in Europe, Vera joined the Red Cross as a nurse, and she was stationed in London in April 1916.

During the Easter Rising, Charles L. Matheson was still residing in No. 20 with his ward, Kathleen Russell, and his son, Arthur, now a qualified barrister. As fighting raged in the city, Arthur wrote an account from No. 20, intended as a letter to his sister Vera. The eleven-page document, now in the possession of Marie Carroll, a relation of Arthur Matheson, is a remarkable artefact, detailing the uncertainty and fear that gripped Dublin's citizens, the hazards of living so close to the gunfire, the daily search for news and household supplies, and the destruction that was visited upon the city.

Arthur began by saying that he was sick over Easter weekend, and so was confined to bed on Easter Monday:

During that Monday morning we had a lot of shooting but did not know what it was until Father went for a stroll in the afternoon and came back and told us that the Sinn Fein Volunteers had risen and seized Stephens Green, the General Post Office and several other buildings.

To some degree he was relying on second hand accounts and rumour. The idea that Sinn Féin was behind the Rising was a common misconception at the time. In the passage below, he mistakenly believes that Francis Sheehy Skeffington was commanding the rebels in St Stephen's Green.

> The Sinn Feiners in the Green were under the command of Sheehy-Skeffington and Countess Markowitz (sic) – the latter was marching about in male clothes and was seen shooting at some officers in Khaki. The Sinn Feiners on Monday shot all soldiers in Khaki who were peacefully walking about the streets, and also a number of civilians both men and women. They probably killed about fifty soldiers that way and anything up to a hundred civilians – the shooting civilians was a great mistake on their part as it turned the popular feeling against them.
>
> . . .
>
> On Tuesday the provision shops were open & it was quite possible to walk about the streets, & I believe there were crowds everywhere, walking & talking quietly and peaceably – but feeling was strong and unanimous against the Sinn Feiners.
>
> . . .
>
> I was up on Wednesday morning and went out with Kathleen to market . . . The fighting then appeared to be getting brisk at the bottom of Harcourt Street (at the Stephens Green end) and also to be coming down from Portobello Barracks. Kathleen got a bit frightened, & no wonder as there was a lot of shooting & noise which sounded very close – so we went down Hatch Street & so home without adventure, except that there were several shots which appeared to be within a few yards of us. That was our last excursion except to market in the mornings. Kathleen fortunately got a good fright which has restrained her curiosity

– & personally I can control my curiosity very easily when there are bullets flying around. Father however goes out exploring constantly – and there are crowds in the streets watching the fighting as if it was a football match. Several have been injured as a consequence, and the wonder is that more have not been killed.

. . .

The Square is quite quiet, people strolling about & chatting, the weather gloriously fine – & all the time within half a mile all round there is almost continuous firing, rifles, machine guns & some artillery.

There has been heavy fighting on Wednesday & Thursday on the bit of Northumberland Road between Haddington Road & the Canal – & a good deal of casualties – & all the time a large crowd on Baggot Street Bridge watching it.

Last night (Thursday-Friday) there was heavy fighting in the city & a huge fire. So far as we can ascertain Sackville Street has been burnt down from Clery's to O Connell Bridge on that (Clery's) side. How much has been burnt on the other side is not known. Practically every shop in the city has been looted. Until last night there were no soldiers in the streets except at a few places where there was actual fighting – & of course no Police – so the scum of the city were free to do their worst. Fortunately they did not come into this District.

(N.B. a bullet whizzed across in front of this my study window a moment ago, not close)

The rebels . . . are a mixture of Socialists, anarchists, disloyal rebels, & visionaries & fanatics. The wonder is that the rebellion did not fail through internal disputes – but in my opinion the rebels do not represent any section of Irish people or opinion except themselves.

I am continuing this on Saturday April 29th.

During the past twenty-four hours our chief anxiety has been "food and how to obtain it". No bakers came round yesterday and we only got two loaves which Father bought by a stroke of luck at Johnston Mooney & O'Brien's bakery

Ballsbridge. I went to the said bakery before breakfast this morning but could get no bread. There was a crowd of about 200 people waiting at the bakery, but it was shut & no bread being sold.

. . .

A curious incident occurred this morning – Kathleen & I were looking out of my bedroom window about eight o'clock when we saw a party of about a dozen (estimates vary considerably) (somebody counted seventeen) Sinn Feiners ride up Upper Fitzwilliam Street on bicycles & go round the North & East sides of the Square & disappear into Upper Pembroke Street. Most of them were in civilian clothes but all had rifles & bandoliers or bags of ammunition. There was nobody about except servant maids cleaning steps etc. & of course there were no soldiers.

Nothing further happened & nobody knows where the Sinn Feiners came from or where they went to – though it is generally believed that they are a party come up from Wicklow or Wexford to join the rebels in Dublin.

. . .

We are getting pretty used to the firing now – personally it does not affect me at all & does not keep me awake – but it is rather getting on Father's nerves, & both he and Kathleen still jump when they hear a shot closer than usual - & it keeps them awake at night.

Once the morning's marketing is over time hangs rather heavy on us as there is nothing to do or see - & there is no use going out to the streets to talk to people as nobody has any reliable news.

. . .

I am continuing this on Sunday 30th April.

Yesterday (Saturday) afternoon about 5.30 we heard that the leaders of the rebels had surrendered unconditionally . . . Though the fighting is not over, the surrender has had a very soothing effect on Father & Kathleen. She slept like a top without taking any drugs, & is quite calm & unexcited this morning – and Father is not so worried or irritable which is a good thing.

. . .

I continue this on Monday 1st May.

Yesterday (Sunday) afternoon, Father, Kathleen and I went into town and Father met a solicitor who gave him a lot of reliable information. What we saw ourselves is, there are only a few bullet holes in the windows of the Shelbourne Hotel and the United Service Club. There are bullet marks all over the College of Surgeons & the windows thereof . . . On the other side of Sackville Street the G.P.O. is burnt down, only the front wall & the pillars are left standing. Every house from Abbey Street to the G.P.O. is burnt down including Mansfield's shoe shop, Eason's and the whole of the Metropole Hotel. We are told a lot of Henry Street is burnt but we did not see it. Stephens Green was locked but we could see the trenches dug at the four corners with rugs & cushions taken from motor cars still in them.

. . .

The Police are about in plain clothes assisting the military – & suspected houses are being visited and searched.

I have been going round the house & stables making all locks & bolts secure & am going to fasten up the window opening on to the roof. We are afraid of wandering Sinn Feiners trying to get in to the house at night for food or shelter.

Tuesday 2nd May.

There was a lot of excitement round here yesterday (Monday) afternoon. There was a lot of shooting quite close to here about lunchtime – and in the afternoon the military stopped all traffic in Fitzwilliam Place and started a thorough search of the block of houses from Littledale's to Sir William Watson's. They entered several houses and went all over the roofs most carefully & apparently searched the stables also . . . Sniping started from somewhere near here and the military fired back & then searched our roofs and the roofs of other blocks round about. There was a lot of shooting for a bit and it continued at intervals until long after dark. I don't know whether they caught the snipers or not, but there are no military around this morning.

...

Everything is quiet today but ordinary life has not yet been resumed. The shops are still shut & the provision shops still have their shutters down & only let customers in by side or wicket doors. Provisions are obtainable in small quantities. We are fortunately alright in that respect. There has been no delivery of bread for several days but we have been able to get plenty of flour and our present cook makes very good bread.

The damage in Sackville Street is more extensive than we thought. On Clery's side everything from & including Lawrence's toy shop to O Connell Bridge is burnt down including unfortunately Robert's office which is very bad luck on him. On the other side the damage extends from Henry Street to Elvery's. There are several shops burnt on both sides of both Middle & Lower Abbey Streets. Also a considerable number of shops in Henry Street including the Coliseum & Hamptom Leedoms but apparently not including any of the big drapery shops.

Father & I and some other members of the Library Committee are going down tomorrow to the Four Courts to take over the Library from the military. I hear that most of the chairs & windows are broken but very little damage.

The destruction in Sackville Street, May 1916

For the past hour (8.0 to 9.0 p.m.) there has been a heavy exchange of shots between a sniper and the military very close behind the house. We heard a bullet 'whining' past just outside the window.

I hear the postal arrangements will be working tomorrow so I will close this 'letter'.

Your loving brother

Arthur.[21]

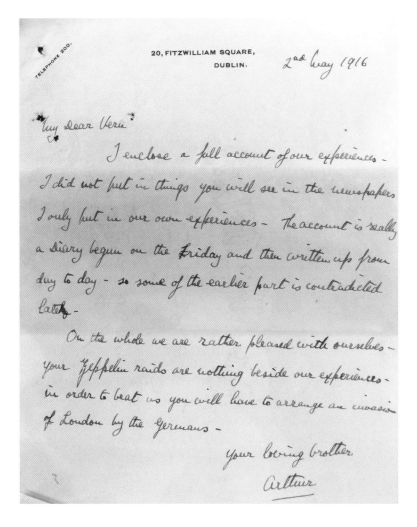

The cover note of Arthur Matheson's eleven-page letter to his sister Vera, 2 May 1916
© Marie Carroll – not to be reproduced without permission

In April 1920, No. 20 was sold at public auction and the remainder of the Mathesons moved away. For the last few years of his life, Charles L Matheson acted as the Recorder, or principal magistrate, of Belfast. He died in that city on 20 May 1921, aged 70.

Arthur Matheson was about to embark on a new career, that of parliamentary draftsman for the Provisional Government of the Irish Free State. An 'appreciation' of Arthur printed in the *Irish Times* following his death in 1948, said, 'When the position was offered to Matheson his inclination must have been to refuse. He belonged to a family whose political traditions were Unionist . . . But his sense of public spirit outweighed these and other merely personal considerations, and he answered the call.'[22]

Matheson's office diaries, covering the years 1923 to 1943, are preserved in the National Archives. Though his main task was in drafting bills and legislation for Dáil Éireann, he was closely involved in the wording of the 1937 Constitution. He had ten conferences with Eamon de Valera that year, and when Matheson retired in 1943, the Taoiseach wrote to him, saying it was, 'recognised in all quarters that from the beginning, you set a very high standard of draftsmanship in our statutes and statutory instruments.' De Valera particularly thanked him for the help that he 'gave so freely in the preparation of the new Constitution.' [23]

Earlier in Matheson's career, Senator Lombard praised his ability and professionalism:

> During six years of rather hurried and most difficult legislation, including the Land Act, the Courts of Justice Act, and the Property Act, that includes patents and copyright and several other things, and hundreds of other Acts that have been passed, and that have gone through our draftsman's office, there has been only one case in which the meaning of a section has had to be interpreted by the Court. That is a wonderful tribute to our draftsman.[24]

In the subsequent years of the War of Independence increasing numbers of flats in Fitzwilliam Square houses saw the infiltration of nationalist conspirators into this unionist stronghold. As we shall see,

No. 5 in particular was a safe house, frequently used by Eamon de Valera. For a brief time the clandestine newspaper of the *Dáil,* the *Irish Bulletin,* was produced from a Fitzwilliam Square flat. The main force behind the publication was Kathleen McKenna Napoli, who kept a typesetter and duplicator in the flat in the months after the truce of July 1921. We can imagine that extraordinary woman cranking out gazettes for the republic's new ministry for publicity in that small apartment. A tightening net of British spies saw the office and printing equipment transported to No. 11 Molesworth Street in October 1921.

Eric J. Arnott wrote about his good friend Gary Trimble, the Irish sculptor, in his book *A New Beginning in Sight*:

> [Trimble's] family was very sympathetic to the Irish cause and, as a boy, he could remember hiding under his parents' dining-room table in Fitzwilliam Square, Dublin, while Michael Collins, one of the great Irish patriots at the time of the revolution, talked to his parents.[25]

However, a quick check reveals that Trimble was born in 1928, so it seems he was pulling his friend's leg. Members of Collins' IRA squad were in Fitzwilliam Square on the morning of Bloody Sunday, 21 November 1920, when British agents were targeted for assassination throughout the city in a coordinated attack. Edward Hyams described the event:

> That the terrorists were not simply killing at random is clear from the case of Captain Crawford whom they found in bed with his wife in their flat in Fitzwilliam Square. They asked him if he was Major Callaghan – the man on their list – being apparently unsure of his identity. He told them his name, and asked them if they were going to kill him to do it downstairs and not in front of his wife. They asked for his papers and from them it was clear that he was a Captain Crawford of the RAMC and that his duties were connected to motor transport. They asked him why he could not have stayed at home in his own country and left the Irish in peace in theirs, returned his papers, and told him if he was not out of Ireland within twenty-four hours they would return and shoot him.[26]

Crawford took them at their word. This was not the only time Collins dispatched his squad to the square. F.O.C. Meenan relates a tale by David Neligan, who was an Irish spy in Dublin Castle:

> Neligan was assigned by the Castle authorities to guard Thomas O'Shaughnessy, the last Recorder of Dublin, who lived at No. 64 Fitzwilliam Square [dubbed "the hangman's friend" by *An Phoblacht*, as described in Chapter 2]. O'Shaughnessy's daughter was marrying a British army officer, and to the reception which was to be held in the house were invited Sir Hamar Greenwood, Sir John Anderson, Generals MacCready and Tudor. Not unnaturally, Michael Collins thought this was an excellent opportunity of getting rid of the Castle authorities at one fell swoop, and his special squad was dispatched to Fitzwilliam Square where they patrolled in two's and three's around the south side waiting for the arrival of the guests. Neligan was to tip them off when they arrived. Apparently Sir Hamar and his colleagues must have smelled a rat or possibly thought that the Recorder's champagne was not worth the risk of a bullet. In any case they only sent their secretaries. Neligan slipped out of the house and informed the squad that the special guests were not coming. It must have been rather an unusual sight to see the squad parading around the square with their hands deep in their pockets and mixing with the ordinary sedate inhabitants of the Square.[27]

If the raid had taken place I wonder what The O'Gorman Mahon might have thought of the resulting bloodbath in his old house at No. 64. Interestingly, Neligan mistakenly believed that three of the killings on Bloody Sunday had taken place at O'Shaughnessy's house. He wrote:

> At breakfast the next morning in the Castle [Chief Inspector of 'G' Division John] Bruton entered. His face was white. "Terrible work in the City", he said, "a crowd of Army men murdered in their beds". I went to O'Shaughnessy's house in Fitzwilliam Square. Two British Army ambulances stood in the Street. R.A.M.C. men brought a stretcher out or the house. On it lay an inert figure. Three

times they entered and emerged with a similar burden. Auxiliaries arrived and held up a crowd of staring loungers. In that house three executions had taken place.[28]

As Meenan mentioned above, Neligan had been assigned to guard Thomas O'Shaughnessy, so he would not have mistaken his house. The bodies he witnessed were most likely victims of the attacks in nearby Pembroke Street and Baggot Street, brought to No. 64 for a short time before their removal.

In the previous chapter we mentioned Dr Denis Coffey of No. 41 Fitzwilliam Square, president of University College Dublin from 1908 to 1940. He was well-known in the locality, particularly for the cab he kept to take him to nearby Earlsfort Terrace, daily. Mark Tierney OSB of Glenstal Abbey grew up in Baggot Street, but played with other children of the locality in the garden of Fitzwilliam Square. He recalled Mr Coffey:

> Dr Denis Coffey went from No. 41 each morning to UCD, where he was President. He had his butler stand at the hall door and call for 'Healy and the mare'. The cab was an enclosed one, well-known to all the residents, and parked most of the time outside the Coffeys' house, though others used the cab betimes.

In 1921 a force of British soldiers descended on UCD to demand the names and addresses of students suspected of IRA activity from the college roll. Mary Macken wrote:

> The President had not yet come in. The O.C. had him summoned. He arrived in the historic horse-cab. He was wearing a tall hat. As a symbol and gesture in an age of tanks and steel helmets, it was perfect. The O.C., asking for the student roll, was told that it was in 41 Fitzwilliam Square. Trust that wise white head! His 'wanted' young men must not be so easily identified.[29]

Meenan wrote that Coffey was simply escorted by armoured car to retrieve the roll, but perhaps the delay was enough to alert those who were to be identified.

The Safe House

LET US RETURN TO NO. 5 FITZWILLIAM SQUARE, once the home of Chief Justice Edward Pennefather. By 1917 the house was owned by Margaret McGarry, a remarkable woman who was one of the founding members of Cumann na mBán, a courier for the Volunteers during the Easter Rising, and later a Sinn Féin Councillor in Dublin Corporation. To give a sense of her personality, in December 1922 a meeting of Dublin Corporation was raided by Auxiliaries looking for IRA man Sean McGarry, who was of no relation. When the police barked out the name 'McGarry', another councillor stated that he wasn't present, at which point Mrs McGarry put up her hand and said, 'Perhaps they meant me.'[30]

At the start of the War of Independence she was asked by ministers of the first Dáil for permission to use No. 5 as a headquarters and meeting place. De Valera in particular used No. 5 as a safe house and office space.

How the MacGarrys came to live in No. 5 was described by Margaret's daughter Maeve in her 1953 witness statement to the Bureau of Military History:

> Before the Rising my mother was negotiating about a house in the Square – No. 5 – and she got possession of it in the autumn of 1917. Countess Plunkett pointed out that she was giving herself an awful lot of trouble because the house was too big. My mother intended to let the top part of the house in flats and to live in the remainder . . . In 1918 and 1919 there were many Sinn Féin and Dáil meetings in No. 5. Joe Reilly [a member of Collins' squad] was a constant visitor and so was Diarmuid Hegarty [IRA Director of Communications], bringing messages. Terence McSwiney [the Sinn Féin Lord Mayor of Cork, who died while on hunger strike in Brixton Prison, 25 October 1920] had lunch there; he was meeting some friends from America; that must have been in 1918. When the Dáil Loan campaign was started, people – priests principally – came from the country with their collections. My mother collected quite a lot of gold. No. 5 was one of the places where the Dáil used to meet, some-

times the whole Dáil and sometimes only the members of the Cabinet.[31]

Some events in No. 5 were not quite so furtive. In May 1919, three members of the American Commission for Irish Independence – Frank Walsh, Edward Dunne, and Michael Ryan – were feted by the Dáil in the Mansion House, followed by a banquet in Fitzwilliam Square. In his witness statement, Maeve's brother Milo McGarry wrote:

> They stayed in our house – No. 5 – because there was a hotel strike on in Dublin and also de Valera occupied a flat there as his office and occasional residence. A large banquet was given in their honour, to which the Dáil Cabinet and members of other public bodies – about eighty in all – were invited. They visited the gaols and they also took evidence from various important people, as a result of which they published a most damning report against the British Government. Lloyd George made this an excuse for refusing to receive them again. It was within a week of their departure from Dublin that de Valera went secretly to England, disguised himself as a stoker, and sailed on a ship bound for America. Griffith did not know of his departure. He called to inquire for him and was astonished not to find him.[32]

Maeve McGarry recalled the night of the banquet:

> This entailed a lot of work and a good deal of it fell on me although I got help from various people. Countess Plunkett and the boys were most helpful. My mother had only two days' notice to prepare the house. We were all shunted out of our bedrooms to make room for the three delegates, their secretary, Mr. Lee, and a Mr. Walsh from Canada, who was a prominent journalist and wanted to report on the Irish situation. He was not very favourable to us when he came first, but he went away very changed, full of admiration for the marvellous movement that was evident in Ireland ... The Dáil gave a reception in the Mansion House and a dinner at our house for the Delegates. We had a great big crowd in the house that night for the dinner which was supplied by Mitchell's. It was I did all the cooking for the rest of their stay. My mother and Frank P. Walsh used to stay

up till three or four in the morning talking about Ireland.
He was a noble character.

No. 5 was also the location where de Valera gave the following famous piece of advice to IRA Chief of Staff Richard Mulcahy. Risteárd
Mulcahy quoted his father:

> Dev was arrested in May 1918 and from that time until he
> returned from America on 24 December 1920, the only re-
> vealing contact I had with him was at 3 Fitzwilliam Square
> [(sic) it was almost certainly No. 5], before he went to
> America, that is say April or May 1919, when out of the blue
> in a casual conversation for a few minutes in the hall of the
> house at Fitzwilliam Square, the president, soon to depart
> for the States said to the chief of staff of the army, "You
> are a young man now going in for politics, I'll give you two
> pieces of advice, study economics and read the Prince".
>
> - Dad became interested in economics in his later parlia-
> mentary years but probably never read "The Prince". At
> least there is no copy of the book in his library![33]

Following de Valera's departure for his American tour in early
June 1919, the space in No. 5 was occasionally used by Michael Collins. Witness statements in the Bureau of Military History tell of men
reporting to Collins in Fitzwilliam Square to receive orders, and a raid
on the office in which IRA intelligence reports were concealed beneath
a hearthrug. Patrick J. Kelly, a 1st Lieutenant in the Dublin Brigade of
the IRA, wrote that in 1920 he and other members of the squad were
dispatched to Fitzwilliam Square to intercept a photographer who had
snapped a picture of Collins.

> We were all on bicycles and patrolled the neighbourhood
> but did not locate the photographer. After contacting Pea-
> dar Clancy we were told the photographer had left for the
> mail boat at Dun Laoghaire. Peadar instructed me to take
> the squad to the mail boat and try to capture the camera.
> We rode from Fitzwilliam Square to Dun Laoghaire in
> thirty minutes. On arrival there we met Peadar Breslin, A
> Company, who told us the boat was about to sail and that
> the photographer had not arrived. Peadar Clancy sent for

Joe Dodd and I next day. He told us that the photographer had got to the Castle with his camera, that he would be leaving there about 4 o'clock p.m. that day with the camera and photographs for British General Headquarters. He was to be on foot and we were to intercept him on Cork Hill. We failed here also.[34]

De Valera returned from his American mission in December 1920, and No. 5 once again became his temporary residence. Its utility as a safe house was demonstrated by an incident in February 1921. De Valera had been staying the night in Loughnavale, Strand Road, Merrion – another residence owned by Margaret McGarry. Maeve McGarry wrote:

> A car came out for him to bring him in to No. 5 Fitzwilliam Square to meet Joe Devlin and Sean McEntee on some important matter. Devlin was staying at the time with some lame doctor in Merrion Square whose name I can't remember. De Valera asked me to accompany him. As we came to Ballsbridge, we saw the military holding up and searching the cars. We asked de Valera to search quickly to see had he anything on him but he hadn't. We slowed down and prayed for guidance in our dilemma. Just before we arrived at the spot, the military decided to stop the searching and moved off. We careered then down Pembroke Road, turned into Wilton Place, got out of the car to walk down Lad Lane and get in through the stables, at No. 5, where somebody was waiting to lead us in. Just then an ambush took place on Leeson Street Bridge. That was one of the routes we could have travelled. The firing was going on as we went down Lad Lane and, when we arrived at the house, my young sister led us in. She gripped De Valera's arm, saying, "You are safe now".

The most significant army raid on No. 5 occurred on 16 April 1921, when members of the 'F' Division of the Auxiliaies descended on the house in armoured vehicles. In her witness statement, Maeve McGarry described how her mother managed to slip from the house unnoticed:

> My mother was in the Corporation and a Councillor for the Fitzwilliam ward since 1919. She had just come home from

a meeting and was having a cup of tea, talking to the house-keeper, when the military broke in. She had an important paper in her bag and wondered where she would hide it. She stuck it down her blouse. She concluded from the intensity of the raids on the Fitzwilliam Street and Square houses that the Castle had some reliable information. Fresh rein-forcements of armoured cars, etc., kept coming along. So she uttered a fervent prayer, put on her hat and coat, walked coolly down the stairs, though the military and Auxiliaries were in every room and on the stairs – they had burst in the back and come up the garden – and she passed through the midst of them out the door. She could not make it out at all. They did not seem to see her. She said herself it was a miracle in answer to her prayer. She went by tram straight out to Loughnavale on the Strand.

Mrs McGarry knew that de Valera, Collins and Cathal Brugha were meeting in the house in Merrion. She warned them of the raid on No. 5, and of the likelihood that some mention of Loughnavale would be found among her papers, and so all the men cleared out.

The McGarrys also owned No. 31 Upper Fitzwilliam Street. Maeve wrote:

> They also searched every room and questioned everyone in the main house of No. 31, but found nothing there, although Fiona Plunkett and I and an engineering student called Har-nett – a brother of Nellie Harnett's – had hidden some gre-nades and ammunition under the boards in the bathroom. I have one of the grenade cases still as a memento.

In the British National Archives in Kew there are a set of papers en-titled 'Easter Rising and Ireland under martial law', including British reports of those same raids on 16 April 1921. An officer from F Com-pany of the Auxiliary Division wrote: 'In accordance with instructions I proceeded with a party of the Company to this address, and in the flat occupied by Mrs McGarry seditious literature was found. This was loaded in one of the tenders and conveyed direct to the Castle.'[35]

Rather sneakily, the same company raided the house again at 10.30 pm that evening to see if anyone had visited in the meantime.

The interaction of Maeve McGarry and the raiding party was detailed in the report:[36]

(7). GENERAL REPORT showing :--

                      To see if anyone had visited these premises.
(a) Reason for Search ;   after the previous raid.
(b) Composition of Search Party ;
(c) Incidents of Search ;   Armoured Car-Officers Cadets "P"Coy
                          Aux Div R.I.C.
(d) Disposal of Persons arrested (if any).
                          Nil.

The room in which we found the documents during the previous raid had been securely fastened up by the occupants of the house. In No 5 Miss McGarry stated that she was glad that we had returne as some jewellery and money had been stolen in the afternoon. When asked to enumerate the articles missing she mentioned a pearl and diamond pendant and £4 in notes.in a wallet. I informed her that I held a receipt for all the jewellery found and took her upstairs to the bedroom and pointed out to her the pendant and notes which were on the table. She then stated that she had not looked in that particular box.

A thorough search of the premises yielded no results.

Mrs McGarry had not returned home

Three days later, an M. McGarry, either Mrs McGarry or her daughter, was required to put in writing that no property had been taken from the house, and no unnecessary damage done. The jotted note also survives in the archives. One wonders if it was written under a certain amount of duress.

> I certify that nothing was taken away a no damage don (except breaking to glass windows + pulling up one floor board)
>
> 19/4/21. M. MacGarry

The use of No. 5 Fitzwilliam Square by Dáil ministers was the subject of a court case settled in 1926. Minister for Finance Ernest Blythe claimed a sum of £2,500 against Mrs McGarry as having been lent to her by Dáil trustees. In the course of the action the use of No. 5 was set out:

> In April 1919 Mr de Valera, Mr Michael Collins and Mr Arthur Griffith, acting on behalf of their Government, requested her to let her house, 5 Fitzwilliam Square, Dublin, as a meeting place for the Ministers of Dáil Éireann and as one of the headquarters of the Government...for the use of the Ministers, their associates and visitors. Board, lodging and attendance were provided for the use of the Ministers and visitors to them from the provinces and America, and also accommodation for associates of the Ministers then "on the run."[37]

In her defence Mrs McGarry claimed the money was not a loan but had been given to her by Collins to cover her expenses. Counsel for the Finance Minister stated that, 'it was never the intention to cast any reflection whatever on the *bona fides* of Mrs McGarry. They appreciated her services to the State, and he desired to say that the action had not been brought with the object of in any way belittling those services'. The case was settled with Mrs McGarry repaying £1,000 to the Dáil.

Conclusion

When Edward Pennefather was retiring to No. 5 each evening, while presiding over the trial of Daniel O'Connell in 1844, he surely could not have imagined the use to which his grand house would eventually be put: a meeting place and safe house for a revolutionary government. It goes to show that any house, street, or square can contain extraordinary and incongruous tales of loyalty and sedition, temperance and revelry, commerce and letters. In various guises Fitzwilliam Square residents were witness to the great set-pieces of Irish history, on the hustings, the battlefield, in the courthouse, the parliament house and the safe house. We followed one unsympathetic landlord to meet his demise on his estates at the hands of his desperate tenants and a humble Fitzwilliam Square cabman who took it upon himself to foil a

Fenian assassination. We followed an agent and his informer into the sanctuary of a locked study where a damning statement was produced in hushed secrecy; and those same pages brandished in the tumult and spectacle of the Parnell Commission and disavowed by the supposed turncoat as pure fabrication. The O'Gorman Mahon residing here in the 1830s, already instrumental in the rise of O'Connell, destined to be unwittingly instrumental in the fall of Parnell. The Young Irelander John Blake Dillon who lived openly in Fitzwilliam Square following his return from exile in the 1850s, and inheritors of that physical force tradition living furtively here in snatches during the War of Independence.

Endnotes

1. Denis Gwynn, *The O'Gorman Mahon* (1934), pp. 24-27.

2. W.J. O'Neill Daunt, *Eighty Five Years of Irish History* (1888), p. 193.

3. Charles Gavan Duffy, *Young Ireland: A Fragment of Irish History, 1840-1850* (1880), pp. 60-61, 47.

4. Brendan O'Cathaoir, *John Blake Dillon, Young Irelander*, pp. 80-81.

5. Ibid., p. 99.

6. *The Nenagh Guardian*, 5 March 1856.

7. *The Nation*, 8 March 1856.

8. *The Nenagh Guardian*, 5 March 1856.

9. Ibid., 19 March 1856.

10. Marie Hughes, 'The Parnell Sisters', *Dublin Historical Record*, Vol. 21, No. 1, p. 15.

11. This and subsequent passages are taken from Emily Monroe Dickenson, *A Patriot's Mistake – Being Personal Recollections of the Parnell Family, by a Daughter of the House* (1905), pp. 34-35; 99-101; 92-94; 88-89.

12. Passages quoted in this section are taken from reports in *The Irish Times* dated 3 November 1875 and 8 December 1877.

13. Katharine O'Shea, *Charles Stewart Parnell; His Love Story and Political Life* (1914), Vol. 1, pp. 123-124.

14. Denis Gwynn, *The O'Gorman Mahon* (1934), pp. 259-261.

15. Charles Villiers Stanford, *Pages from an Unwritten Diary* (1914), pp. 254-255.

16. Passages quoted in this section are taken from a report in *The Irish Times* dated 14 February 1889.

17. This and subsequent passages are taken from John McDonald, *Diary of the Parnell Commission* (1890), pp. 69; 72-74.

18. F.S.L. Lyons, 'Parnellism and Crime', *Transactions of the Royal Historical Society*, Fifth Series, Vol. 24 (1974), p. 138.

19. *The Irish Times*, 4 November 1891.

20. James M. Whistler, copy telegram sent to Alfred McDermott [meant for Tudor McDermott], 43 Fitzwilliam Square, 10 November 1891; MS Whistler M33; *The Correspondence of James McNeill Whistler*, Glasgow University Library, On-line edition.

21 Letter from Arthur Matheson to Vera Matheson, 21 April 1921, in the possessoin of Marie Carroll.

22 *The Irish Times*, 30 December 1948.

23 Eamon de Valera to Arthur Matheson, 25 May 1943, National Archives of Ireland (TSCH/3/S9494).

24 Seanad Debates, Vol. 11, Col. 225 (20 December 1928).

25 Eric J. Arnott, *A New Beginning in Sight*, p. 108.

26 Edward Hyams, *Terrorists and Terrorism* (1975), p. 107.

27 F.O.C. Meenan, *The Georgian Squares of Dublin and the Professions, Studies: An Irish Quarterly Review*, Vol. 58, No. 232 (Winter, 1969), pp. 412-413.

28 Bureau of Military History 1913-21 – Witness Statement No. 380: David Neligan.

29 Mary Macken, 'Dr. Denis J. Coffey President of University College, Dublin, 1909-1940', *Studies: An Irish Quarterly Review*, Vol. 29, No. 114 (1940), p. 185.

30 *The Irish Times*, 7 December 1922.

31 This and subsequent passages taken from Bureau of Military History 1913-21 – Witness Statement No. 826: Maeve McGarry.

32 Bureau of Military History 1913-21 – Witness Statement No. 356: Milo McGarry.

33 Risteárd Mulcahy, *Richard Mulcahy (1886-1971); A Family Memoir* (1999), p. 132.

34 Bureau of Military History 1913-21 – Witness Statement No. 781: Patrick J. Kelly.

35 Easter Rising & Ireland Under Martial Law 1916-1921; WO 35/78/818.

36 Easter Rising & Ireland Under Martial Law 1916-1921; WO 35/78/817.

37 *The Irish Times*, 9 June 1926.

9

Conclusion

While compiling this book, the author has strolled around Fitz-william Square several times, been invited into some of the homes and wandered the central garden. It's uncanny that everyone mentioned throughout these pages looked on the same houses, lived out their own dramas in these same rooms, walked the enclosed paths at their own leisure. The fabric of the city has changed without, the fabric of the house interiors is much changed within. But if any one of those featured were to look out from the centre of the garden they would encounter a familiar vista. Trevelyan's quote is apt:

> The poetry of history lies in the quasi-miraculous fact that once...on this familiar spot of ground, walked other men and women, as actual as we are today, thinking their own thoughts, swayed by their own passions, but now all gone, one generation vanishing after another.[1]

Of course, a thousand other residents have had no mention, content enough, or lucky enough, to live out their lives without a brush with history. Some of those unnamed may have struggled, some prospered, some no doubt had tales that would fill chapters of their own, had the author been but diligent enough to discover them. Still, the Fitzwilliam Square lives less ordinary that left their mark in historical records have proved an eclectic bunch.

Though mentioned above, the central garden hasn't received much notice in these pages. Unchanged in 200 years, it's still sadly inaccessible and remote for most – which perhaps could be understood if the houses were still filled with families; instead, the garden always appears bereft. Historically, it is most notable for hosting the first Irish tennis open championships in the late nineteenth century, which invariably provided great excitement and spectacle. The first open was staged in 1879, its first champion was Vere Thomas St. Leger Goold. Imagine a young man, racquet aloft, beaming to an appreciative crowd within the park and those looking down from windows surrounding the square. In subsequent years he retired from the game and fell into alcoholism. In 1891, he married a French widow named Marie Violet. They wound up in Monte Carlo where they became heavily indebted to a wealthy Danish woman, Emma Liven. In August 1907, Vere and his wife caught the train from Monte Carlo to Marseilles. They deposited two large trunks in a cloak room to be forwarded to London. However, officials became concerned by the distressing odour that emerged from the cases, ordered them opened and discovered the dismembered remains of Ms Liven. Vere St. Leger died in a prison on Devil's Island, French Guiana in 1909, thirty years after accepting the acclaim of a sun-drenched Fitzwilliam Square.

For the most part, the garden was a play area for the square's children, supervised by nannies gossiping on benches, or keeping a watchful eye from upper-storey windows. We saw that No. 34 on the south side was the Swiss Private Hotel in the 1920s, run by Emma and Ernst Naher, immigrants from Switzerland. Their young son George was left by his parents to while his lonely hours within the central garden. His daughter Gaby, who wrote a book about her family's experiences, visited the square and imagined him:

> I peer through the tall iron bars of the gate into Fitzwilliam Park....To a five-year-old this would have been a vast garden and George would have looked small and alone, standing all the way in there on the grass, or on a leafy path beneath one of the Square's plane or beech trees. I feel a curious desire to protect him from the hurt of that abandonment, to hold his hand as he wanders the great garden.[2]

George befriended the elderly gardener who tended the lawns, shrubs and courts of Fitzwilliam Square. This fellow was also recalled to the author by Fr. Tierney of Glenstal Abbey, who played in the garden when he was a child in the 1920s:

> There was a wonderful grounds-man called 'Freddy', who kept the tennis courts immaculately trimmed and rolled. He was a freemason and once showed me his mason kit, including a little skirt or apron. He also acted as supervisor of us wild young people.

Anthony O'Brien of No. 65 played as a youngster in the square several decades later. He recalled the excitement that ensued when children from the neighbouring Pembroke Street tenements, 'the Pembo Gang', vaulted the railing to horseplay with their (supposedly) well-heeled fellows.

Today, the shouts of children at play rarely ring from the enclosed park. The conversion of houses to non-residential use after the 1920s was quite rapid. Meenan's 1969 study of the Georgian squares provides the figures.[3] In 1928, eleven of Fitzwilliam Square's sixty-nine houses were no longer places of abode for single families living alone. Twenty years later, that number had jumped to forty houses. By 1968, the transformation into a non-residential square was almost complete, when sixty-three of the houses were no longer family homes. As noted in Chapter 7, Fitzwilliam Square was inundated with doctors in the mid-twentieth century, many of whom kept their consulting rooms there. Meenan's figures show that between 1908 and 1968 houses occupied by doctors had increased from twelve to sixty-one. Yet another seismic shift in usage came just a year after Meenan's study, when St. Vincent's Hospital relocated from St. Stephen's Green farther south to Elm Park, and the doctors drifted away, their consulting and waiting rooms replaced by office suites.

The lease on the central garden had expired in 1963 and some of the houses began to sit vacant and fall into dereliction. Mary Bryan wrote:

> The shadow of the happenings on the northside squares loomed large.... Fortunately the threat to the square posed by the changes of the 1960s/1970s was averted. The inherent perception of Fitzwilliam Square as a prestigious location prevailed and, if the doctors had gone, there were still

lawyers and barristers attracted to the square, together with architects and accountants, as well as language institutes and financial institutions. The conversion of entire houses to apartments never became popular but the move to multi-office use became prevalent, and was the norm for the rest of the century.[4]

Inevitably, many original details and design features have been lost, but the essence and fabric of the square remains largely intact. The protection of this intrinsic character was boosted by the designation of Fitzwilliam Square and environs as an architectural conservation area (ACA) by Dublin City Council in 2009. Thus future developments and changes will be managed by a framework of protective policies, but we'll leave those details to architectural historians and conservationists.

It's time we took our leave of the many and varied residents of Fitzwilliam Square. Turn away from the tall, handsome houses – graceful family homes for the most part, though we remember the apothecary shop, the private hospital, the assembly rooms for evangelical brethren, the guest-houses, school-houses and safe-houses. Bid farewell to the maids and governesses, butlers and coachmen. Hear the echo of carriages and footsteps and children at play, as the hum of conversation and gentle music that spill from first floor windows all recede. We can glance once more across the granite steps; columned doorcases and elaborate fanlights; the tall sash windows, some still with their original pane pattern; the wrought iron balconies, railings and boot-scrapers; the enclosed park, its dwarf wall and iron fence, the trees that overhang and obscure the view of the manicured lawns; the distinctive red brick facades, some with granite cladding on the lower floor. Above all, we remember the people who lived within – Lady Branden and The O'Gorman Mahon, Justice Monahan and J.B. Dillon, Mainie Jellett, Jack Yeats, and all the rest. No more to be gleaned, we turn to depart Fitzwilliam Square, step around a corner and away along the Georgian mile.

Endnotes

1. George Macaulay Trevelyan, *An Autobiography and Other Essays* (1949), p. 13.

2. Gaby Naher, *The Truth about My Fathers*, pp. 106-107.

3. F.O.C. Meenan, 'The Georgian Squares of Dublin and the Professions', *Studies: An Irish Quarterly Review*, Vol. 58, No. 232 (Winter, 1969), pp. 407-408.

4. Mary Bryan, *The Georgian Squares of Dublin*, p. 109.

Index

Index

Picture Credits

Page 2: A Plan of Merrion Square with the Intended New Streets Being Part of the Estate of the Rt. Hon. Lord Viscount Fitzwilliam (1764) by Jonathan Barker. NAI Pembroke Estate Papers 2011/2/2/10. Courtesy of the National Archives of Ireland. Photo copyright Davison & Associates.

Page 3: A Map of that Part of the Estate of The Rt. Hon. Richard Lord Viscount Fitzwilliam Within the Circular Rd (1789) by Pat and John Roe. NAI Pembroke Estate Papers 2011/2/1/12. Courtesy of the National Archives of Ireland. Photo copyright the author.

Page 7: 'Oh! Che Boccone!' or 'Oh! What a Mouthful!': 1789 print purporting to show Richard Fitzwilliam in the garb of a clown in the dressing room of Mademoiselle Zacharie.

Pages 10, 98: A Map of Part of the Estate of The Rt. Hon. The Earl of Pembroke and Montgomery Situate in the County of the City of Dublin (1822) by John Roe. NAI Pembroke Estate Papers 2011/2/1/28. Courtesy of the National Archives of Ireland. Photo copyright Davison & Associates.

Page 37: Four drawings in ink on one sheet of the poet James Clarence Mangan. PD 2159 TX (26) 1. Courtesy of the National Library of Ireland. Photo copyright the author.

Page 43: Edward Pennefather by Daniel Drawsure. EP PENN-ED (1) II. Courtesy of the National Library of Ireland.

Page 45: The State Trial Portraits. PD HP (1844) 6. Courtesy of the National Library of Ireland. Photo copyright the author.

Page 99: Lady Dufferin. EP DUFF-HE (1) II. Courtesy of the National Library of Ireland. Photo copyright the author.

Page 114: A.P. Graves by V.L. O'Connor. PD 2159 TX (34) 4. Courtesy of the National Library of Ireland. Photo copyright the author.

Page 126: Copyright Gaby Naher.

Page 136: Willcocks Huband. Critical and Familiar Notices on the Art of Etching upon Copper. Courtesy of the Early Printed Books Library, Trinity College Dublin. Photo copyright the author.

Pages 158, 159, 162: Copyright Anthony O'Brien.

Page 208: Bartholomew Lloyd by Campanile, oil on canvas, 79 x 68.5 cm. Reproduced by kind permission from the board of Trinity College Dublin.

Page 216: Humphrey Lloyd by William Gorman Wills, oil on canvas, 70.5 x 59.5 cm. Reproduced by kind permission from the board of Trinity College Dublin.

Page 225: Charles H. Benson by Stephen Catterson. Courtesy of the Royal College of Surgeons in Ireland.

Page 226: Dr J.H. Benson. Reproduced by kind permission of the Royal College of Physicians of Ireland.

Page 229: John William Moore by Sean O'Sullivan. RCPI 151. Reproduced by kind permission of the Royal College of Physicians of Ireland.

Page 234: William Ireland De Courcy Wheeler. Courtesy of the Royal College of Surgeons in Ireland.

Page 235: Bethel Solomons by Estella Frances Solomons. RCPI 32. Reproduced by kind permission of the Royal College of Physicians of Ireland.

Page 240: Group portrait of Daniel O'Connell, M.P., (1775-1847), statesman, Charles O'Gorman Mahon, M.P., (1800-1891), and Thomas Steele, (1788-1848), repealer. PD 2120 TX (1) 3. Courtesy of the National Library of Ireland. Photo copyright the author.

Page 262: The Parnell Inquiry Commission. PD HP (1889) 1. Courtesy of the National Library of Ireland. Photo copyright the author.

Colour Image 1: A Map of Part of the Estate of The Rt. Hon. The Earl of Pembroke and Montgomery Situate in the County of the City of Dublin (1822) by John Roe. Photo copyright Davison & Associates.

Colour Image 3: Going to the Levée at Dublin Castle by Rose Barton, 1865-1929 (1897). NGI 2989. Watercolour on paper. Unframed: 35.6 x 26.6 cm. National Gallery of Ireland Collection. Photo copyright National Gallery of Ireland.

Colour Image 4 (i): Centre Hall of Great Industrial Exhibition, Dublin 1853. PD HP (1853) 1. Courtesy of the National Library of Ireland. Photo copyright the author.

Colour Image 4 (ii): Nursery Tea (1918) by Mainie Jellett. Private Collection. Copyright Jellett Estate. Photo copyright the author.

Colour Image 5: NGI 1326. Decoration (1923) by Mainie Jellett (1897-1944). Tempera on wood panel, 89 x 53 cm. National Gallery of Ireland Collection. Copyright Jellett Estate. Photo copyright National Gallery of Ireland.

Colour Image 6 (i) and (ii): Two views of Poulaphouca by Dermod O'Brien. Copyright the Estate of Dermod O'Brien. Photos copyright Anthony O'Brien.

Colour Image 7: Fitzwilliam Square in May by Kitty Wilmer O'Brien. Copyright the Estate of Kitty Wilmer O'Brien. Photo copyright Anthony O'Brien.

Colour Image 8: Fitzwilliam Square by Charles Ginner. Copyright the Estate of Charles Ginner. Courtesy of the British Council Collection. Photo copyright Rodney Todd-White & Son.

Photos on pages 9, 47 and 82 are copyright the author. All other images are in the public domain.